International Law and the Global South

Perspectives from the Rest of the World

Series Editor

Leïla Choukroune, International Law and University Research, Portsmouth University, New Delhi, India

This book series aims to promote a complex vision of contemporary legal developments from the perspective of emerging or developing countries and/or authors integrating these elements into their approach. While focusing on today's law and international economic law in particular, it brings together contributions from, or influenced by, other social sciences disciplines. Written in both technical and non-technical language and addressing topics of contemporary importance to a general audience, the series will be of interest to legal researchers as well as non-lawyers. In referring to the "rest of the world", the book series puts forward new and alternative visions of today's law not only from emerging and developing countries, but also from authors who deliberately integrate this perspective into their thinking. The series approach is not only comparative, post-colonial or critical, but also truly universal in the sense that it places a plurality of well-informed visions at its center.

The Series

- Provides a truly global coverage of the world in reflecting cutting-edge developments and thinking in law and international law
- Focuses on the transformations of international and comparative law with an emphasis on international economic law (investment, trade and development)
- Welcomes contributions on comparative and/or domestic legal evolutions

More information about this series at https://link.springer.com/bookseries/13447

Amitendu Palit
Editor

Globalisation Impacts

Countries, Institutions and COVID19

 Springer

Editor
Amitendu Palit
Trade and Economics
National University of Singapore
Singapore, Singapore

ISSN 2510-1420 ISSN 2510-1439 (electronic)
International Law and the Global South
ISBN 978-981-16-7184-5 ISBN 978-981-16-7185-2 (eBook)
https://doi.org/10.1007/978-981-16-7185-2

© The Editor(s) (if applicable) and The Author(s), under exclusive license to Springer Nature
Singapore Pte Ltd. 2022, corrected publication 2022
This work is subject to copyright. All rights are solely and exclusively licensed by the Publisher, whether
the whole or part of the material is concerned, specifically the rights of translation, reprinting, reuse
of illustrations, recitation, broadcasting, reproduction on microfilms or in any other physical way, and
transmission or information storage and retrieval, electronic adaptation, computer software, or by similar
or dissimilar methodology now known or hereafter developed.
The use of general descriptive names, registered names, trademarks, service marks, etc. in this publication
does not imply, even in the absence of a specific statement, that such names are exempt from the relevant
protective laws and regulations and therefore free for general use.
The publisher, the authors and the editors are safe to assume that the advice and information in this book
are believed to be true and accurate at the date of publication. Neither the publisher nor the authors or
the editors give a warranty, expressed or implied, with respect to the material contained herein or for any
errors or omissions that may have been made. The publisher remains neutral with regard to jurisdictional
claims in published maps and institutional affiliations.

This Springer imprint is published by the registered company Springer Nature Singapore Pte Ltd.
The registered company address is: 152 Beach Road, #21-01/04 Gateway East, Singapore 189721,
Singapore

Preface

Since the outbreak of the global financial crisis in 2008, numerous anxieties and concerns have been expressed over globalisation. These range from the discriminatory benefits that economic globalisation has delivered to certain countries and social groups; the growth of 'champions' of globalisation, primarily the liberal pro-market, pro-trade political, business, policy and academic elites who have allegedly exploited globalisation for self-gains while suppressing alternative critiques; and the profuse cross-border mobility of people and the cultural assimilation encouraged by economic globalisation that has marginalised many local populations and indigenous practices.

Consternations over globalisation have been accompanied by rise of hostile political narratives and 'anti-globalisation' champions criticising globalisation and its proponents. These include, the flourishing and maturing of the Brexit movement in the United Kingdom (UK) leading to formal separation of the UK from the European Union (EU) and the election of President Donald Trump in the USA. Both these developments in the last decade mark pushbacks experienced by pro-globalisation politics and its encouragement of greater integration of national economies, systems and societies across the world.

The trends of the pushback are also visible in political changes that have occurred across Asia, Europe and the Americas during the last decade. India is a notable example. One of the largest emerging markets and populous developing countries, India, after persisting with gradual adoption of market forces in institutions and regulations, is turning inward, by adopting trade-disengaging external policies, rationalised by the quest for self-reliance. China, on the other hand, is reconstructing regional economic development spaces through mechanisms of tighter state control, and greater prominence of state agencies in supply of global public goods through expansive, but conspicuously hegemonic projects like the Belt and Road Initiative (BRI). These nuanced efforts by China and India to 'manage' integration with the global economy for enabling maximisation of benefits, without sacrificing strategic national interests, might become a prominent trait of modern globalisation among the global South.

In the globalisation discourse, much attention has been devoted to institutions, particularly those spearheading economic globalisation, like the World Trade Organization (WTO). Since its birth in 1995, the WTO has administered a multilateral rules-based order for running global trade. Since the last decade, far-reaching developments have been challenging the WTO's writ and credibility. These include the growth of large, comprehensive mega free trade agreements (FTAs) covering a wide spectrum of trade-related issues, including labour, environment and data standards, among specific groups of countries. These mega FTAs, and bilateral trade deals with identical wide coverage, challenge the functional scope and structural inflexibilities of the WTO in advancing a modern global trade agenda. The WTO's existential fundamentals, particularly its inclusive character, has been heavily attacked, most notably by the Trump Administration in the US, highlighting WTO's 'discriminations'—vis-à-vis the US and other large developing economies, ostensibly, China, India, Brazil, Indonesia and several others.[1] The US proclivity to repeatedly question 'flexibilities' granted by the WTO to 'others', arguably, creates precedents, which can embolden many WTO members, notably other prominent global powers, to disregard the WTO at ease. The tendency also sparks unwanted fissures in world trade leading to pushback of the multilateral trade order by smaller blocs of trade coalitions, bound by identical economic structures, capacities, institutions and agendas, under the rubric of overarching political coalitions.

The latest challenge to globalisation is inflicted by COVID19. The pandemic is fundamentally recasting the global economic and political orders through critical anti-globalisation shifts. Deep political mistrust among countries following the outbreak, organised around the US–China strategic divide, the resultant geopolitical hostilities and concomitant country alignments, are restructuring the global economic order into distinct, unconnected trade and business spaces carved out by geopolitics. The disconnection among these spaces will be accentuated by the race between the US and China to dominate global tech industries, and the national anxieties to secure access to public health supplies, particularly vaccines for tackling the unabating COVID19. Technology and pandemic mitigation are likely to become defining elements of a new global order post-COVID19 as the world struggles to adjust to 'new normal's in security, strategic, political and economic spheres.

This volume begins by reflecting on the remarkable political and economic developments of the last decade that have centred around the discourse on globalisation and shaped its contours. Noting the significant outcomes from these developments, manifesting in anti-globalisation leaders and their agendas securing political legitimacy in the US, Europe and Asia, the book focuses on the political economy context of the backlash against globalisation. Sonia and Vinod Aggarwal's chapter situates the context by analysing causes leading to the backlash. The paper addresses one of the key frailties of the popular construct of globalisation: the sweeping neo-liberal assumption that withdrawal of state and subsequent perpetuity of markets in production and distribution, would assure greater welfare across societies and communities.

---

[1] 'Trump ramps up attack against WTO', Politico, 26 July 2019; https://www.politico.com/story/2019/07/26/trump-world-trade-organization-1623192.

Preface

A more grounded political economy interpretation, factoring in concerns of development, and the complementary role of the state, needs far greater academic attention. The scope of the narrative, bringing in markets, states, institutions and communities, in ensuring effective distribution of public goods in a globalised world, as envisaged by the influential Washington Consensus, is explored by Amitendu Palit in the chapter on revisiting globalisation in the context of COVID19. While many argue the pandemic acquired catastrophic proportions due to porous borders and rapid movements of people across them, a globalised response to managing pandemics and similar outbreaks in future remain critical, given the urgent need of several parts of the world in accessing medicines and food, and their shortages exacerbated by COVID19. COVID19 also accentuates challenges for global institutions in the post-liberal world order that is experiencing intense rivalry among major powers.

Moving ahead, the book reflects deeper on institutions, and their contributions to globalisation. The specific focus in this regard is on international economic laws and the role of the WTO. Leila Choukroune's chapter explores three specific verticals of international economic law—trade & investment; labour & human rights; and judicial activism. The chapter delves into the scoping of the three spectrums, in the empirical context of China and India—the world's largest developing countries—working on normative internationalisation through globalisation, and the processes of modernisation, democratisation and resistances generated by such efforts. The experiences offer deep insights given the ongoing struggles of both countries to simultaneously benefit from, and minimise, hardships of adjusting to globalisation. Further on institutions, equity and inclusiveness are identified central to the struggle to make them deliver, as explored at length through a robust empirical approach by Abhijit Das, researching the key episodes of protests against globalisation, particularly trade-related issues at the GATT/WTO[2]. The functioning of the WTO, as mentioned before, has been a key source of friction and unhappiness among its stakeholders. The reasons contributing to the unhappiness are essential for evaluating the wider perspective of what a future global trade and economic order might look like given the escalating trade tensions and the overall lack of conviction in the WTO's ability to manage world trade.

China occupies a prominent position in the contemporary narrative on globalisation. Proponents of economic globalisation point to China's remarkable commercial success, particularly its achievements in lifting millions out of poverty, as an example of the benefits economic globalisation can produce. With several Western nations, particularly the US, pushing back on globalisation, China has volunteered to lead the next phase of globalisation[3]. Is this largely rhetoric? Obtaining clearer insights in this regard is crucial as China expands its strategic influence around the world, through

---

[2] GATT, abbreviated for the General Agreement on Tariffs and Trade, was the framework for global trade till it was replaced by the WTO from 1995. The GATT took shape right after the end of the 2nd World War. 'The GATT years: from Havana to Marrakesh', World Trade Organization (WTO). https://www.wto.org/english/thewto_e/whatis_e/tif_e/fact4_e.htm.

[3] 'China's Xi Jinping defends globalisation from the Davos stage', World Economic Forum, 17 January 2017. https://www.weforum.org/agenda/2017/01/chinas-xi-jinping-defends-globalization-from-the-davos-stage/.

grand projects like the Belt and Road Initiative (BRI). Jean Marc Blanchard's assessment of China's performance, strategies and posturing are followed by the book in transitioning to closer country perspectives. This entails the experience analysis of two small countries with contrasting backgrounds to benefit from economic globalisation. Mohammad Razzaque discusses the experience of Bangladesh, a populous and poor least developed country, which has successfully scaled economic and social development ladders by maximising exports. Yet, as Bangladesh graduates out of its Least Developed Country (LDC) status, it hesitates to embrace economic globalisation more closely. The attitude is in marked contrast to that of Ireland, another small economy from Europe discussed by Louis Brennan, which has prospered by exploiting cultural, administrative, geographic and economic similarities and differences for its greater benefits and national advantage. Both experiences, in their entireties, are critical in understanding why globalisation has not always been welcomed as a comprehensive process in many parts of the world, and why studying it as a composite process, is a major academic challenge.

Objective assessment of globalisation remains incomplete without reflecting on regionalism. In doing so, it is customary to look at the European experience to serve as a benchmark. Such a benchmark overlooks the differences and complexities associated with Asian regionalism. Jayant Menon studies these differences with respect to ASEAN and identifies the very different motivations and objectives of the two regional programs. ASEAN's success lies in its almost unique achievement of using regionalism for globalisation. The metrics used for assessing regionalism must reflect true objectives, even if they lie below the surface. These metrics and objectives, though, are encountering challenges as Asian regionalism struggles to come to terms with the repositioning of regional supply chains in the aftermath of COVID19. Amitendu Palit and Preety Bhogal explore the factors driving the urge to make supply chains resilient. Multi-country resiliency initiatives need to be apprised in the light of the difficulty of economic decoupling, much as the same is encouraged by the post-COVID19 regional politics. India's challenges in this regard viewed with respect to a strategic industry like pharmaceuticals have much to reveal in this regard.

The volume concludes by reflecting on what globalisation might metamorphose into in the years and decades to come as the world gets gripped by the phenomenal advances in technology, characterising globalisation 4.0. Access to technology and the ability to use it effectively, is the key to abilities of countries in exerting global influence to 'dominate'. It is hardly surprising that the new Cold War between the US and China is essentially a war around technology. Along with technology, great advancements have been made in digitalisation, national and global economic functions turn substantially digital. The process would hasten in the post COVID19 era, which emphasises contactless distribution and digital deliveries. However, technological prowess and rapid digitalisation raise questions on whether their advances would result in enlarging inequalities among countries, regions and societies. Amitendu

Palit's final chapter describes these contexts and revisits the critique underpinning globalisation's discriminatory character, and reflects further on whether such a character might forcefully manifest in the emerging world order.

Singapore, Singapore   Amitendu Palit

Acknowledgements

This volume comprises several papers that were presented at a workshop organized by the Institute of South Asian Studies (ISAS) in the National University of Singapore (NUS), in October 2017, in collaboration with the APEC Study Center at the University of California at Berkeley. I take this opportunity to thank the contributors for the papers and their steadfast commitment to this volume. I'm grateful to ISAS-NUS – particularly Professor C Raja Mohan, Director ISAS; Professor Subrata K. Mitra, former Director ISAS; and Hernaikh Singh, Deputy Director, ISAS, for their cooperation and support. I'm deeply thankful to Mekhla Jha for providing excellent research assistance and editorial support. Finally, my special thanks to Nupoor Singh at Springer Nature and Leila Choukroune at the University of Portsmouth UK for their support and guidance in the project.

Contents

1 Robots Versus Aliens: The Backlash Against Globalization 1
Sonia N. Aggarwal and Vinod K. Aggarwal

2 Revisiting Globalization: A Post-COVID19 Perspective 25
Amitendu Palit

**3 Normative Internationalization Through Globalization:
India and China Between Modernization, Democratization,
and Authoritarian Resistances** 43
Leïla Choukroune

4 Discontent Against Globalization: Reasons and Remedies 65
Abhijit Das

**5 China and the Impact of Economic Globalization: A Complex
Tale of Gains and Losses Viewed Through the Lenses of FDI** 87
Jean-Marc F. Blanchard

**6 Geo-economics, Globalization and the Covid-19 Pandemic:
Trade and Development Perspectives from Bangladesh** 105
Mohammad A. Razzaque

**7 Managing Globalization to National Advantage: The Case
of Ireland** 127
Louis Brennan

8 Multilateralising Regionalism: The ASEAN Experience 145
Jayant Menon

**9 COVID19, Supply Chain Resilience, and India: Prospects
of the Pharmaceutical Industry** 159
Amitendu Palit and Preety Bhogal

10 Globalization and New Developments: Towards a More Fragmented World? 183
Amitendu Palit

Correction to: Geo-economics, Globalization and the Covid-19 Pandemic: Trade and Development Perspectives from Bangladesh C1
Mohammad A. Razzaque

Editor and Contributors

About the Editor

Amitendu Palit is Senior Research Fellow and Research Lead (trade and economics) in the Institute of South Asian Studies (ISAS) in the National University of Singapore (NUS). An economist with nearly three decades of policy and academic experience, he works on international trade and investment, political economy of public policies, India & Asia-Pacific. Prior to NUS, he spent several years in India's Ministry of Finance. He has authored and edited several books with leading international publishers, including 'China India Economics: Challenges, Competition and Collaboration' (2011), 'The Trans Pacific Partnership, China and India: Economic and Political Implications' (2014), 'Special Economic Zones in India: Myths and Realities' (2008; co-authored), 'Seeking Middle Ground: Land, Markets and Public Policy' (2019; co-edited), 'Seven Decades of Independent India' (2018; co-edited) and 'Employment Policy in Emerging Economies' (2017; co-edited). Author of several peer-reviewed academic journals, he is member of the World Economic Forum's Global Future Council on Trade and Investment, a columnist for India's Financial Express, and a commentator for BBC, Bloomberg News, Channel News Asia and CNBC.

Contributors

Sonia N. Aggarwal Berkeley APEC Study Center, UC Berkeley, Berkeley, CA, USA

Vinod K. Aggarwal Berkeley APEC Study Center, UC Berkeley, Berkeley, CA, USA

Preety Bhogal Economics, Kansas State University, Manhattan, USA

Jean-Marc F. Blanchard Mr. and Mrs. S.H. Wong Center for the Study of Multinational Corporations, Los Gatos, CA, USA

Louis Brennan Trinity Business School, Trinity College, Dublin, Ireland

Leïla Choukroune Professor of International Law and Director of the University's Thematic Area in Democratic Citizenship, University of Portsmouth (UoP), Portsmouth, UK

Abhijit Das Centre for WTO Studies, Indian Institute of Foreign Trade, New Delhi, India

Jayant Menon Visiting Senior Fellow, ISEAS-Yusof Ishak Institute, Singapore, Singapore

Amitendu Palit Institute of South Asian Studies (ISAS), National University of Singapore, Singapore, Singapore;
National University of Singapore, Singapore, Singapore;
Trade and Economics, National University of Singapore, Singapore, Singapore

Mohammad A. Razzaque Research and Policy Integration for Development (RAPID), Dhaka, Bangladesh

Chapter 1
Robots Versus Aliens: The Backlash Against Globalization

Sonia N. Aggarwal and Vinod K. Aggarwal

1 Introduction

The rise of anti-globalization has stimulated thinking about the root cause and remedies for the turn toward nationalism and protectionism and away from trade liberalization. For neoliberal economists with a belief in the miracle of the unfettered market, the answer is simple: Keep the state out of the private sector and everything will be fine.[1] But with a backlash against globalization growing throughout both the developed and developing world, and worsening in many cases with the COVID19 crisis, this answer is not only overly simplistic but also detrimental. Politicians have identified "aliens" in terms of foreign investment, trade, and immigration as negatives for workers, but have generally failed to address the major cause of job losses—the impact of technology and automation ("robots"). To address such an impact stemming from increasing globalization, a more significant intelligent activist state must be pursued. In addition, one must pay attention to the global and institutional impact of the pursuit of industrial policies by countries such as China—rather than simply claiming that such policies are "inefficient". This chapter explores these issues from a broad political economy context.

Section II of the chapter begins by tracing trends in globalization, pointing to both economic data that depict a slowing of benefits reaped from globalization as well as some recent political events that illustrate the turn toward protectionism. Section III discusses neoclassical economic theory and then contrasts it with neomercantilist thought. Section IV considers the efforts by the United States (U.S). to address

---

[1] Parts of this paragraph draw on the Forward by Vinod Aggarwal in Choi et al. (2017).

S. N. Aggarwal
Berkeley APEC Study Center, UC Berkeley, 552 Barrows Hall, Berkeley, CA, USA

V. K. Aggarwal (✉)
Berkeley APEC Study Center, UC Berkeley, 552 Barrows Hall, Berkeley, CA, USA
e-mail: vinod@berkeley.edu

© The Author(s), under exclusive license to Springer Nature Singapore Pte Ltd. 2022
A. Palit (ed.), *Globalisation Impacts*, International Law and the Global South,
https://doi.org/10.1007/978-981-16-7185-2_1

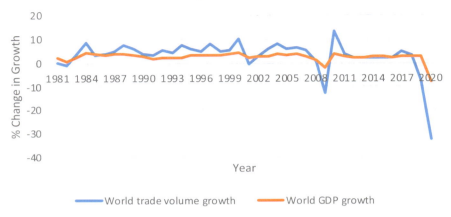

Fig. 1 Global Trade Growth. *Source* https://www.wto.org/english/news_e/pres20_e/pr855_e.htm

job losses and the impact on firms and shows how the measures to this point have been inadequate. Section V concludes by discussing alternatives to current U.S. neoclassical economic policies with both a domestic and global focus.

2 Trends in Globalization

In terms of recent economic trends, the financial crisis of 2008 appears to have had a persistent effect on globalization trends, followed by the COVID19 crisis. In trade, for example, before 2008, global trade volumes were steadily higher than GDP growth. But as Fig. 1 shows, this trend dipped in 2008 in connection with the global financial crisis.

After 2016, trade growth was on the path to recovery, until plummeting in connection with the 2020 pandemic. The Brexit referendum, closely followed by the election of Donald Trump and significant U.S. protectionist actions, suggests that anti-globalization trends remain strong. With a loss of nearly six million jobs in a 12-year period (1999–2011) and coupled with a rise in China's manufacturing industry that mirrors America's decline, the arguments for protectionism and anti-globalization echoed by Donald Trump gained traction.[2] Looking to the future, the Biden administration is unlikely to reverse many of these protectionist policies given concerns by and about American workers who believe their jobs have been sent overseas and the continuing bipartisan concern about China's industrial policy and intellectual property rights, or lack thereof.

---

[2] BBC (2016).

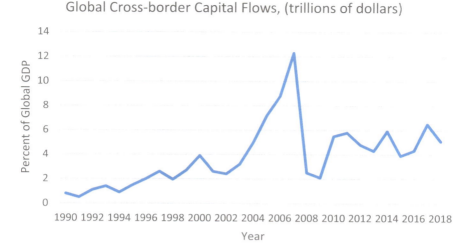

Fig. 2 Global cross-border flows. *Sources* https://www.mckinsey.com/industries/financial-ser vices/our-insights/the-new-dynamics-of-financial-globalization, https://www.mckinsey.com/~/ media/McKinsey/Industries/Financial%20Services/Our%20Insights/The%20new%20dynamics% 20of%20financial%20globalization/Financial%20globalization_Full%20Report_August_29_ 2017%20(1).pdf, https://unctad.org/system/files/official-document/wir2019_en.pdf

In addition, as Fig. 2 shows, international financial flows have also declined sharply since the 2008 crisis. While the 1980s were a period characterized an 8% average annual increase in international trade, following the 2008 financial crisis, such growth has stagnated. Referred to as "The Great Retrenchment", cross-border financial flows have declined to less than half the rate seen in 2009.[3]

In terms of immigration, despite rhetoric to the contrary, many Mexican immigrants have been returning to Mexico from the United States. Figure 3 shows that net migration has dropped sharply with the Trump Administration.

From a political perspective, the backlash against globalization is often seen as a recent phenomenon, tied to the 2016 U.S. presidential election elevating President Trump, the June 2016 Brexit vote, and the Syrian refugee crisis that has led to a backlash against immigration in Europe. But the 2011 Singapore election and 2014 Swiss anti-immigration referendum were also harbingers of anti-globalization sentiment. Both of these countries have been extremely successful in their economic performance and have been highly globalized. Yet if significant parts of the population of small rich countries have become skeptical of globalization, could others be far behind?

The rise of post WWII anti-globalization in the U.S. can be traced back to the period prior to negotiations over the North American Free Trade Agreement (NAFTA), which has usually been seen to be an important turning point. In the early

---

[3] Eichengreen (2016).

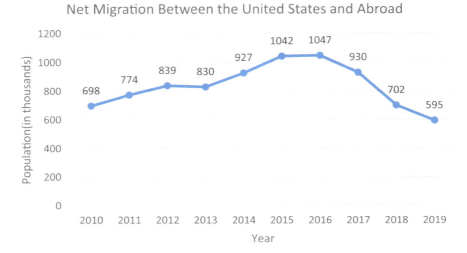

Fig. 3 Net Migration for the United States. *Source* https://www.census.gov/library/stories/2019/12/net-international-migration-projected-to-fall-lowest-levels-this-decade.html

1980s, efforts to renew the Generalized System of Preferences (GSP) acted as an important precursor to linkage efforts in NAFTA. Labor and religious and human rights activists reframed their protectionist efforts by linking trade substantively to workers' rights.[4] This reframing led to the inclusion of a labor rights clause in a fall 1984 bill to renew GSP. However, the Reagan administration was concerned that such a linkage could negatively impact the United States' relations with crucial oil-supplying Muslim countries that had a history of discriminating against women. The administration was also concerned that this linkage could raise concerns about how Israel treated Palestinian workers. Thus, President Reagan pushed for presidential discretion in implementing sanctions in cases where the rules were not complied with.

In the 1992 election and debate over NAFTA, labor saw an opportunity to link trade and labor.[5] Candidate Ross Perot exaggerated claims that NAFTA would create a "giant sucking sound" as jobs moved to Mexico. In contrast, President Bush strongly advocated its ratification, having led NAFTA negotiations. On the other hand, candidate Bill Clinton supported NAFTA but argued that he would not agree to the treaty without further side agreements clauses that included labor and the environment. Environmentalists were also active in the formation of NAFTA. Friends of the Earth, a U.S. NGO, and a coalition from the U.S., Canada, and Mexico had been pressing President Bush to include environmental provisions in trade accords.[6] In response,

---

[4] The remainder of the paragraph further draws on the discussion of Compa and Vogt (2001).

[5] See Aggarwal (1983) for a discussion of NAFTA trade linkages in the negotiations.

[6] The review of facts in this paragraph and the next paragraph draws on Vogel (1999) but not the interpretation of linkages. See Aggarwal (2013) on linkages.

Bush instituted a USTR advisory committee that included climate change activists from various NGOs. However, while Bush made this move likely to simply secure NAFTA's passage, the creation of such an advisory committee led to pressures to include a link to the environment. Particularly, environmental activists pushed Congressional members to support such a linkage in NAFTA's final form.

Candidate Clinton's stance that he neither supported nor opposed NAFTA, but if elected would fix it, proved to be a winning election strategy. Through this strategy, he garnered support from both big business and endorsements from labor and environmental groups. However, once elected, President Clinton's side agreements were inadequate for both labor and environmental groups. Thus, in order to secure NAFTA's passage, Clinton turned to Republicans to gain their support. Though Democrats largely continued to oppose NAFTA, Congress ultimately passed the agreement in November 2003, and it took effect on January 1, 1994. The battle to pass NAFTA proved to be a turning point in trade politics. However, both labor and environmental groups continued to press the U.S. government to include linkages to labor and environmental policies in future trade agreements.

3 Theories of the Global Political Economy

Underlying the post-WWII economic order has been a strong commitment to theories of economic liberalism. Here, we very briefly review liberalism before turning to neomercantilist approaches to the global economy.

Given the dominance of neoclassical international economic theory, very little needs to be said about it. The key tenet in this philosophy is that wealth is not finite. In reaction to classical mercantilist thought, Adam Smith argued that all nations could benefit by allowing the competitive market system to prevail—both domestically and internationally. Increasing efficiency and wealth would come from the best use of labor and capital. The maximum efficiency of the economy would come from the greatest degree of specialization arising from a division of labor. And to get to this specialization, the invisible hand should be allowed to operate. In short, this suggested that as everyone sought to increase their profits from the production of goods, everyone would benefit since products would be produced cheaply and would be sold at the lowest price that would cover costs plus a normal profit.

On the whole, economists have generally given short shrift to the possible problems of neoclassical trade theory, with some exceptions.[7] What are some of these critiques? Because an increase in aggregate welfare does not eliminate struggles over who will gain most from the increase of the pie, countries have incentives to use various restrictions to increase their own welfare—to the detriment of other countries. This is the notion of an optimum tariff.[8] The basic idea is that if there is no retaliation, countries may be able to impose restrictions on trade that will increase

---

[7] See the work of Paul Krugman and Dani Rodrik.

[8] Bowen (2015).

their welfare to the detriment of others. In this situation, countries can act as monopolists or monopsonists and affect the price at which goods are traded. In some cases, even if there is retaliation, countries may be better off with trade restrictions. Hence, harmony is not assured with global gains.[9]

Second, there are severe problems in attempting to implement a policy of free trade and free exchange. Since there is no single world government that can determine policies, nations must bargain over the setting up of a free exchange regime. And of course, in bargaining, countries will always seek to improve their relative and absolute positions through various linkages.

Third, the idea of efficiency as the most important goal has come under increasing attack. Numerous other considerations such as distribution, the environment, economic security, and employment can also be suggested as being of critical importance. Before turning to a discussion of these other possible goals, let us first look at some of the problems associated with the notion of efficiency.

If there are market imperfections such as inefficient international capital markets or other "imperfections" such as oligopolies and monopolies, the theories of how free exchange will lead to increasing efficiency are susceptible to attack. And as we know, imperfections are very common in the international economy. The idea that economies will benefit from trade and capital flows is also based on the notion that resources can be moved without cost. Auto workers in Detroit seem to have trouble believing this. People and plants are not as easily mobile as is often assumed. Finally, with respect to efficiency, free trade has generally been very static, focusing on existing comparative advantage. But if one conceives of comparative advantage from a dynamic standpoint, then it may be useful to have temporary restrictions which allow one's industry to develop sufficiently to gain advantage in the production of that product. This is the idea of protection for so-called infant industries.

Aside from the problem with efficiency and free exchange, states may have other goals that are not fulfilled by the "invisible hand". For example, with respect to employment, we have already seen that with trade, people may find their jobs lost to industrial automation or outsourcing. State interests would have such employees retrained sufficiently quickly and be given other jobs, but corporate efficiency leads to their unemployment, with few incentives for companies to retrain workers who may no longer possess competitive skills for an evolving market.[10]

With respect to income distribution, free trade may lead to benefits for all but lead to relative disparities and even absolute disparities in income of groups unless an efficient transfer mechanism exists to compensate actors who do not directly have a stake in the corporations that are succeeding in the economy. And as we know, governments are not all that efficient in transferring resources from one group to another without nasty fights, as evidenced by not only fights over taxation and any type of economic redistribution but even as seen within corporate organizations, as evidenced by Uber and Lyft's unwillingness to classify drivers, the backbone of

---

[9] Humphrey (1987).

[10] Federal Reserve Bank of San Francisco (2001).

1 Robots Versus Aliens: The Backlash Against Globalization

their business, as employees who would have traditionally received benefits prior to Reagan-era deregulation.[11]

Finally, as we shall see, this is where neomercantilists have the most to say: economic security may be impaired by increasing specialization and an international division of labor. While economists recognize the national security argument as a possible exception to the pursuit of specialization (if your opponent specialized in nuclear weapons and you specialize in wine, you may have some political problems), as they note correctly, security arguments are often abused by protectionist interests. In the 1950s, the wool industry argued for the protection of domestic production, claiming that "there is a need for 150 million to 200 million woolen blankets to ensure survival in case of an atomic war."[12]

Let us now turn to neomercantilist thought. Neoliberal theory was actually a reaction to mercantilist thinking. Popular in the seventeenth and eighteenth centuries, as Jacob Viner notes, mercantilists focused on three claims[13]: (1) the idea of what constitutes wealth; (2) the idea of what constitutes power; and (3) the relationship between wealth and power from the point of view of countries.

For mercantilists, wealth was the possession of gold. Gold could be exchanged for other goods since it was the accepted medium of exchange. Possession of gold, then, was equivalent to the possession of wealth since it could be used to obtain other goods and services. Since the quantity of gold was fixed except for new discoveries, a zero-sum game was being played by states. With respect to power, this was clearly thought of in zero-sum terms, implying that conflict and disharmony would characterize a relationship between any two parties. All states would be enemies of each other.

Viner's theories on mercantilist thought are conceived of in terms of the national interest and, and tie together the notions of wealth and power and the maximization of a country's position and national interest[14]: (1) to gain power, it is absolutely essential to accumulate wealth; (2) to acquire wealth, power is essential; (3) the primary purpose of state policy is achieving wealth and power; and (4) there is a long run equilibrium between achieving wealth and power, but in the short run, military security takes precedent and thus may lead to some economic sacrifices.

Given that wealth and power share an interdependence and a zero-sum relationship, the state tries to increase its autonomy in order to keep dependencies at a minimum and increase its leverage.[15] The mercantilists recognized that if the relationship between wealth and power was asymmetrical even in the slightest then it could be subjected to manipulation. Indeed, this approach was the central theme of Albert Hirschman's classic work on German trade policy, *National Power and the Structure of Foreign Trade*.[16]

---

[11] Burtless (1996).

[12] 1959 Pastore Senate Committee on Trade discussed in Aggarwal (1985).

[13] Viner (1948).

[14] *Ibid.*

[15] *Ibid.*

[16] Hirschman (1945).

States are better positioned to achieve the medium-term goal of self-sufficiency and the long-run goal of more wealth and power if they[17]: (1) stimulated domestic production through various aids such as subsidies and grants; (2) reduced dependence by importing as little as possible; and (3) increased their surplus and gained leverage over other states by actively promoting exports.

Mercantilism makes a clear distinction between the domestic economy and the international economy (unlike in liberalism). In the domestic economy, free trade led to efficiency and growth which served to increase one's power. But internationally, trade was regulated in a manner which benefitted the nation state. This could create a potential conflict between the domestic and international order. Domestic entrepreneurs could only buy and sell in accord with what is in the best interest of the state—not necessarily what they perceived to benefit their short run interest.

Neomercantilism can be seen as a response to liberal thought—just as liberalism was a response to old style mercantilism. What are these differences between mercantilism and neomercantilism? First, neomercantilists accept that there is a potential for a large pie in the international economy. Wealth is no longer seen as fixed. Yet as I noted, this does not rule out conflict. And the result is that according to neomercantilist thought, everyone tries to seek a surplus in their balance of trade.

A second difference in neomercantilist versus mercantilist thought is the type of instruments utilized to pursue state interests. These methods have become more varied. Rather than simple quotas in trade, development states have sought to use a host of measures including development financing, currency manipulation, government procurement, technological standards, and a host of other non-tariff barriers.[18]

Neomercantilism is not just of theoretical interest. As we shall see, China's "Made in China 2025" set of industrial policies that targets 10 sectors have been described by a host of analysts as being a mercantilist strategy. How such a strategy can be reconciled with a neoliberal WTO based trade order remains an open question.

We next turn to U.S. historical and current economic responses to the displacement caused by shifts in globalization.

4 U.S. Domestic Responses to the Challenges of Globalization

Although nationalist politicians have focused on the downsides of trade, outsourcing, and immigration as the source of job losses for the middle class, they have generally ignored the significant impact of technological change and automation. Most careful studies show that domestic employment losses are due to technological changes,

---

[17] Viner (1948).

[18] See Aggarwal and Aggarwal (2016). For discriminatory trade measures since the 2008 financial crisis, see globaltradealert.org.

1 Robots Versus Aliens: The Backlash Against Globalization

rather than to these other factors such as immigration—a misconception that right-wing parties have exploited to promote white nationalism. For example, in the manufacturing industry, employment has dropped by one-third from 2000 to 2010, equating to a loss of 5.6 million jobs, echoing a similar decline in the 1990s that continues today—a decline that is a direct result of increased automation in manufacturing.[19] Yet little has been done, as we shall see, to address the problem of technological change. Almost all U.S. efforts for both firms and workers have revolved around providing adjustment assistance only if affected parties can demonstrate firm problems or job losses due to trade. To consider existing U.S. trade adjustment programs, we first look at the history behind their establishment and then examine existing policies and their efficacy. We begin by looking at policies toward firms, then move on to individual workers and communities.

4.1 An Overview of Trade Adjustment Policies

Congress instituted the first official trade adjustment assistance (TAA) programs in 1962 as a response to the tensions created by trade liberalization in the context of the Kennedy Round of the GATT. TAA's earliest iteration authorized two programs: covering workers using programs such as retraining, relocation allowances, and extended unemployment benefits; and covering firms through loans, loan guarantees, technical assistance, and tax benefits.[20]

TAA proponents argued that programs should address three crucial areas of post-war II industrialization: economic efficiency, equity, and political pragmatism. Adjustment programs increased economic efficiency by allowing for more rapid transition of displaced workers to newly competitive jobs. Although subsidies were criticized for decreasing incentives to relocate or take different jobs, such programs still enabled greater retraining that otherwise would have been expensive and potentially unattainable. Equity, criticized as being discriminatory against workers who had been laid off for non-trade reasons, was intended to spread the wealth from trade to those who had lost income. Finally, and most relevant today, adjustment programs were designed to prevent backlash from trade. By offsetting the "losers" displaced as a result of greater liberalization, Congress sought to create new opportunities to prevent negative reactions that would be more sustainable than protectionism.[21]

Both Democrats and Republicans focused on expanding trade in 1960, with Democrats placing a priority on creating TAA as an integral part of expanding trade liberalization.[22] Yet securing actual assistance under TAA was a complex multi-step

---

[19] Sherk (2010).

[20] Community programs creating loans and grants were created in 1974, but have since been discontinued. All TAA programs are generally reauthorized under one bill, most recently in June 2015 under President Obama. Hornbeck (2013), The White House Blog (2015).

[21] Hornbeck (2013).

[22] *Ibid.*

process and the eligibility criteria was difficult to meet, requiring that one show that an increase in imported goods was "caused in major part" by tariff reductions, and that such an increase was a "major cause" of injury to the firm or the worker.[23] TAA, as a result of onerous restrictions, was rejected by the AFL-CIO and organized labor for its ineffectiveness in retraining or relocating workers or providing any real assistance to firms.[24]

By 1974, burdened by an ineffective program that only functionally served to provide some additional unemployment insurance, Congress redesigned TAA. Eligibility requirements were made significantly less stringent, and Congress implemented increased benefits as well as created assistance for older displaced workers.[25] Still, TAA's effectiveness continued to fluctuate until the NAFTA was passed, when President Clinton reinvigorated TAA but only with regards to jobs lost to Canada and Mexico rather than responding to the context of the ongoing Uruguay Round of the GATT.

Despite continued extensions, TAA languished at various points until 2002, when the Trade Act was reformed to meet the increasing challenges of globalization—but with mixed results. The Bush Administration, while supportive of TAA reauthorization, failed to create effective changes to the program. Democrats suggested broadening eligibility to service works and firms, public sector works, and applicants based on industry. It also recommended more flexible training and better health benefits. Republicans blocked these efforts, merely agreeing to keeping the program running, rather than implementing meaningful reforms.[26]

President Obama passed the most comprehensive TAA program since the 1970s in 2011, which was extended in June 2015.[27] The revitalized program made service workers eligible, covered service workers retroactively, and expanded eligibility to cover workers whose jobs were threatened not only by trade agreements but also by imports from countries that did not have standing agreements with the U.S., most notably, China.[28]

By 2019, the Trump administration made promises to expand the TAA Program by increasing the number of workers eligible to apply for job search and relocation allowances, increase allowances and create more flexibility for apprenticeships and staffing flexibility, and streamline the application process.[29] Although such policies were not implemented by the outcome of the 2020 U.S. presidential election, the U.S. Department of Commerce provided $13 million in funding to Trade Adjustment Assistance Centers (TAACs) in multiple states, which, while signaling an increased focus on such programs, is unlikely to make a significant difference.[30] President-Elect

---

[23] Lawrence (1977).

[24] Hornbeck (2013).

[25] *Ibid.*

[26] *Ibid.*

[27] Collins (2018), Fefer (2020)

[28] White House Blog (2015).

[29] U.S. Department of Labor (2019). https://www.dol.gov/newsroom/releases/eta/eta20191106.

[30] U.S. Department of Commerce (2019).

Biden has indicated his intention to revitalize the Trade Adjustment and Assistance Community College and Career Training (TAACCCT), which was initially created by President Obama after the 2008 financial crisis to create a $1.9 billion workforce development program.[31]

4.2 Current Worker-Related Programs

As part of the June 2015 TAA extension, TAA for Workers (TAAW) was reauthorized in June 2015 as well. TAAW is deployed under the Department of Labor and cooperates with state agencies. The annual appropriations, supported through a mandatory program, were $861 million in 2016.[32] TAAW's eligibility standards were revised and now require workers to establish that their jobs shifted to outside the U.S. or they were lost as a result of an increase in imports that were directly competitive. Workers that are upstream suppliers or downstream producers of TAAW-impacted firms may also be eligible for such benefits.[33] The USITC also publicly identifies firms whose workers are eligible for TAA due to a market disruption or other "qualified action".[34] After a group is certified by the Department of Labor, individuals apply for state-administered benefits at American Job Centers, available throughout the country.[35] The states with the greatest allocations are Texas, Pennsylvania, California, and Michigan.[36]

In 2015, TAAW programs covered 57,000 workers, 65% of whom are white.[37] Twelve percent had a bachelor's degree or more advanced education, and the median age was 50 with 11 years of employment at previous job.[38] Of the 413 petitions certified for impacted groups, 320 were in manufacturing (77.5%).[39]

TAAW creates four types of benefits: training and reemployment services, Trade Readjustment Allowance (TRA), Reemployment Trade Adjustment Assistance (RTAA), and the Health Coverage Tax Credit, the latter being relatively minor.

Training and Reemployment Services

TAAW's training and reemployment services help workers prepare and procure new employment. The bulk of these subsidies are for training, which enable workers to learn new skills to pursue employment in a new sector. Workers are also eligible

---

[31] U.S. Department of Labor (2018).

[32] Lynch (2016).

[33] *Ibid.*

[34] *Ibid.*

[35] *Ibid.*

[36] U.S. Department of Labor (2015). See Table 26.

[37] *Ibid.*

[38] *Ibid.*

[39] *Ibid.*

for case management services to find a job and may by given relocation allowances if pursuing employment outside their local community.[40] Funds for these services go up to $450 million a year and are allocated to states through a formula that looks at past and anticipated future data on program usage. Administrative costs for this program are capped at 10% to ensure appropriate use of funds by states.[41] There are no federal limitations on how much training an individual can receive, and these programs are decentralized and range from occupational skills training in classrooms to remedial and customized training. The top sectors for post-TAAW employment are manufacturing (aircraft, plastic products, and pressed and blown glassware), administrative support, and healthcare and social assistance. Popular jobs in the service industry include temporary help services, general medical and hospital services, elementary and secondary schools, and skilled nursing facilities.[42]

Despite relatively liberal regulations for retraining, the training and reemployment, services offered through TAAW have faced criticism for failing to adequately prepare workers for jobs that would pay comparable salaries to their previous positions. Those who were employed after completing training earned an average of $29,884 a year.[43] While this was an overall wage replacement of 80.9%, older workers had significantly inferior results. The average worker over 60 only recouped 55.2% of his or her salary.[44] Thirty percent of program participants in 2015 failed to complete their training.[45] Interestingly, the wage replacement rate even for those who did not complete or even enroll in training programs was the same 80% as for those who did, with similar median salaries to those who completed such programs.[46] These numbers only apply to the 57,000 workers who are approved under TAAW—not all employees who are laid off.

Trade Readjustment Allowance (TRA)

The Trade Readjustment Allowance program provides weekly income support to TAAW-certified workers who have used up unemployment compensation and are also enrolled in training programs. TRA is administered through state unemployment insurance systems, and is an individual entitlement. Payments are equal to the worker's final unemployment compensation check, which is calculated based on previous wages. The highest maximum weekly benefits from unemployment compensation were $698 (in Massachusetts) and the lowest was $240 (in Arizona).[47]

TRA in its current iteration has been criticized for creating poor incentives—for instance, extended unemployment compensation pays workers for prolonged periods

---

[40] Lynch (2016).

[41] *Ibid.*, p. 3.

[42] U.S. Department of Labor (2015).

[43] *Ibid.*, Table 18.

[44] *Ibid.*, Table 20.

[45] *Ibid.*, Table 10.

[46] *Ibid.*, Table 24.

[47] Lynch (2016).

of joblessness, which keeps workers out of the labor force and leads to lost experience in the interim.[48] Workers are eligible a total of 130 weeks of unemployment compensation and TRA benefits.[49]

Reemployment Trade Adjustment Assistance (RTAA)

RTAA, a wage insurance program for workers over age 50, provides cash payments to those who obtain reemployment at a lower wage. The program provides cash payments equal to 50% of the difference between the worker's previous, trade-affected job and the new job. The maximum is $10,000 over a 2-year period.

4.3 Firm-Related Programs

The rise of multinational corporations has created global value chains, which now account for 70% of global trade in goods, services, and capital goods.[50] The emergence of these value chains, while enabling U.S. firms to produce higher value-added products, has also led to certain firms becoming less competitive in the increasingly open global economy. TAA for Firms (TAAF) is designed to help trade-impacted firms improve performance.

The primary focus of TAAF is on struggling small and medium enterprises (SMEs). SMEs make up 98% of exporters in the U.S., and accounted for $471 billion in known value of good exports.[51] Despite manufacturing being responsible for 60% of U.S. exports, manufacturing for SMEs only account for less than 25% of exports—non-manufacturing and service companies create the majority of exports instead.[52] Despite strong ties to SMEs who add value to MNC exports, their positions may become increasingly precarious as foreign competitors move up the value chain and the U.S. continues to adopt liberalized trade policies.

TAAF and TAACs

The TAAF program is governed by the Economic Development Administration (EDA) in the U.S. Department of Commerce, and operates through eleven regional TAACs, which provide technical assistance to firms.[53] TAACs are comprised of consultants who can help firms identify resources and develop strategies to turn businesses around.[54] TAACs are granted funds to operate their programs. Neither funds nor direct financial assistance may be given to firms.

---

[48] Irwin (2016).

[49] Lynch (2016).

[50] Harrison (2014).

[51] Scott (2015).

[52] *Ibid.*

[53] Harrison (2014).

[54] *Ibid.*

To be granted assistance for TAAC consultants, firms must go through three stages: petition for certification, recovery planning, and business recovery plan implementation. In the first phase, the firm must document that it is impacted by trade through a three-factor test. First, a firm must show that "a significant number or proportion of workers in the firm," have or may have lost jobs.[55] Second, sales or production of at least 25% of goods have decreased significantly, and third, increased imports or competitive articles have "contributed importantly" to layoffs and the decline in sales and production.[56]

In the second phase of TAAF, the firm has 2 years to create and present a business recovery plan, called the Adjustment Proposal (AP). APs must first, reasonably "materially contribute" to the economic adjustment of the firm. Second, they must provide adequate consideration of the firm's workers. Finally, the AP must confirm that the firm will use its own resources for adjustment. TAACs assist with every step of the process.

Finally, in the third phase, the firm has up to 5 years to fully implement their projects, unless granted an extension. The EDA may provide financial assistance for project implementation of up to 75%, capped at $75,000.[57]

TAACs often pursue a variety of strategies to help firms, such as marketing and sales strategies, new products, or promotional initiatives. They also target production inefficiencies and can also develop debt-restructuring strategies.[58]

TAAF Results

In 2015, 113 out of 1,418 inquiries on TAAF were approved for the program.[59] All 113 companies were in the manufacturing sector. The states with the highest number of certified firms were Pennsylvania (12), Illinois (10), and Missouri (9).[60] Only 60% of firms completed the program in 2015, with others failing to move forward with their APs or going bankrupt.[61] Of the firms that completed the program, after 1 year, firms reported average sales increases of 20.8% and increased productivity of 18.1%. Despite these increases, average employment only increased by an average of 2.3%.[62]

As one can see, U.S. TAA policies are somewhat fragmented from other social welfare and infrastructure policies. TAA only addresses workers and firms who have been directly impacted by trade and do not consider those who are displaced by automation.

---

[55] The lesser of five percent of the work force or 50 workers. 13 C.F.R. 315.2.

[56] *Ibid.*

[57] U.S. Department of Commerce (2015).

[58] Harrison (2014).

[59] U.S. Department of Commerce (2015). See Exhibit 4.

[60] *Ibid.*

[61] *Ibid.*

[62] *Ibid.*

5 Beyond Liberal Economic Palliatives: A Policy Agenda

The essential logic of American policy to cope with globalization has been focused on weak efforts to assuage labor concerns, and to a lesser extent domestically affected firms, through the TAA program. Yet despite the possibility of TAA creating a compelling framework to help workers, firms, and communities, most parties fail to gain eligibility to take part in the program. In 2015, fewer than 20,000 displaced workers were ever enrolled in TAAW, and a significant number still resorted to lower paying jobs even after completing training programs. In addition, only 113 firms, all in manufacturing, were enrolled in TAAF, and while they saw around 20% increases in productivity and sales, there was only an average of 2.3% in job increases at these firms, despite a significant number of jobs having been lost (a criterion for initial eligibility).

Given the ineffectiveness of current U.S. economic policy in helping workers and firms cope with displacement caused by globalization, what types of strategies work? In our view, the U.S. should pursue four methods for revitalizing trade-displaced firms, workers, and communities. First, the USTR should pursue agreements that are more beneficial to Americans more broadly (and not just American MNCs), and should enforce the rules of free trade against competitors who are using protectionist policies and currency manipulation to the detriment of U.S. producers.

Second, the government should devote more resources to labor-centric TAA and transition the program from only addressing jobs lost to trade to also addressing jobs lost due to automation. Even with TAA programs, the U.S. lacks comprehensive social programs that create a safety net for workers and communities looking for new sources of income. Without universal education, housing, and healthcare, families face fewer options when impacted by trade and automation. In contrast to countries such as Germany and the Netherlands, which both have relatively similar policies in labor adjustment to the U.S., but significant social welfare and infrastructure investment programs, the U.S. remains far behind in helping its firms and workers.

Third, investing in human capital can reduce frictional unemployment and help better manage churning, rapidly employing displaced workers through giving them relevant skills. Here, differentiating by age is crucial. Existing programs use the same training resources for all displaced labor, which can be beneficial to the younger generation but a challenge for older people.

Finally, the U.S. should focus on creating better programs to phase out inefficient firms and keeping communities strong after they undergo massive job losses.

5.1 Better Trade Agreements

Although pulling out of trade agreements and trade deals may not be the optimal way to improve American labor conditions, the U.S. government still must regulate the global trade arena to ensure fair competition. The U.S. remains highly competitive in several areas—software, hardware, services, and agriculture to name a few—and pulling out of agreements would harm innovation and competitiveness in these areas.[63] Top U.S. exports (outside of services) include refined machines, engines and pumps, electronic equipment, and spacecraft, helicopters and airplanes.[64]

Protectionism is also not a sustainable solution. While occasionally effective in fostering growth for nascent industries in developing countries, import substitution industrialization and other forms of protectionism are often not conducive to sustained development. As evidenced by past attempts to impose tariffs, when one country is barred from importing to the U.S., others fill the void—for instance, when President Obama imposed duties on automobile tires from China, these jobs did not shift to the U.S. Instead, they went to Indonesia and Thailand, with little impact on American labor.[65]

Industrial policy, when deployed with precision, can still foster industries that are struggling and reduce lead-time for workers switching jobs from languishing sectors. China has effectively picked winners in their economy and invested in human capital and infrastructure growth to enable increased innovation. The announcement of it's Made in 2025 program that targets ten key industries through aggressive industrial policy measures clearly demonstrates that some type of neoclassical convergence among countries in their economic policies is a naïve hope.

The U.S. should push back against trading partners that have engaged in non-competitive practices as it has been doing, but without adequate support from its allies. China has heavily subsidized a range of industries such as steel, wind turbines, solar panels, and textile manufacturing.[66] Using discriminatory regulations to foster growth in these sectors, China has given its companies an advantage in production, enabling China to sell products for lower prices and harming otherwise competitive companies in the U.S. and Europe.[67] By questioning these practices, the U.S. can restore free market capitalism rather than placing its own industries in peril by failing to address the industrial policies employed by other countries. These policies will not only help struggling companies but also dominant American companies—trade barriers remain in several service sectors such as telecommunications, architecture, engineering, and financial services, which are significant areas of U.S. export dominance.[68] These business service sectors employ 25% of Americans already, despite trade barriers, as compared to manufacturing's 9%.[69]

Beyond questioning the highly protectionist policies used by its foreign competitors, the U.S. should demand that its trading partners uphold the labor, environmental,

---

[63] Irwin (2016).

[64] MIT (2015).

[65] Irwin (2016).

[66] See the special issue on industrial policy edited by Vinod K. Aggarwal and Simon J. Evenett, Industrial Policy in the Post-Crisis Era, *Business and Politics*, December 2014.

[67] Alden and Litan (2016).

[68] *Ibid.*

[69] *Ibid.*

and IP regulations that the WTO calls for in its rules. Beyond the WTO dispute settlement system, the government must initiate investigations and use U.S. trade laws to protect companies and employees from unfair trade practices more quickly.[70]

5.2 Labor Adjustment

The U.S. government must also invest in human capital to regain a competitive labor market. By creating a more dynamic workforce, the U.S. can enable its labor force to better adjust to economic trends. As a result of job displacement through trade, ICITE calls for supportive policies—stable macroeconomic policies, adequate property rights, effective regulation, and well-designed public investments to offset the results of trade, creating policies to "help workers to move more quickly into new, higher productivity jobs" and "attenuate human costs of normal job transitions and unemployment arising from economic shocks as well as lay the foundation for more rapid growth."[71]

Beyond creating this safety net, the federal government should create targeted programs for three generations of American workers whose jobs have been lost to either trade or technology: workers near retirement (50+), middle age (40–60), and younger people starting their careers (18–40). These figures are based on the U.S. Department of Labor's averages for retraining. Workers from under 30 to late 30 s who received TAA training replaced wages by 92.5–106.7%. Those from 40 to 50 received 80%, and workers over 50 received significantly less, with workers over 60 only regaining 55%. As a result, the three groups are the older generation (50+) the middle generation (35–50), and the younger generation (under 35). We can divide each group based on their wage replacement rate, age, and work experience to consider how to create a comprehensive program that both protects displaced workers but also creates new opportunities for those who may pursue new careers.

Of all workers who have been displaced, trade adjustment has most significantly failed the older generation nearing retirement. These workers often have families and relied on a pension, and no longer have the resources to retrain into a new profession or move to a new area where jobs are more plentiful. As a result, displaced workers over 50 should be provided with a more comprehensive safety net if their jobs are displaced not only as a result of trade but also by automation or other unemployment challenges. Such provisions should include universal healthcare and potentially income supplement support. Current RTAA, or supplemental wage insurance, is capped at $10,000 over 2 years. This does not provide enough for workers who previously made significantly more and were responsible for supporting their families.

A more controversial solution would be to create a guaranteed minimum income, funded by reductions in unemployment benefits, social security, or food stamps. This

---

[70] *Ibid.*

[71] Newfarmer and Sztajerowska (2012).

method has been advocated by some economists, and while it would be an effective safety net, it may disincentivize future generations from pursuing education and employment.[72] Instead, a pilot program could have two components: enacting an age minimum and tying income received to a purpose. In this case, the age minimum would be 50, and the wages could be tied to traditionally unpaid services—volunteering at schools through coaching teams, leading scout trips; volunteering at shelters; taking classes; pursuing and creating art; or caretaking by delivering meals to the elderly or helping them run errands. Such programs would ensure that recipients still have work, even without jobs, and would create purpose.

Middle-aged workers between 35 and 50 present the greatest challenge for labor adjustment policy. Most low-skilled and uneducated workers in this category did not go to college and are now seeing jobs they believed they would keep after high school becoming increasingly irrelevant. Workers in this group also often have families who rely on their income and children who may no longer be able to afford public higher education as a result of this unemployment.

Because these workers are younger than their 50 plus counterparts, pushing them into retirement is premature and unproductive. Instead, TAA should expand retraining programs for this generation and help them find service-oriented jobs that remain in the community are sustainable. One method of creating incentives to find new jobs is to expand RTAA to younger workers who lost their jobs due to automation and trade. The inclusion of workers whose jobs are lost to automation is crucial in changing perceptions on trade—while exports and trade are often blamed for job losses, as we have seen in manufacturing, automation can play an even greater role. A newer approach to covering these Americans must be conceived to bolster labor and communities.

The U.S. should provide more comprehensive training programs for its workers to enter non-tradable jobs such as healthcare, services, and education. To incentivize entry into these training programs, the U.S. should sponsor employees undergoing these programs to provide basic income while training is in progress. Through subsiding education for middle-aged workers, those who face layoffs as a result of trade or automation are less likely to give up on their jobs searches and exit the labor market and instead pursue new opportunities.

Investing in primary and secondary education for the younger generation is a crucial element to human capital development—the American education system is far behind Germany and the Netherlands, falling behind other countries especially in math and science. College and university level education is also becoming increasingly out of reach for many Americans—with cuts to scholarship programs and academic grants, students are unable to afford tuition. The U.S. should look to both Germany and the Netherlands on how to offset education costs, devoting a higher percentage of GDP to education. Although cutting tuition completely seems unlikely, offsetting some costs to promote increased access to education would create significant benefits. Another option is community colleges and vocational schools—these

---

[72] Murray (2016).

1 Robots Versus Aliens: The Backlash Against Globalization

institutions are already lower cost than their 4-year counterparts, and if they were made free, would provide access for students without the sharp increase to taxpayers.

In addition to creating more social programs that defray the cost of higher education, the U.S. Department of Labor and Department of Education should pursue public–private partnerships in this area. Either department could create tax incentives for companies to create paid apprenticeships for students—either while in college or as summer internship, or post-college. By guaranteeing employment after college and aiding with scholarships, companies can create their own pipeline for bright students and create new opportunities for younger people now entering the labor market, discouraging students from avoiding college and trying to work at factories or other jobs that require fewer expenses to enter but are more likely to be displaced by trade or automation in the future. Instead, students and younger workers can pursue jobs in engineering, healthcare, business services, and other high value industries that are U.S. export strengths.

5.3 Firm Adjustment

Firms are a more complex challenge than labor—subsidizing failing industries is not as effective as picking winners, as China has done, and instead, the government should enable firms to pivot into more profitable areas. Our first strategy of restoring truly fair and competitive market practices would help in this area—the U.S. is more efficient in several areas, but not against the heavily subsidized companies that are able to offer lower prices.

Aiding struggling firms, while successful under TAAF in increasing profits and productivity by 20%, still do not lead to returned jobs. Instead, the U.S., in addition to helping struggling companies create more lean and efficient companies, should provide incentives for these companies to expand into more lucrative industries either through expanding products or moving up the supply chain, and create incentives for hiring more employees. Manufacturing companies make up all of the firms aided under TAAF, and while manufacturing jobs are becoming rapidly automated, there are still value options higher on the supply chain, particularly looking to Germany as an example. Even in the U.S., high value manufacturing remains a strong export. For instance, aircraft and spacecraft exports have increased by 49.4% since 2011.[73]

5.4 Communities

Community development is also a priority in rural areas where towns are reliant on one or two industries for employment, such as coalmining or steel. Every additional trade-displaced worker is associated with other lost jobs in the community—when

---

[73] World's Top Exports (2017).

firms and individuals are displaced and jobs are moved to non-commutable areas, workers in non-tradable jobs face similar losses as a result of population decreases.[74] In less productive areas, fewer jobs are created as a result of falling demand for local goods, leading to lower prices. As a result, relocation elasticity, or the ability to find jobs in different sectors within the same community, are low and the least productive locations face their residents migrating away.

One area where Germany and the Netherlands significantly devote resources as compared to the U.S. is through their community development programs. Beyond investing in human capital through education and healthcare, both countries foster infrastructure development and local incentives to draw new business.

Infrastructure development serves two purposes: First, rebuilding communities requires a significant investment of labor and resources. As a result, promoting direct infrastructure development through building roads, bridges, schools, and other public institutions can create jobs within a community and employ firms that may be struggling as the result of an exodus of workers.

Second, revitalizing communities can draw other businesses into town. The U.S. should also look to creating a more robust digital infrastructure system, similar to the Dutch, establishing more internet access points and opportunities for exchanges, which could increase education—training programs can be offered online, allowing students and displaced workers both learn new skills that are increasingly relevant in the global economy. Having strong educational institutions creates a better work-force, which can create network effects—better students draw better universities, and better universities create students who look to start innovative companies—this can be seen in Ann Arbor and Durham, where having strong educational institutions nearby encourages companies to establish hubs near strong research centers.

Finally, the U.S. must establish better social welfare programs. One of these goals is to standardize its education system. Although compulsory education mandates that all students attend schools until 18, the quality of this education varies wildly, creating students who are underprepared for college or vocational programs. In addition, universal healthcare, which was threatened by the Trump administration, has saved thousands with preexisting conditions and millions who previously were unable to afford healthcare.[75]

Not every rural town has access to world-class universities like the University of Michigan and Duke, however. An alternative is creating local incentives to establish new businesses. This can be seen in Akron, Ohio, which has developed incuba-tors to create new "Silicon Valley" style growth and networks.[76] Examples of these incentives include creating incubators that provide cities with Wi-Fi and technology classes, as well as tax incentives for bringing business. Given that land is significantly cheaper in these areas than in San Francisco and New York, the Midwest can draw significant companies to establish regional offices with stronger physical and digital infrastructure.

---

[74] Federal Reserve Board (2017).

[75] CNN (2016).

[76] Huffington Post (2011).

6 Conclusion

The backlash against globalization is not simply a temporary phenomenon, led by venal politicians.[77] With changing patterns in technology, trade, outsourcing, and immigration, current U.S. policy designed to address the domestic fallout of globalization and its discontents, and to prevent national backslash, has proved wanting. This chapter has argued that much of this lack of attention to coping with both the displacement of firms and labor has been driven by an unwarranted faith in the smooth adjustment of production factors that is the bread and butter of neoliberal economics. By engaging in apolitical analysis because of the complexity of including political factors in economic modeling, economists have been blind-sided by the rise of anti-globalization. By rushing to catch up with the newfound appeal of populism, but being still wedded to a fallacious neoclassical economic paradigm that ignores the role of the state and the importance of political lobbying, economists have generally recommended policies that are simply more of the same. As we have suggested, attention to neomercantilist thinking may help us to better understand new political pressures in the global economy. To be clear: the point is not that neoclassical prescriptions and hopes would not be optimal—but rather that the models of how the real world works are simply wrong.

Our examination of U.S. policies with respect to workers and firms demonstrates that the palliative that the U.S. government has pursued has been unable to cope with the displacements resulting from trends in technology, outsourcing, immigration, and trade. Policies that could lead to better outcomes, as we argue, should not be seen as being on the left or being on the right. An enhanced approach to helping workers and firms, policies that countries such as Germany and the Netherlands, among others, have pursued with greater success, show that there are better alternatives. And it is also time to recognize that having a "heavy rider" such as China in the global liberal trading order will spell the death knell of the post-WWII international economic order. Ironically, the collateral damage in this game will not only be in the U.S. and China, but the rest of the world as well.

Acknowledgement An earlier version of this chapter was prepared for presentation at the ISAS Workshop: "Revisiting Globalization: Comparing Country Experiences from South Asia and the World", 12 October 2017, Singapore. We would like to thank Arnav Singhvi and Zhenyu Zhang for valuable research assistance. For comments, we are grateful to Jerry Ding, Lilac Peterson, and Anastasia Pyrinis. Vinod Aggarwal would like to thank the Ministry of Education and the National Research Foundation of the Republic of Korea (NRF-2017S1A3A2067636) and the UC National Laboratory Fees Research Program. Sonia Aggarwal is a lawyer at a fintech firm in San Francisco but has written this chapter in her personal capacity.

---

[77] Aggarwal (2016).

References

Aggarwal, Sonia N. and Vinod K. Aggarwal. 2016. "The Political Economy of Industrial Policy." Working Paper. 16 (1). Berkeley, CA: Berkeley APEC Study Center.

Aggarwal, Vinod K. 1983. "The Domestic and International Politics of Protection in the U.S. Textile and Apparel Industries." In John Zysman and Laura Tyson, eds., American Industry In International Competition (Ithaca: Cornell University Press, 1983), pp. 249–312.

Aggarwal, Vinod K. 1985. *Liberal Protectionism: The International Politics of Organized Textile Trade.* Berkeley, California: University of California Press.

Aggarwal, Vinod K. 2013. US Free Trade agreements and Linkages. *International Negotiation* 18 (1): 89–110.

Aggarwal, Vinod K. 2016. "The Liberal Trading Order Under Assault: A US Perspective." *Global Asia* 11 (4): 11–0–113.

Aggarwal, Vinod K. and Simon J. Evenett. 2014. "Industrial Policy in the Post-Crisis Era." *Business and Politics*, 16(4).

Alden, Edward and Robert Litan. 2016. "A Winning Trade Policy for the United States." *TheCouncil on Foreign Relations.* https://www.cfr.org/report/winning-trade-policy-united-states

BBC News. 2016. "Why is globalization under attack?" http://www.bbc.com/news/business-375 54634

Bowen, Laura. 2015. "Rethinking the optimal tariff theory." *Chicago Policy Review.* http://chicag opolicyreview.org/2015/01/15/rethinking-the-optimal-tariff-theory/

Burtless, Gary. 1996. "Worsening American Income: Inequality: Is world trade to blame?" *Brookings Institution.* https://www.brookings.edu/articles/worsening-american-income-inequality-is-world-trade-to-blame/

Choi, Jongwon, Huck-ju Kwon, and Min Gyo Koo. 2017. *The Korean Government and Public Policies in a Development Nexus,* Volume 2. Springer.

CNN. 2016. "Who would lose coverage under Obamacare repeal? Trump supporters." http://money.cnn.com/2016/12/07/news/economy/obamacare-uninsured-trump/index.html

Collins, Benjamin. 2018. "Trade Adjustment Assistance for Workers and the TAA Reauthorization Act of 2015." *Congressional Research Service.*

Compa, Lance, and Jeffrey S. Vogt. 2001. Labor Rights in the Generalized System ofPreferences: A 20-Year Review. *Comparative Labor Law and Policy Journal* 22 (2/3): 199–238.

Eichengreen, Barry. 2016. "Will Globalization go into reverse." *Prospect Magazine.* https://www.prospectmagazine.co.uk/magazine/will-globalisation-go-into-reverse-brexit-donald-trump

Federal Reserve Bank of San Francisco. 2001. "FRBSF Economic Letter."http://www.frbsf.org/economic-research/publications/economicletter/2001/october/unemployment-and-productivity/.

Federal Reserve Board. 2017. "The Unequal Reallocation of Trade-Induced Job Losses: Evidence-from the U.S. Trade Adjustment Assistance."

Fefer, Rachel F. 2020. "Trade Adjustment Assistance for Firms." *Congressional Research Service.*

Harrison, Glenn. 2014. "Trade Adjustment Assistance for Firms: Economic, Program, and PolicyIssues." *Congressional Research Service.*

Hirschman, Jacob. 1945. *National Power and the Structure of Foreign Trade.* University ofCalifornia Press.

Hornbeck, J.F. 2013. "Trade Adjustment Assistance and Its Role in U.S. Trade Policy."*Congressional Research Service.* https://fas.org/sgp/crs/misc/R41922.pdf

Huffington Post. 2011. "Will the Midwest Become the Next Silicon Valley?" http://www.huffingtonpost.com/ray-leach/is-midwest-us-the-next-si_b_820032.html

Humphrey, Thomas. 1987. "Classical and Neoclassical Roots of the Theory of Optimum Tariffs". *Federal Reserve Bank of Richmond Economic Review* 73(4): 17–28.

Irwin, Douglas. 2016. "The Truth About Trade." *Foreign Affairs.* 95 (84). https://www.foreignaffairs.com/articles/2016-06-13/truth-about-trade

Lawrence, Robert Z. 1977. "An Analysis of the 1977 U.S. Trade Deficit." *Brookings Institution.*https://www.brookings.edu/bpea-articles/an-analysis-of-the-1977-u-s-trade-deficit/

1 Robots Versus Aliens: The Backlash Against Globalization

Lynch, Karen E. et al. 2016. "Labor, Health and Human Services, and Education: FY2016 Appropriations." *Congressional Research Service.*

Massachusetts Institute of Technology. 2015.http://atlas.media.mit.edu/en/profile/country/usa/

Murray, Charles. 2016. "A Guaranteed Income for Every American." *The Wall Street Journal*.www. wsj.com/articles/a-guaranteed-income-for-every-american-1464969586

Newfarmer, Richard and Monika Sztajerowska. 2012. "Trade and Employment in a Fast-Changing World." In *Policy Priorities for International Trade and Jobs,* edited by DouglasLippoldt. Paris: Organization for Economic Cooperation and Development.

Scott, Lauren. 2015. "Profile of U.S. Exporters Highlights Contributions of Small- and Medium-Sized Businesses." *Tradeology: The Official Blog of the ITA.* https://blog.trade.gov/2015/04/08/profile-of-u-s-exporters-highlights-contributions-of-small-and-medium-sized-businesses/

Sherk, James. 2010. "Technology Explains Drop in Manufacturing Jobs." *The Heritage Foundation.* http://www.heritage.org/jobs-and-labor/report/technology-explains-dropmanufacturing-jobs.

U.S. Department of Commerce. 2015. "Fiscal Year 2015 Annual Report to Congress: TradeAdjustment Assistance for Firms Program." *Economic Development Administration.* https://www.eda.gov/pdf/annual-reports/taaf/FY15-TAAF-Annual-Report-to-Congress.pdf

U.S. Department of Commerce. 2019. "Press Release." https://www.eda.gov/news/pressreleases/2019/10/23/taac.htm..

U.S. Department of Labor. 2015. "Trade Adjustment Assistance for Workers Program: FiscalYear 2015." https://www.doleta.gov/tradeact/docs/AnnualReport15.pdf

U.S. Department of Labor. 2018. "TAACCCT: Program Fact Sheet." https://www.dol.gov/sites/dol gov/files/ETA/TAACCCT/pdfs/TAACCCT-Fact-Sheet-Program-Information.pdf.

U.S. Department of Labor. 2019. "Notice of Proposed Rule Making by the Department of Labor." https://www.dol.gov/newsroom/releases/eta/eta20191106

Viner, Jacob. 1948. Power Versus Plenty as Objectives of Foreign Policy in the Seventeenth andEighteenth Centuries. *World Politics* 1 (1): 1–29.

Vogel, David. 1999. "The Politics of Trade and Environment in the United States." Working Paper94. Berkeley, CA: Berkeley Roundtable on the International Economy, UC Berkeley.

White House Blog. 2015. On Trade, Here's What the President Signed into Law. https://obamaw hitehouse.archives.gov/blog/2015/06/29/trade-here-s-what-president-signed-law.

World's Top Exports. 2017. http://www.worldstopexports.com.

Chapter 2
Revisiting Globalization: A Post-COVID19 Perspective

Amitendu Palit

1 The Washington Consensus, US–China Divide, and De-Globalization: Lessons from the Post-Liberal World Order

The outbreak of COVID19 from early 2020 occurred just about three decades after the collapse of the Berlin Wall in November 1989 and the reunification of Germany in October 1990. The unification of East and West Germany, and the disintegration of the Soviet Union in December 1991, marked the formal end of the Cold War that had characterized a bipolar global order for more than four decades after the end of the Second World War. As the ideological polarization of the world, symbolized by the American and Soviet blocs and their respective allies, ceased to exist, so did, by a large measure, policies, and institutions shaping socialist economic systems. The spirit of market-based economic policies reflected in the unrestricted flow of goods and services across national borders, easier cross-country movement of people, enabling policies facilitating cross-border movement of capital, and championing of private entrepreneurship, were emphasized across continents and regions by a unipolar world order headed by the US. These were largely symbolized through the much-discussed and debated 'Washington Consensus'—a set of policies and economic reforms articulated by economist John Williamson—with large buy-in from the Bretton Woods institutions (International Monetary Fund and World Bank) and US government agencies.[1] While the construct was primarily an effort to shift political consensus from heavy state control of national economies to greater role of private enterprise and management, it did, on occasions, encourage the growth

---

[1] Irwin (2020).

A. Palit (✉)
Institute of South Asian Studies (ISAS), National University of Singapore, 29 Heng Mui Keng Terrace, Singapore, Singapore
e-mail: isasap@nus.edu.sg

© The Author(s), under exclusive license to Springer Nature Singapore Pte Ltd. 2022
A. Palit (ed.), *Globalisation Impacts*, International Law and the Global South,
https://doi.org/10.1007/978-981-16-7185-2_2

of extreme positions advocating minimalist governments and excessive focus on markets, defeating the original intent of the Consensus.[2]

1.1 Economic Globalization and Washington Consensus: Trials and Tribulations

The Washington Consensus included, inter alia, policies encouraging the privatization of state-owned enterprises, better targeting of public expenditure by reducing wasteful subsidies, enhancing fiscal discipline, liberalizing exchange rates, allowing foreign investments in sectors of the economy hitherto closed to foreign capital, and advancing trade liberalization by rationalizing on-border import tariffs.[3] The policies were pushed actively by the International Monetary Fund (IMF) and World Bank in various countries of the world in support of higher economic growth and stronger macroeconomic fundamentals. Structural reforms gathered pace in several countries, including in large emerging market developing countries like China and India. China, which had begun gradually liberalizing its economy from 1978, embarked on an aggressive restructuring of its state-owned enterprises, while allowing foreign investment in several sectors of the economy. It also embraced large-scale trade liberalization involving lowering tariff protection on domestic agriculture as part of its 'reform' commitments in joining the WTO. India, on the other hand, embraced market-oriented economic policies from the early 1990s by cutting import tariffs, devaluating its currency, allowing private enterprise and foreign investment in domestic industry, liberalizing the capital market, and beginning divestment of government equity in state enterprises. Several other economies adopted similar policies with the core principles of the 'Washington Consensus' remaining the preferred approach for economic management well into the first decade of the current century.

Economic globalization, as spearheaded by the Consensus, encountered a major setback following the global financial crisis of 2008. The crisis invited sharp criticism of liberal market-oriented economic policies for exacerbating inequalities among countries, communities, and economic classes. Interestingly, the criticism of globalization was particularly trenchant in several advanced, high-income Western economies, notably the US, the UK, and Europe. The anger and frustration over economic policies legitimized by the Washington Consensus, and strongly advanced by institutions and experts from the West, notably the US and the UK, was ironic. The irony was experienced strongly through electoral outcomes influenced by divisive votes in the US and the UK in 2016, leading to the entry of President Donald Trump in office in the US, and the formalization of the UK's separation from the European Union through Brexit. These far-reaching political outcomes, however, were by no means sufficient for obliterating the anger against globalization. Indeed, surveys carried out in the US and the UK of specific demographic focus groups in

---

[2] Ibid.

[3] Williamson (2002).

2 Revisiting Globalization: A Post-COVID19 Perspective

2019, before the outbreak of COVID19, point to the prevalence of 'left behind' and 'swept up' opinions harboring strong sentiments against economic globalization.[4] Most of these opinions, including those of the 'left behind' lamenting the loss of jobs due to deindustrialization as local industries closed and jobs were outsourced elsewhere, and the 'swept up' suffering dislocation from local roots and communities upon responding to opportunities created by globalization, were identical in their feelings of alienation and loss.[5] Similar feelings were noted in the rise of populist nationalist political groups in Europe, which, while not being able to win elections, did nevertheless underscore their prevalence in the continent.[6]

The larger global outlook, before the outbreak of COVID19, was conspicuous by the prominence of angry voices in the West chastising economic globalization. Much of the ire was directed at China. In this respect, the fault line between the West, and China, which looks bottomless and unbridgeable more than a year after the outbreak of COVID19 in January 2020, had its depth dug well, even before the pandemic struck. The early seeds were sown after identifying China as the main beneficiary of economic globalization at the expense of the US and other Western economies.

The key narrative in this regard pointed to the tremendous benefits China obtained by 'taking away' production from the West. Multinational firms, managing various cross-border production networks and supply chains, were quick to realize and act upon the efficiency gains offered by China, and several other developing and emerging market economies that had cheap skilled workers for carrying out a variety of labor-intensive industrial functions. The more labor-intensive parts of various manufacturing supply chains moved out of their original hubs in the West as a result. China was a huge beneficiary of this outsourcing as it combined the advantages of cheap labor with the ability to produce large volumes in a short time. As discontent over lost jobs in major industries—automobiles, metals, textiles, chemicals, machinery—galvanized into political movements, China became widely identified as the villain by many of these. Along with China, India too was held responsible for job losses in the West, particularly over IT jobs in the US getting to be entirely dominated by Indian professionals.[7]

---

[4] Silver et al. (2020).

[5] Ibid. Clearly, assessing globalization through its impacts on immediate local communities and neighborhoods, often generate more adverse feelings, as opposed to more macro and big perspective visualizations of how economic globalization has impacted countries and their populations as a whole. The sharp chasm between the negative and positive views on globalization are easy to comprehend if viewed through such lenses.

[6] Cuperus (2017).

[7] Sengupta (2018).

1.2 US-China Divide and the Post-Liberal World Order: Rivalry Hastening De-Globalization

In the years leading to the pandemic, especially the later years of the decade of the 2020s, the world witnessed a remarkable twist in perspectives toward globalization emanating from the US and China, respectively. China emerged as the strongest global voice defending economic globalization. Addressing the world's largest and most influential gathering of business leaders at the annual meeting of the World Economic Forum in January 2017, Chinese President Xi Jinping described economic globalization as the 'Pandora's Box' and argued that it cannot be held responsible for global challenges like the plight of refugees. In an interesting counterpoint to the narrative of blaming economic globalization for the financial crisis of 2008, he mentioned the latter was not 'an inevitable outcome' of the former, but was the consequence of chase for-profit and imperfect regulations. Painting China as the poster-boy of economic globalization, he underlined his country as both a beneficiary of and a contributor to, globalization.[8] The speech delivered a few days before Donald Trump took office as the US president on 20 January 2017, was in marked contrast to the cynicism of globalization evident in the US president's inaugural speech. The speech was replete with sentiments of the 'left behind in its emphasis on lost jobs and closed factories. Without naming China and other countries, the 'exploitation' of America by others was made abundantly clear by President Trump: "We must protect our borders from the ravages of other countries making our products, stealing our companies and destroying our jobs".[9] The contrast between the two speeches made a noted commentator describe the Chinese president's speech as the one that would have been expected from the US president![10]

By the end of the last decade, the global order was visibly split among the US and China with their respective allies. The US allies included the world's major democracies, which had grown increasingly wary of China's efforts to use economic clout for geopolitical control. Such efforts by China were most conspicuous in its articulation of the Belt and Road Initiative (BRI). A humongous multi-modal connectivity project, the BRI promises to revolutionize connectivity between Asia, Africa, and Europe. Its land corridors aim to connect China to Europe and Africa, through contiguous landmasses of Central Asia, Russia, West Asia, South Asia, and Southeast Asia. The initiative also includes the twenty-first-century Maritime Silk Road, for connecting China and the Far East, to Africa and Europe, through the waters of the South China Sea, the South Pacific Ocean, the Bay of Bengal, the Indian Ocean, the Arabian Sea, the Persian Gulf, and the Mediterranean Sea. The final connectivity component of

---

[8] 'China's Xi Jinping defends globalization from the Davos stage', World Economic Forum, 17 January 2017; https://www.weforum.org/agenda/2017/01/chinas-xi-jinping-defends-globalization-from-the-davos-stage/. Accessed on 23 March 2021.

[9] 'Full text: 2017 Donald Trump Inauguration speech transcript', Politico; 20 January 2017; https://www.politico.com/story/2017/01/full-text-donald-trump-inauguration-speech-transcript-233907. Accessed on 23 March 2021.

[10] Wolf (2017).

2 Revisiting Globalization: A Post-COVID19 Perspective

the project is its digital arm, the 'Information Silk Road', for linking countries and regions of the BRI brought together by land and sea, through cyberspace.[11]

For China, the BRI is an initiative to promote a world order different from that weaved around alliances and dynamics between the US, Europe, and Russia after the Second World War. Such a construct, arguably, is President Xi's vision for enabling China to generate new power relations through new partnerships and alliances.[12] The ambition is intimidating, given the strong possibility of China 'weaponizing' economic clout for geopolitical gains. The BRI has created widespread apprehensions of China's ability to do so, as an inevitable impact of the generous soft loans and investments on easy terms to various countries for building connectivity infrastructure. Several countries, while eager to receive support for building infrastructure, are arguably not financially robust enough to repay the financial obligations. They, therefore, can get 'beholden' to China in a manner that leads to compromising their geopolitical autonomies.[13] India, which has been particularly wary of the deleterious consequences of expanding the Chinese strategic footprint in its neighborhood, has drawn specific attention to indebtedness caused by BRI and its consequent ramifications.[14] China's ostensible efforts to weaponize its ability to fund infrastructure development in infrastructure-deficient countries, as well as the control it has on global supply chains[15] (a point looked at in closer detail in the next section) does not, however, make it exceptional. A similar tendency has been noted for the US during the Trump Administration. The unilateral trade actions initiated by the Trump Administration against trade partners with whom it runs large bilateral trade deficits reflected a policy stance where the US was unhesitant to use its dominant position in the international economic, and geopolitical global order, for coercing countries to adjust trade and economic relations in a manner suiting its national interests.[16]

A survey of the global economic and political landscape before the outbreak of COVID19 makes it distinctly clear that the outlook for economic globalization is hardly comparable to what it was in the early 1990s. Washington Consensus policies, while not entirely relegated to the background, have encountered strong resistance, in countries that were its active promoters. Indeed, these policies are no longer being owned by the US, whose experts and institutions were their foremost backers. Many among the latter, such as the IMF and World Bank, might still be supporting these policies. However, the Trump Administration's emphasis on 'America First' and obvious disapproval of economic globalization has left US pro-globalization institutions bereft of the mighty heft that American political patronage to globalization always provided.

While not advocating ownership of the Washington Consensus, China has emerged as the most vocal supporter of economic globalization. While pronouncing

---

[11] Kadi (2019).

[12] Kondapalli (2017).

[13] In Asia, such concerns have been particularly strong for Sri Lanka, Pakistan, and Maldives.

[14] Palit (2017).

[15] Braw (2020).

[16] Mullan (2020).

the support, China has left no doubts about its perspectives on globalization, which, notwithstanding similarities with the Washington Consensus, is nonetheless seasoned by the Chinese vision of a 'socialist market economy'. The original Washington Consensus, and the fundamentals of economic globalization, therefore, while not being formally abandoned, does face a severe crisis of commitment. This crisis for economic globalization, in terms of lack of strong political commitment, is compounded by a crisis for political globalization arising from the US–China rift. The rivalries between the world's largest economies and major powers escalated to a point of serious hostilities even before the outbreak of COVID19. These tensions and confrontations aggravated due to the COVID19 as discussed in the next section.

2 COVID19 and Its Aftermath: Challenged Institutions, New Supply Chains, and the Overarching Politics

A tendency toward de-globalization had gathered considerable strength in the last decade and just before the outbreak of COVID19. The tendency was being fostered by two prominent drivers. The first of these, as discussed in the previous section, was the growth of positions in the West, particularly in the US, of current global trade and business rules working against country-specific national interests and benefitting China and several other developing countries.[17] The sharpest manifestation of the US's unhappiness over global trade rules was its demand to 'reform' the WTO by reviewing flexibilities available for developing countries.[18] The demand, and earlier US actions of imposing unilateral tariffs on steel and aluminum imports along with several imports specifically from China, outlined the US determination to act against China's perceived 'advantages' in what according to it was a deeply flawed global system of trade rules. These actions by the Trump Administration sent a strong signal to the world over the world's largest economy, and champion of economic globalization for decades, looking to destabilize a trade order that had expanded based on in-built flexibilities for developing countries. The signal was intended not just for China but also large emerging market developing countries like India and Turkey, for both of which the US withdrew preferential access for exports under its Generalized System of Preferences (GSP). It was clear that from a US perspective the global trade order of the WTO, along with special and differential conditions that had become an integral part of global trade rules, as well as those in bilateral relations between the developed 'North' and the developing 'South', needed to change. Economic

---

[17] Trump lashes out at rich economies' 'unfair' WTO advantage, The Straits Times, 28 July 2019; https://www.straitstimes.com/world/united-states/trump-targets-china-in-call-for-wto-to-ref orm-developing-country-status. Accessed on 29 March 2021.

[18] Trump targets China in call for WTO to reform 'developing' country status, Reuters, 27 July 2019; https://www.reuters.com/article/us-usa-trade-wto-idUSKCN1UL2G6. Accessed on 29 March 2021.

globalization, facilitated through the WTO's rules for years, faced the huge challenge of lack of acceptability, threatening its core.

The second driver of the tendency toward de-globalization, again as outlined in the earlier section, was the deep cleavage of mistrust emerging between the US and China. The context of the mistrust has been explained. But what is perhaps important to note is that the mistrust had much to do with the exceptional economic rise of China and the geopolitical influence that it has been able to command from the rise.[19] China's ability to challenge the US and its allies on major global issues, and claim leadership on global public concerns (e.g., climate change), business (e.g., the WEF address by President Xi mentioned earlier) and international development (e.g., through the leadership of development financial institutions like the Asian Infrastructure Investment Bank (AIIB) and New Development Bank (NDB)) has had profound implications on US–China ties. Healthy and stable ties between the US and China are imperative for the smooth functioning of the global economic and political orders. However, these ties are diverging rapidly making it exceptionally difficult for global rules-based institutions to function effectively.

The outbreak of COVID19 further damaged US–China relations. The impacts of the damage have led to several far-reaching developments. Notable among these, are the strains on global institutions such as the World Health Organisation (WHO) and the WTO; and efforts to recast existing production networks in form of regional and global supply chains into new ones identified by security partnerships. The impacts will be far-reaching for the world as it struggles to cope with the damages inflicted by COVID19.

2.1 Institutional Impacts: Wither WHO, WTO?

No other global institution has been as much in the spotlight after the outbreak of the COVID19 as the WHO. Under normal circumstances, such attention wouldn't have been surprising. As the leading multilateral body for addressing global health concerns, the WHO is expected to be at the forefront of global struggles for containing pandemics. It has unfailingly done so in the past during outbreaks caused by the H1N1, Zika, and Ebola viruses, as well as during the Severe Acute Respiratory Syndrome (SARS) outbreak in the early years of the century. During the COVID19 outbreak, which began from its identification in the Wuhan province of China in early January 2020, WHO has been in news for various reasons. Apart from its role in monitoring the global status of the pandemic and working with various countries for its management, the WHO has also been a victim of the tensions between China and the US.

---

[19] The US–China competition has been described as 'the struggle of the generation between democracy and autocracy' with US apprehensions over China extending beyond its economic power and influence to greater fears about the purported spread and appeal of the Chinese political systems. Dealing with a China that's not like us; EastAsiaForum, 29 March 2021; https://www.eastasiaf orum.org/2021/03/29/dealing-with-a-china-thats-not-like-us/. Accessed on 29 March 2021.

From the time COVID19 was identified, and the WHO's eventual declaration of its outbreak as a pandemic, a great amount of public opinion was expressed on articulating conspiracy theories around China's role in the spread of the virus, and the WHO's perceived reluctance to blame China for the catastrophe. The criticism of the WHO led to the demand for it conducting an independent inquiry into the origins of the virus in China. The demand was moved by the European Union and Australia and supported by a large number of WHO members.[20] But the most serious allegation against the WHO was leveled by President Trump who accused it of working with China in covering up the incidence of the virus in its early days, and threatened to pull the US out of the WHO[21] leading China to expectedly retaliate and accuse the US of spreading conspiracies.[22] Indeed, the plight of the world's most significant health agency, in the middle of vicious invectives being traded by the US and China,[23] reflected an emerging, and likely to become enduring, the character of the current global world order: the heightened geopolitical power rivalries between the US and China in the post-liberal global order of the twenty-first century. War-like phrases and casting of aspersions characterize the rivalry making it difficult for an organization like the WHO to perform its core responsibilities of managing global health.[24]

The WHO didn't distinguish itself in the early stages of the pandemic, most notably by underestimating the severity of the contagion. At the same time, it was also relying largely on China, which till then was the epicenter of the pandemic, in learning more about the nature of the virus and its impacts. COVID19's identification as a novel strain of the SARS group of viruses might have influenced the WHO's delays in declaring a pandemic. It did rely heavily on the feedback from China on the virus and erred in not urging countries to resort to curbs faster, particularly on international travel.[25] The error, though, cannot be described as its complicity in working with

---

[20] 'Coalition of 62 countries backs joint Australian EU push for independent enquiry into coronavirus outbreak' Australian Broadcasting Corporation (ABC), 17 May 2020; https://www.abc.net.au/news/2020-05-17/coronavirus-inquiry-world-health-assembly-china-covid-19/12256910. Accessed on 29 March 2021.

[21] 'Blaming China for Pandemic, Trump says US will leave the WHO', The New York Times, 29 May 2020; https://www.nytimes.com/2020/05/29/health/virus-who.html. Accessed on 29 March 2021.

[22] 'Coronavirus: China accuses US of spreading conspiracies', BBC, 24 may 2020. https://www.bbc.com/news/world-asia-china-52790634. Accessed on 29 March 2021.

[23] While President Trump accused China of 'mass worldwide killing' (Trump blames China for mass worldwide killing, ChannelNewsAsia, 20 May 2020; https://www.channelnewsasia.com/news/world/trump-blames-china-mass-worldwide-killing-covid-19-coronavirus-12753604), Chinese foreign minister ang Yi accused the US of being infected by 'political virus' (as in 22 earlier).

[24] Cole and Dodds (2020).

[25] In its first assessment of the situation in China issued on 9 January 2020, the WHO referred to 'pneumonia' cases in the Wuhan province of China. Its statement further mentioned the assessment of Chinese authorities that the virus '..does not transmit readily between people'. It did also advise against 'application of travel or trade restrictions on China'. https://www.who.int/china/news/detail/09-01-2020-who-statement-regarding-cluster-of-pneumonia-cases-in-wuhan-china. Accessed on 29 March 2021.

China. More than anything else, the shortcoming reflected the WHO's functional weaknesses that do not empower it to regulate rules for handling a pandemic of the scale and severity of COVID19. Indeed, the WHO's strengthening as an institution for tackling future incidences of pandemics was a thought that was expressed early on by India in the G20 summit on Coronavirus held in March 2020.[26] Similar sentiments have more recently been echoed by Dr Anthony Fauci, the current Chief Medical Adviser to US President Joe Biden.[27]

The impact of the power rivalry between the US and China that has affected the WHO is, in several ways, similar to the resonance experienced at the WTO. As mentioned earlier, the Trump Administration was trenchantly critical of the global rules-based trade order of the WTO being biased in favor of large developing countries like China. President Trump's threat of pulling the US out of the WHO was similar to his earlier threat of pulling the US out of the WTO.[28] While not living up with the threat, the Trump administration succeeded in disrupting the working of the WTO by blocking the appointment of members to the appellate panel of the WTO's dispute settlement body. Making the WTO's dispute settlement mechanism partly dysfunctional was a reflection of the US's intention to make the WTO fall in line with US interests. Such a 'fall in line' attitude was also visible in President Trump's decision to halt US funding to the WHO.[29] The WHO's capacities would have been severely reduced if the US—its largest donor—had withdrawn funding, more so at a time when its role needed to be enlarged, as opposed to being limited, for fighting the pandemic.[30] The Trump Administration was convinced about international organizations, particularly the UN bodies, working in ways that benefitted China at the expense of the US and weren't hesitant to resort to 'threats' of US withdrawal for making its displeasure clear. In a world, where the two largest powers are engaged in intense rivalry, their spat was expected to spill over on to other forums, as it did in the UN General Assembly.[31] Among many other contributions of the Coronavirus, the damage that it has to US–China relations—what experts describe as a 'historic low' since both countries resumed diplomatic engagement in 1979[32]—is remarkable. The

---

[26] 'At G20 Summit, Narendra Modi calls for a stronger WHO to fight Coronavirus, say reports', Scroll.in; 27 March 2020. https://scroll.in/latest/957391/at-g20-summit-narendra-modi-calls-for-a-stronger-who-to-fight-coronavirus-say-reports. Accessed on 29 March 2021.

[27] Dr. Anthony S Fauci remarks at the World Health Organisation Executive Board Meeting', HHS Press Office, 21 January 2021. https://www.hhs.gov/about/news/2021/01/21/dr-anthony-s-fauci-remarks-world-health-organization-executive-board-meeting.html. Accessed on 29 March 2021.

[28] 'Trump threatens to pull US out of World Trade Organiation', BBC, 31 August 2018. https://www.bbc.com/news/world-us-canada-45364150.

[29] 'WHO officials respond to US funding halt: 'We regret the decision', World Economic Forum, 15 April 2020. https://www.weforum.org/agenda/2020/04/04152020-who-briefing/. Accessed on 29 March 2021.

[30] The Biden Administration has reversed its predecessor's decision and retained US funding for WHO.

[31] 'UN General Assembly: US-China tensions flare over coronavirus', BBC, 22 September 2020. https://www.bbc.com/news/world-54253408. Accessed on 30 March 2021.

[32] Putz et al. (2021).

inevitable fallout of such damage coming on the back of already frosty bilateral ties, and deep mistrust of each other in a competitive world order shifting rapidly from unipolarity to unmistakable bipolarity, will be witnessed in the troubled functioning of institutions. This will be unavoidable as both the US and China gather allies around each other for building competitive coalitions. Such competitive alliance-building is visible in the efforts to reorganize and reposition supply chains in the aftermath of COVID19.

2.2 Reorganization of Global Supply Chains: Economics and Politics

The power rivalry in the post-liberal world order has manifested in the frequent use of harsh phrases around the outbreak of COVID19. This, already mentioned in the context of the WHO's role in managing (or mismanaging) the spread of COVID19, is not the only demonstrative example of the unhealthy global consequences of power rivalry. Concerns about supply chain dependencies are also the result of such rivalry.[33] Considerable apprehensions have been expressed on such dependencies in the aftermath of COVID19 and multi-country efforts have been launched for reducing these dependencies.

The outbreak of COVID19 in the Wuhan province of China and the stringent lockdowns announced thereafter led to significant disruptions in several industrial supply chains.[34] As sourcing of key raw materials and other intermediates from China got affected, businesses and countries realized the vulnerabilities for supply chains, in the event of disruptions in China. Asian regional supply chains had got disrupted earlier due to natural calamities like the Fukushima earthquake and tsunami in Japan in March 2011, and the widespread monsoon floods in Thailand later in the year.[35] But the COVID19 triggered disruptions were of a much larger scale, primarily because of their location being in China. The disorders were a stark reminder for various countries, including large regional economies like India, Japan, and Australia, about the organic dependence their countries have on China for sourcing. As the largest source of imports for all three countries, China, over the years, has become indispensable in the supply of industrial capital goods and intermediate inputs required by these countries (e.g., machinery, mechanical appliances, bulk drugs, electrical items, chemicals, steel, and vehicle parts). These chains cracked as supplies from China halted. Supplies of a large number of consumer goods procured from China by these countries too were at risk of running into shortages. The US, and the EU which also have China as their largest source of imports, were equally concerned

---

[33] Cole and Dodds (2020).

[34] Nearly a thousand Fortune 500 companies have strong supply links with the Wuhan province. Braw (2020).

[35] The floods in Thailand caused a breakdown in Toyota's Lexus cars as a critical component used in assembling of Lexus was sourced exclusively from Thailand.

over the supply chain disruptions. In this regard, the early weeks after the outbreak found several of the world's major economies converging on the common anxiety of vulnerabilities for their economies caused by the heavy dependence on China.

The economic concerns, while necessary conditions for encouraging supply chain realignments post-COVID19, wouldn't have, by themselves, been sufficient for institutionalizing efforts for doing so. The sufficiency was provided by the geopolitics that unfolded after COVID19. Compounded with economic factors, the geopolitics led to unusual proactivity on part of several countries to work together for reducing supply chain dependencies on China. A key driver of this decisive geopolitics was the steep decline in US–China relations following COVID19 that has already been discussed. It is noteworthy that along with deterioration in ties with the US, China's relations with India, Australia, and Japan also deteriorated sharply as the COVID19 pandemic spread across the world. India's ties with China dropped to their lowest point in recent history after violent clashes between armed forces on the disputed borders of the two countries in the high Himalayas led to several casualties, in June 2020.[36] Australia's bilateral ties with China soured over a bitter trade war and sharp exchanges in social media over alleged atrocities committed in Afghanistan.[37] Japan, whose relations with China come with considerable historical baggage carried forward from the jarring memories of conflict during the Second World War, found ties with China getting further complicated on claims over disputed territories in the South pacific.

The sharp deterioration in US–China ties, accompanied by the simultaneous dips in bilateral ties between China and some of the US's major allies and close partners in the region, was sufficient ground for providing a political driver for reorganizing supply chains.[38] The outcome was the announcement of the Resilient Supply Chain Initiative by Japan, Australia, and India in September 2021.[39] The initiative is significant as it expressed the joint intention of three of the Asian region's largest economies with a combined economic size of more than $9 trillion declaring their intent to enhance the resiliency of supply chains in the Indo-Pacific region. The allusion to the COVID19 crisis and resultant changes in the region's economic and technological landscape and the importance of cooperating for ensuring resilient supply chains marked an unusual multi-country effort in managing supply chains.

---

[36] 'India and China See Most Violent Clash In Decades At Himalayan Border', npr, 17 June 2020; https://www.npr.org/2020/06/17/879041059/india-and-china-see-most-violent-clash-in-dec ades-at-himalayan-border. Accessed on 31 March 2021.

[37] (a) How China's trade restrictions are affecting the Australian economy', BT, 26 November 2020; https://www.bt.com.au/insights/perspectives/2020/australia-china-relations.html. Accessed on 31 March 2021. (b) "Australia demands China apologise for posting 'repugnant' fake image," BBC, 30 November 2020, https://www.bbc.com/news/world-australia-55126569. Accessed on 31 March 2021.

[38] Palit (2021).

[39] 'Australia-India-Japan Economic Ministers' Joint Statement on Supply Chain', Australian Government, Department of Foreign Affairs and Trade. 1 September 2020. https://www.dfat.gov. au/news/media-release/australia-india-japan-economic-ministers-joint-statement-supply-chain. Accessed on 31 March 2021.

The context of the announcement left no doubt over the intention of the countries to pursue economic delinking from China.

The efforts to reposition regional production networks for minimizing their vulnerabilities to disruptions is in contrast to the earlier efforts that encouraged the growth of these very same chains. Economic globalization, backed by low trade barriers, easy investment rules, and convenient movement of people, has encouraged the growth of supply chains by enabling businesses to take advantage of the core strengths of specific locations. The West and the East had joined forces in this regard. More and more production, including sourcing of raw materials, intermediates, and their final assembling, has moved out from mature industrial economies in the US and Europe to Asia and the Americas. With goods moving seamlessly across borders, supported by easy investment rules and flexible movement of workers, Asia, was able to emerge as the global hub of critical manufacturing industries. China was a distinct beneficiary of the process as, over the three decades following its economic transformation from 1978, it emerged as the manufacturing powerhouse of the world. The overwhelming focus of supply chains on cost efficiency deflected attention from the prominent concentrations these chains had developed, in their linkages with China. Such concentration was an understood, but understated characteristic of the economic globalization that supply chains have facilitated for years. An initiative like the RSCI aims to fundamentally de-characterize globalization in this regard.

The de-characterization of globalization through the reorganization of supply chains is not limited to the RSCI alone. In one of his earliest far-reaching economic policy decisions, President Joe Biden of the US has announced a far-reaching initiative on review of American supply chains for increasing their resilience.[40] The review was announced just before the US and Chinese leaders met in Alaska in March 2021, the first occasions of such a meeting after COVID19 and in the Biden Presidency. The meeting exposed the rifts between the two sides on several issues leaving little doubt over the US–China divide being too significant to be patched up in the foreseeable future.[41] The US initiative, and the RSCI, are primarily efforts to reposition supply chains out of China for reducing China's ability to weaponize the economic dependence of other nations on it.[42] The concerns are not unfounded given China's increasing assertiveness and clear efforts to use its economic clout for geopolitical gains, as witnessed in the BRI initiative.

The emergence of the 'Quad' between the US, Australia, India, and Japan, primarily as a security grouping for counterbalancing China, is likely to reflect in the longer term an economic reordering of supply chains bringing together the common concern of resiliency, as gleaned in terms of reducing dependence on China. The Quad has picked up great energy in the aftermath of COVID19 with the Summit

---

[40] Executive Order on America's Supply Chains, The White House, Briefing Room, 24 February 2021. https://www.whitehouse.gov/briefing-room/presidential-actions/2021/02/24/exe cutive-order-on-americas-supply-chains/. Accessed on 31 March 2021.

[41] How it happened: Transcript of the US-China opening remarks in Alaska', Nikkei Asia, 19 March 2021. https://asia.nikkei.com/Politics/International-relations/US-China-tensions/How-it-happened-Transcript-of-the-US-China-opening-remarks-in-Alaska. Accessed on 31 March 2021.

[42] Oya (2021).

between its Heads of States in March 2021 affirming to work together for securing an Indo-Pacific region that is 'unconstrained by coercion'. The alliance is not just positioning itself as a security partnership, or economic club for containing China; it is also fully committing to strengthening 'democratic resilience'. The emphasis leaves little doubt over the fight against China also turning value-based—in terms of the struggle being that of democratic and liberal principles against autocratic ideas and practices.[43] Such a struggle might increasingly become the defining rift in the world order going ahead, as global production networks try to organize themselves around the conflict between the US and China, on commercial, political, and strategic grounds.

3 India in the New World

India exemplifies the manifestation of multiple complexities arising from the disruptions in the world order.

Over the last three decades, India has enlarged economically, to become one of the largest economies in the world, backed by a robust and rising trajectory of GDP growth facilitated by market-oriented economic policies, including external sector liberalization. Despite such a notable economic performance, India has always been hesitant to openly embrace economic globalization. This is largely due to apprehensions over the impact of such globalization on several sections of its domestic economy and the likely adversities inflicted by such impacts. Indeed, while gradually opening up its economy to allow the market to play a bigger role in production, India continued emphasizing strongly the interests of developing economies at the WTO, including providing forceful leadership of developing country coalitions at the WTO for safeguarding their interests in the Doha Development Agenda.[44]

India's transition to a more market-oriented economy began from the early 1990s, the time from when Washington Consensus policies became popular among global policymakers. In the early years of India's economic transition, the influence of Washington Consensus agencies like the IMF and the World Bank were evident in the pattern and approach to economic restructuring. Several policies belonging to the Consensus, such as competitive determination of the exchange rate, market-based fixing of the interest rates or capital prices, fiscal discipline, restructuring of the

---

[43] 'Quad Leaders Joint Statement: "The Spirit of the Quad", The White House, Briefing Room, 12 March 2021. https://www.whitehouse.gov/briefing-room/statements-releases/2021/03/12/quad-leaders-joint-statement-the-spirit-of-the-quad/. Accessed on 31 March 2021.

[44] The two most important coalitions of WTO members led by India were the G-33 and G-20. While the G33 focused on safeguarding market access in domestic agriculture sectors, G20's objective was greater liberalization of domestic agricultural markets in developed countries. More details on these group, including their current members, are available at https://www.wto.org/english/tratop_e/dda_e/negotiating_groups_maps_e.htm?group_selected=GRP017 and https://www.wto.org/english/tratop_e/dda_e/negotiating_groups_maps_e.htm?group_selected=GRP017. Accessed on 1 April 2021.

public sector enterprises, better targeting of subsidies, and deregulation of controls on private investment in production, were implemented across various sectors of the economy. Such implementation, however, did not obliterate opinions that were cynical of these policies. These mainly included those critical of open trade policies, withdrawal of government controls from agriculture pricing and marketing, and privatization of state-owned enterprises, particularly those in prominent services like banks, insurance, transport, and education. Over the last few years, the prominence of these opinions has become more significant. One of the most important implications of such prominence has been India's withdrawal from wide-ranging discussions on regional trade liberalization, most notably the Regional Comprehensive Economic Partnership (a 16-member grouping comprising 10 economies of Southeast Asia, Australia, New Zealand, Japan, India, Korea, and China) in November 2019.

Notwithstanding wide-ranging economic reforms, including exhaustive liberalization of industrial investment policies welcoming private domestic and foreign investment, Indian manufacturing has failed to enlarge its share in the national economy. As a result, the expected transition of labor-intensive industries absorbing surplus labor from agriculture hasn't happened to the desired extent. Agriculture and farm-sector occupations continue to provide livelihoods to nearly two-thirds of the population. The services sector, spearheaded by domestic market-oriented services like transport, education, finance, health, communications, and more recently online retail, has offered employment to those with relevant skills. The skill mismatch with respect to requirements of flourishing sectors and those of the workforce, primarily those engaged in low-skilled agriculture and rural occupations, have created large chunks of unemployment. Matters haven't been helped by the steady transformation of labor-intensive industries like textiles, chemicals, and automobiles, to technology-intensive functioning with obvious labor-displacing implications. The plights and distress of the 'have nots' comprising the jobless and displaced have become significant in India during the last decade, as industrial transformation, and a noticeably lower trajectory of GDP growth in the second half of the last decade, have highlighted the exigencies of both 'jobless growth' and 'growth less jobs'. The public policy response has been to expand welfare programs for supporting rural and marginal incomes and ensuring support for access to a wide range of basic services like cooking gas, health insurance, and free schooling. However, in the absence of an overall robust expansion in economic growth, the state's fiscal capacities to support such welfare are limited over time.

The outbreak of COVID19, like in most other major economies except China, has led to India experiencing a contraction in the rate of growth of GDP. The contraction is not expected to be lasting with economic activity pulling back GDP growth to positive, as more and more sectors begin functioning at normal capacities. Much though will depend on the prolongation of the pandemic. India, though, has utilized the context of COVID19 to push through a series of pending far-reaching reforms. These include reforms in the labor market, agriculture marketing and distribution, and privatization of state-owned enterprises. Indeed, in this respect, India has been noticeably prominent among emerging market economies in using the pandemic and its aftermath as a suitable context for pushing deeper structural reforms.[45]

The announcement of the new economic reform policies, does not, however, mean that opposition to such reforms has receded within the country. New agricultural laws have encountered stiff resistance. The other policies too are encountering opposition. But it could well be that the Indian government is keen on obtaining as much policy gains as possible in an atmosphere that makes growth-oriented policies imperative for getting economies back on track. In this respect, it is interesting that some of the 'hard' reforms entailed in the Washington Consensus, such as privatization of state-owned enterprises, might find unexpected salience in major emerging markets like India.

In the post-pandemic scenario, India reflects a policy dilemma being experienced by several emerging market developing economies: balancing welfare support for poor and economically vulnerable sections with the necessity of generating high economic growth. Exclusive focus on the former objective, while fetching popular support, is impossible to be sustained over a long period as state coffers become depleted. On the other hand, turning pro-market by choosing growth as the core goal, is likely to overlook inclusivity and ignore many 'have not's. India is looking to incline more towards the latter objective, and adopting far-reaching reforms for doing so, without apparently sacrificing the commitment to the former. Inclusive measures, such as the focus on social security and working conditions in the new labor laws, expanding universal health insurance coverage, assuring the supply of food grains at affordable prices to poor people, expanding digital literacy, and escalating financial inclusion by bringing the poor within the formal banking system, are measures that are expected to cushion many of the 'have not's from possible disruptions caused by radical structural reforms.

Balancing the objectives will be a critical challenge for India. But it is important to note that empirical cross-country evidence pointing to the long-term economic damage caused by populist policies is substantial.[46] In contrast, Washington Consensus appears to have delivered relatively better outcomes, particularly if noted with respect to the counterfactual of comparable outcomes in countries that have stayed away from such policies.[47]

An interesting aspect of India's post-COVID19 economic efforts is its linkage with the evolving global and regional geopolitics. India has utilized its 'bad' ties with China to highlight the importance of reducing economic dependence on the country. The emphasis on 'self-reliance' articulated by Prime Minister Modi in the

---

[45] Brazil's structural reforms were put off course by COVID19. OECD reports underline the importance of continuing with these reforms, more so after COVID19, which has increased the imperative. Brazil Economic Snapshot. http://www.oecd.org/economy/brazil-economic-snapshot/. Accessed on 1 April 2021. The context for reform, and its legitimacy has been noticed to have risen for South Africa too. 'South Africa's COVID19 strengthens Ramaphosa's economic reforms hand', Reuters, 23 April 2020. https://www.reuters.com/article/us-health-coronavirus-safrica-politics-a-idUSKCN2252EG. Accessed on 1 April 2021.

[46] Funke et al. (2020).

[47] Grier (2021).

aftermath of COVID19,[48] and the organization of new economic policies and their management around the notion of self-reliance, strikes a strong resonance in today's India that is too aware of the rough edges of coexisting with an assertive neighbor prone on using economic dependence for strategic advantage. India's difficulties with China have stretched beyond their bilateral domain to the greater international space, where China's rise has created strong ripples, more so given the strategic ambitions of India to play larger regional and global roles, creating sufficient grounds for competition and potential conflict. The growth of a prominent international anti-China narrative post-COVID19 over the origins and spread of the pandemic, aided in large measure by President Trump's frequent allusion to the 'China virus', had already created considerable misgivings in India about China. The military clashes in the Himalayas in June 2020, the worst since the military conflict of 1962, created huge backlashes on China in India. The fact that COVID19 and its outbreak also found the US–China divide enlarging, and several Asian and Western economies finding ties with China getting seriously estranged, created conducive conditions for India to step into an emerging framework comprising countries looking to economically and strategically reduce dependence on China. India's active role in the pronouncement of the RSCI, and the maturing of the Quad framework, are indications of India decisively committing to power configurations and alignments in the post-liberal world order.

India's substantive goal would be to utilize its geopolitical alliances in a manner that contributes to its economic goals, by bringing in new investments and institutional linkages, as well as linkages with some of the world's major markets. The interesting question in this regard would be to ascertain that in a world fracturing around US–China competition, and moving into a new phase of de-globalization, the combination of economic and political upsides and downsides that taking 'positions' implies. India's national interests have pushed it in the direction of specific geopolitical partnerships and commitments. The key test of such commitments is their impact on economic outcomes for a country that is projected to become the world's most populous in the foreseeable future.[49] COVID19 has specifically exposed the vulnerabilities for a country like India, which has large economically marginal populations with limited access to basic facilities and is at serious risk of further marginalization from further growth of the pandemic. India's aspirations of playing a prominent role in the emerging world order, and being noted as a credible stakeholder in advancing global and regional stability, depend significantly upon outcomes it achieves for its people in a fast-changing and complex global order.

---

[48] 'Biggest lesson from COVID19 is to be self-reliant, says PM Modi', mint, 24 April 2020. https://www.livemint.com/news/india/pm-modi-says-biggest-lesson-from-covid-19-is-being-self-reliant-11587711644303.html. Accessed on 1 April 2021.

[49] 'India likely to surpass China as world's most populous country in next 8 years: UN', Healthworld.com, 19 June 2019; https://health.economictimes.indiatimes.com/news/industry/india-likely-to-surpass-china-as-worlds-most-populous-country-in-next-8-years-un/69850344. Accessed on 1 April 2021.

4 Looking Ahead

Washington Consensus policies continue to guide economic management in various countries, notwithstanding their trenchant criticism by various opinions. Such policies are likely to retain their greater appeal in encouraging market-oriented economic growth programs. The alternative, that of the state playing the pivotal role in promoting economic growth, is unlikely to create much resonance among national policymakers, given the huge responsibilities of mobilizing resources and their distribution for governments. Most governments across the world, developed and developing alike, appear more focused on the latter, preferring a more active role by market and private actors in the former. Even China, over the years, has allowed private enterprises, including foreign capital and technology, to play incrementally larger roles in its development. India, as discussed in the chapter, is pursuing an interesting mix of private enterprise-driven economic transformation models while putting the state firmly in the key role of efficient allocation of spoils of economic growth. In many ways, this strategy reflects what economic globalization was missing and was criticized for: a mechanism for ensuring egalitarian distribution of benefits. The state needs to step in for delivering a balanced outcome. But whether for India or many other countries where state presence in the economy is growing (accelerated further by the economic stimulus and social sector management responses entailed by COVID19) would this approach mean a comeback of overarching state presence in different garbs, would be revealed only over time.

In the meantime, notwithstanding its appeal for policymakers, the challenge for Washington Consensus-premised globalization to progress arises from the friction in the global order. The US–China divide and its attendant implications on the reorganization of global production, and country alliances, are pressurizing global rules, institutions, and systems. The divide is unlikely to obliterate. Perpetuation of the chasm will continue to produce impulses forcing countries to look at collective global engagement skeptically. The skepticism will spill over to the management and functioning of global institutions such as the WHO and WTO and also on global cooperation for addressing critical global challenges like climate change and pandemic prevention. The underpinning is as strong an obstacle for collective efforts to ensure global economic recovery as there could be.

References

Braw, Elisabeth. 2020. Blindsided on the supply side. *Foreign Policy*. https://foreignpolicy.com/2020/03/04/blindsided-on-the-supply-side/. Accessed on 25 March 2021

Cole, Jennnifer, and Klaus, Dodds. 2020. Unhealthy geopolitics: can the response to COVID-19 reform climate change policy? *Policy and Practice, Bulletin of the World Health Organization (WHO)*. https://www.who.int/bulletin/volumes/99/2/20-269068/en/. Accessed on 29 March 2021

Cuperus, René. 2017. The populist revolt against globalization, Clingendael Spectator. vol. 71, 3. https://www.clingendael.org/pub/2017/3/the-populist-revolt-against-globalisation/. Accessed on 23 March 2021

Funke, Manuel, Schularick, Moritz, and Trebesch, Christoph. 2020. Populist leaders and the economy. Discussion Paper. DP 15405. Centre for Economic Policy Research (CEPR), London, 24 October. https://ae624e09-a-62cb3a1a-s-sites.googlegroups.com/site/christophtrebesch/MFT_PopulismMacroeconomy.pdf?attachauth=ANoY7coNJKFt0Y_wuN8CNGHZGfTpds odkDP7xGfdTHMMZMrUV_xOig5Fl36Sx2UjWddnSXGwoSNbgX3VpRazP5J_uTsrNRegx UAmvY1a5K2vsNsHyCqrRbtuACN-nvxNlNVXugxNwgDK16urisvzr1oswZz_EJ64J3tFpz zxMKnp8EBpTK4KgbVLIdjl4OKYTCyQm_ewZjWanZk0_YN-Y2YyZHyJ4zzL33TiSwHA-MvNSkLAt9EcYgM%3D&attredirects=0. Accessed on 1 April 2021

Grier, Kevin B. and Grier, Robin, M. 2021. The Washington consensus works: Causal effects of reform, 1970–2015. *Journal of Comparative Economics*. 49(1):59–72. https://doi.org/10.1016/j.jce.2020.09.001. Accessed on 1 April 2021

Kadi, Tin Hinane El. 2019. The promise and Peril of the digital silk road, Chatham House, 6 June. https://www.chathamhouse.org/expert/comment/promise-and-peril-digital-silk-road. Accessed on 24 March 2021

Kondapalli, Srikanth. 2017. Why India is not a part of the belt and road initiative summit. Indian Express, 15 May. https://indianexpress.com/article/opinion/why-india-is-not-part-of-the-belt-and-road-initiative-summit-4656150/. Accessed on 25 March 2021

Oya, Shin. 2021. It's time to reduce the world's trade dependence on China. The Japan Times, 26 January. https://www.japantimes.co.jp/opinion/2021/01/26/commentary/worldcommentary/api-china-trade/. Accessed on 31 March 2021

Irwin, Douglas A. 2020. *The Washington consensus stands the test of time better than populist policies.* Washington DC, USA: Peterson Institute for International Economics (PIIE), December 4. https://www.piie.com/blogs/realtime-economic-issues-watch/washington-consen sus-stands-test-time-better-populist-policies. Accessed 21 March 2021

Terrence, Mullan. 2020. The corrosion of world order in the age of Donald Trump, Council on Foreign Relations, 13 February. https://www.cfr.org/blog/corrosion-world-order-age-donald-trump. Accessed on 25 March 2021

Palit, Amitendu. 2017. The Maritime Silk Road Initiative (MSRI): Why India is worried, What China can Do. *Global Policy*, 31 May. https://www.globalpolicyjournal.com/blog/31/05/2017/maritime-silk-road-initiative-msri-why-india-worried-what-china-can-do. Accessed on 25 March 2021

Palit, Amitendu. 2021. Resilient supply chain initiative: A political driver to revive Asian regional growth. Georgetown Journal of International Affairs, Walsh School of Foreign Service, Georgetown University, 30 January. https://gjia.georgetown.edu/2021/01/30/resilient-supply-chain-ini tiative-a-political-driver-to-revive-asian-regional-growth/. Accessed on 31 March 2021

Putz, Catherine, Rej Abhijnan, Strangio, Sebastian, and Tiezzi, Shannon. 2021. How COVID19 changed Asia. *The Diplomat*, 12 March. https://thediplomat.com/2021/03/how-covid-19-cha nged-asia/. Accessed on 29 March 2021

Sengupta, Jayshree. 2018. Anti-globalization wave to affect all, including US and EU, Observer Research Foundation (ORF). *Raisina Debates*, 28 March. https://www.orfonline.org/expert-speak/anti-globalisation-wave-affect-including-us-eu/. Accessed on 23 March 2021

Silver, Laura, Schumacher, Shannon, Mordecai, Mara, Greenwood, Shannon, and Keegan, Micahel. 2020. *In U.S. and UK, Globalization Leaves Some Feeling 'Left Behind' or 'Swept Up'.* Pew Research Center, October 5. https://www.pewresearch.org/global/2020/10/05/in-u-s-and-uk-glo balization-leaves-some-feeling-left-behind-or-swept-up/. Accessed 23 March 2021

Williamson, John. 2002. What Washington means by policy reform. Washington DC, USA: Peterson Institute for International Economics (PIIE), November 1. https://www.piie.com/commentary/spe eches-papers/what-washington-means-policy-reform. Accessed 21 March 2021

Wolf, Martin. 2017. Donald Trump and Xi Jinping's battle over globalization. Financial Times, January 25. https://www.ft.com/content/74b42cd8-e171-11e6-8405-9e5580d6e5fb. Accessed on 23 March 2021

Chapter 3
Normative Internationalization Through Globalization: India and China Between Modernization, Democratization, and Authoritarian Resistances

Leïla Choukroune

1 Introduction

The internationalization of law is not a new phenomenon. Internationalization has been discussed in academic literature from the fall of the Berlin wall and probably reached a pic in the production of conceptual analysis in the mid-2000s with a series of intellectual debates around the integration of international law by domestic courts and the pro-active role of the Judge, in the United States and Europe, through what

---

I would like to express my sincere gratitude to the organizers of the international conference *"Revisiting Globalization: Comparing Country Experiences from South Asia and the World",* which took place on the 12 October 2017, at the National University of Singapore (NUS). I am especially thankful to the Institute of South Asian Studies (ISAS), and Dr Amitendu Palit, Senior Research Fellow and Research Lead (Trade and Economic Policy) for leading this fascinating project.

This chapter is largely based on years of field work and interviews in China and India. I would also like to thank all the interviewees from Academia, Government, Businesses, and Civil Society who have accepted to answer my questions and participated to the study of the global South in critically unveiling its contribution to a genuinely "international" law.

This chapter draws upon previous and parallel studies published by the author in the past few years, namely, Leïla Choukroune "From without to Within: Indian International Law as Modernizer", in Leïla Choukroune and Parul Bhandari (eds), *Exploring Indian Modernities*, Springer, 2018, pp. 37–57; Leïla Choukroune, "Indian and Chinese FDI in developing Asia, the Standard Battle Beyond Trade", *The Indian Journal of International Law,* Vol. VII, 2015, pp. 89–116; Leïla Choukroune, "The Language of Rights and the Politics of Law: Perspectives on China's Last Legal Ditch Struggle", *International Journal of the Semiotic of Law,* Vol. 29, 2015, pp. 779–803. Content re-used here with permissions.

L. Choukroune (✉)
Professor of International Law and Director of the University's Thematic Area in Democratic Citizenship, University of Portsmouth (UoP), Portsmouth, UK
e-mail: Leila.choukroune@port.ac.uk

© The Author(s), under exclusive license to Springer Nature Singapore Pte Ltd. 2022
A. Palit (ed.), *Globalisation Impacts*, International Law and the Global South,
https://doi.org/10.1007/978-981-16-7185-2_3

some called a judicial dialogue leading to the "cross fertilization" of norms.[1] This rather optimistic approach to a positive internationalization was later balanced with distantiated perspectives on the challenges and other damages of an economic globalization questioning the State's normative autonomy and impacting its regulatory freedom. International investment law is, for example, at the forefront of today's thinking on globalization and the merits it truly entails in terms of normative internationalization.[2] Recent political developments from the Brexit to US-led trade wars directly challenge a somehow too naïve perception of a not fully democratic regulatory harmonization, which was naturally to produce more democracy and freedom as in an idealized European Union. Questioning globalization and its normative benefits is indeed a way to reclaim national identities, not only in the populist and xenophobic variations such an enterprise could generate, but also in search for a genuine cosmopolitanism better integrating the diversity of unique national realities.

At the same time, without challenging the very basis of globalization nor even the rules of international law, developing Asia has managed to benefit from it through a selective and strategic acculturation. As such, developing Asia presents a rather different image of globalization than Europe or North America. While globalization is producing its lot of injustices, from economic exploitation to political subjugation, and contestation is certainly not absent from the public sphere, developing Asia's rapport and perception of globalization is generally seen as more positive and empowering than in developed countries. The COVID19 Pandemic, despite its temporary nationalistic calls and border closures, has not really changed the done. The latest UNCTAD investment figures have indeed revealed that both China and India have received the most part of the greatly collapsed Foreign Direct Investment (FDI) flows. In 2020, FDI fell by 42%. This dramatic decline has mostly affected developed countries and Europe in particular. On the contrary to this trend, FDI in China increased by 4% while they rose by 13% in India boosted by the digital economy sector.[3]

Complexities are central to the globalization process and its possible slow down, if not contestation. The Global South, although underrepresented in the scholarly debate and still poorly studied in a rather Western centric research, is now better placed to bring challenging conceptual developments as well as meaningful explanations.[4] For

---

[1] Anne-Marie Slaughter had probably set the tone with the concept of "cross-fertilization" of law, see, for example, Slaughter (2000); while others have made remarked contributions, see Benvenisti (2008); and some have tried to systematize the trend in an ambitious project, see André Nollkaemper's Oxford project on International Law in Domestic Courts: http://opil.ouplaw.com/page/ILDC/oxford-reports-on-international-law-in-domestic-courts#Contributors. On internationalization, see as well, Delmas (2003). *Critique de l'intégration normative* (Paris: PUF, 2004); Loquin and Kessedjian (2000), Morand (2001), Arnaud (1998), Auby (2003). For a recent synthetical approach rightly integrating English and non-English language sources, see Varella (2014).

[2] See Choukroune (2016).
See as well, Chaisse (2020–21).

[3] See UNCTAD (2021).

[4] On the complexities in the internationalization of law, "post-national law" and the challenges to Universalism and a "World Constitution", see notably, Habermas (2001, 2008).

countries like China and India, this international law, which they hardly had a hand in creating, has not reduced their normative autonomy but, on the contrary, participated to their empowerment and wise recourse to dispute settlement in a large variety of fields, internationally, but also internally. On a positive note, the de-territorialization of norms has enabled their true integration in domestic law in a journey, which eventually re-territorialized fundamental rights. From without to within and vice versa, internal law and/or Asian globalized international law have participated to the democratization process in often empowering the weakest, while social progress was challenged, and genuine democracy and the rule of law kept at bay by domestic pressures if not oppositions. And yet, 2020 has seen Hong Kong de facto taken over by mainland China with the adoption of a security law greatly limiting the Basic Law (Hong Kong's mini constitution) and the local judicial system. India, on its side, showed its less democratic nature in first imposing a very oppressive lockdown and later repressing farmers' demonstrations while leaving the Kashmir issue unresolved. There is nothing like a rosy picture or an overwhelming acceptance of international norms conducive to democratization but a path towards a socio-political change, which is as expected as contested, as established as challenged.

On the basis of three case studies, Trade and investment law and disputes (I), Labour and Human Rights (II), and Judicial Activism (III), this chapter addresses the issue of normative internationalization through globalization in China and India as well as the processes of modernization and democratization and the resistances it has generated.

2 Trade and Investments: A Progressive yet Distant Adhesion

2.1 Rules Integrators

In trade as well as in international investment law, India and China have taken a rather heterodox path, which might appear for many as an alternative to "Western rules". They have integrated a *sui generis* model mixed with norms imported and reinterpreted in light of creative practices embedded in contrasted histories and political regimes. As we will see below, some signs of exportation of a sort of Chinese or Indian globalized international law are now perceptible when looking at the most recent geopolitical developments from the new Silk Road, to the EU-China investment deal or Indian and Chinese mergers and acquisition policies. But to understand this Asian journey, one first needs to recall important historical moments.

India was one of the 23 original Contracting parties of the General Agreement on Tariffs and Trade (GATT) and founding Member of the World Trade Organization (WTO), but China has only acceded to the WTO, in December 2001, after more than 15 years of complex negotiations questioning the very nature of its "socialist market economy". While India has played a central role in the introduction of development issues within the GATT and was one of the main negotiators of the Generalized System of Preferences (GSP) adopted in 1968 in the context of the second United Nations Conference on Trade and Development (UNCTAD), China has long been a *"rule taker"* more than *"rule maker"*.[5] In the recent past again, India has often resisted certain trade evolutions in relation to agriculture, services, or intellectual property with, for example, along with Brazil and South Africa, the drafting of the Doha Declaration on the Trade Related Aspects of Intellectual Property Rights (TRIPS) agreement and public health of November 2001, and the Protocol amending the TRIPS agreement in 2005.[6,7] In the COVID19 pandemic context, it is, together with South Africa, lobbying for temporarily suspensions of intellectual property rights for better access to new technologies and vaccines for the developing world.

Far from being a passive actor in normative integration, China has learned to act by observing the strategy of other Members and is now at the very forefront of WTO dispute settlement, not only as far as the number of disputes is concerned, but also with regard to the legal strategy it develops to juggle with the flexibilities envisaged in the WTO Agreement hence surprisingly managing to reactivate the customary principle of "permanent sovereignty over natural resources".[8] These arguments, together with the principles of "equity and common but differentiated responsibilities" as applied to climate change negotiations, now find a real echo among developing countries.[9] In the context of the US disengagement from multilateral organizations and the WTO Dispute Settlement Body (DSB) in particular, China appears as the greatest defender of the organization. The Chinese garden donated by China and opening the gate to the Geneva-based institution for multilateral trade is highly symbolic of a presence which is here to remain for symbols matter very much in Chinese culture.

A similar independent path was somehow taken in investment law. As far as China is concerned, one generally identifies three moments, if not three generations of International Investment Agreements (IIAs). The initial phase started with China's

---

[5] See Choukroune (2014); and Leïla Choukroune, Special Issue of *China Perspective* (editor), *China's WTO Decade*, http://chinaperspectives.revues.org/5770.

[6] See: https://www.wto.org/english/thewto_e/minist_e/min01_e/mindecl_trips_e.htm.

[7] See: https://www.wto.org/english/tratop_e/trips_e/wtl641_e.htm.

[8] See in cases DS394 *China—Measures Related to the Exportation of Various Raw Materials* (https://www.wto.org/english/tratop_e/dispu_e/cases_e/ds394_e.htm) and DS *431China— Measures Related to the Exportation of Rare Earths, Tungsten and Molybdenum* (https://www. wto.org/english/tratop_e/dispu_e/cases_e/ds431_e.htm).

[9] See the BRICS 2015 Environment Ministers Declaration available at: http://www.brics.utoronto. ca/docs/150422-environment.html: "We recognize that sustainable development should comprehensively address the key challenges of today, in particular, poverty eradication, changing unsustainable and promoting sustainable patterns of consumption and production, protecting and managing the natural resource base of economic and social development and effectively addressing climate change. We reaffirm our commitment to implement the Rio Declaration, Agenda 21, the Johannesburg Plan of Implementation (JPOI), and the outcomes of the Rio + 20 Conference in our respective countries, and through our cooperation within the framework of BRICS in accordance with the Rio principles, including the principle of common but differentiated responsibilities".

first BIT with Sweden, in 1982, and lasted until the late 1990s.[10] It was largely characterized by a prudent if not reluctant approach to normative internationalization with National Treatment (NT) seldom granted and international dispute settlement limited to the determination of the amount of compensation for expropriation. From 1998 on, with the China-Barbados BIT of July 1998 that offered, for the first time, foreign investors unrestricted access to international arbitration, China entered into a new phase of BIT drafting inspired by EU model treaties and framing NT in a less restrictive and somehow personalized manner depending on whether the country was a developed or developing nation. The last phase, starting from 2007 and the China-Korea BIT, is generally described as a more liberal one partly inspired by NAFTA in the sense that Chinese treaties granted Fair and Equitable Treatment (FET) in de facto accepting certain customary international law features, but also the national treatment and MFN often defined in using the now generalized yet difficult to interpret "in like circumstances" terminology.[11] To these three generations, one could add a fourth one corresponding to today's mega-regional trade and investment negotiations and China's expansion as a global investor. This fourth generation may well be characterized—and this is not China specific—by a certain distantiation from the late 1990s NAFTA model in relation to today's new investment issues. In addition, it integrates the lessons learned from China's accession and participation to the WTO. Lastly, the recent wave of Foreign Trade Agreements (FTAs) drafting does not seem to add much to China's general BIT approach on the contrary to some thesis often put forward and according to which a regional negotiation's aim is to further liberalize trade in introducing greater protection and flexibilities. In this context, it is interesting to look at the recently concluded, although not yet adopted, EU-China Comprehensive Agreement on Investment.[12] A rather strange instrument already criticized for its very minimal human rights content, it shows the result of a natural compromise between the parties, but also the growing influence of China in the drafting style of a number of provisions. The central presence of the WTO in the Section V (Dispute Settlement), Article 21 (Choice of Forum) is quite revealing as well. It remains to be seen if the Agreement is supported by the EU parliament and how it is implemented, but the astute observer of Chinese BITs is already able to denote a form of reverse internationalization, be it only through the weight of the power (un)balance between the EU and China.

Although a relatively latecomer on the BIT scene with a first treaty signed with the UK in 1994, India has progressively developed a very large number of treaties with developed and developing countries all over the world. While it restricted itself to BIT until 2004, it then accepted to enter into regional negotiations and FTA with countries such as Japan, Korea, and Malaysia. Interestingly, India took an opposite stance to China as far as NT and MFN are concerned. While it generally granted the

---

[10] Agreement Between the Government of the People's Republic of China and the Government of the Kingdom of Sweden on the Mutual Protection of Investments, 29 March 1982.

[11] On China's investment treaties evolution, see for example the recent researches of Hadley (2013), and Berger (2013).

[12] See the text of the Agreement at: https://trade.ec.europa.eu/doclib/press/index.cfm?id=2237.

two standards of treatment (as well as FET) in most of its 1990s and 2000s treaties, its recent attempts show a real suspicion against the MFN. This, of course, is a direct result of its recent—and first—condemnation by an arbitral tribunal in the *White Industries case*. While based on the India-Australia BIT, the large interpretation of the MFN standard by the investment tribunal resulted in finding that standard of *"effective means of asserting claims and enforcing rights"* could be found in India-Kuwait BIT through the MFN indeed....[13] It then concluded that: *"The Republic of India has breached its obligation to provide effective means of asserting and enforcing rights" with respect to the White Industries Australia Limited's investment pursuant to the article 4(2) of the BIT incorporating the article 4(5) of the India Kuwait BIT"*.[14] For these reasons, and because many other relatively similar (tax related) cases are underway (see below), the Indian government has decided to review its BIT policy including its BIT model, the latest draft having no mention of the MFN standard, which may prove problematic for Indian investors going global.[15] India illustrates itself by a multitude of recent developments on the ISDS front with now 25 cases as a respondent and 8 as a claimant.[16] In addition, its Corporate Social Responsibility (CSR) approach remains quite unique and is reflected in its BIT policy. Very few countries have yet adopted a legally binding definition of Corporate Social Responsibility (CSR) with clear obligations for foreign investors. India was the first ever country to make CSR mandatory with the Section 135 of its *2013 Companies Act and, a few years later, the* Article 12 of its 2015 model BIT and the 2019 and 2020 new amendments to the Companies Act and the Companies (Corporate Social Responsibility Policy) Rules, respectively.[17]

China and India FDI heterodox strategy eventually revealed positive as it gave space for regulatory autonomy and gradual economic liberalization in supporting the development of national champions now "going global" as they claim, in turn, the national treatment standard of protection.[18,19] One has to bear in mind the revolutionary nature of standards of treatment directly impacting on States' regulatory autonomy and domestic constitution.

---

[13] Article 4(5) of the India-Kuwait BIT provided that: "Each party shall … provide effective means of asserting claims and enforcing rights with regard to investments …". Each Contracting State shall maintain a favourable environment for investments in its territory by investors of the other Contracting State. Each Contracting State shall in accordance with its applicable laws and regulations provide effective means of MFN.

[14] See The *White Industries* Final Award at 16.1.1. available at: https://www.italaw.com/cases/doc uments/1170.

[15] On the recent developments and pros and cons of an MFN insertion, see Rajan (2015), Online test issue.

[16] See UNCTAD ISDS statistics and update at: https://investmentpolicy.unctad.org/investment-dis pute-settlement/country/96/india.

[17] See Choukroune (2021).

[18] See Sornarajah (2010).

[19] On Chinese Outward Investment Policies, see, for example, International Institute for Sustainable Development, (IISD), Chinese Outward Investment, an Emerging Policy Framework (compilation of primary sources), 2012.

With shrewd negotiating skills and strategic advocacy, India and China have been able to use the existing trade and investment regime as a tool of their might. Shunning the paths marked by regulated liberalism of the 1990s, they affirm a heterodox model, which partly stands out and appeals to developing countries seeking alternatives to a Washington consensus, which has failed to bring the development benefits expected. At a chosen pace, their selective and critical normative integration has contributed to their political autonomy and this is particularly true in the area of international investment law, a key domain of sovereign independence now at the centre of a renewed international attention and for which, India and to a lesser extent China are also facing the consequences of particular policy choices as explained below.[20]

2.2 Dispute Makers and Settlers

With 21 disputes as complainant, 45 as respondent, and 186 as a third party, China, has within only a few years, accumulated a vast experience close to that of the United States or Europe.[21] On the contrary to all that was envisaged at the time of China's entry into the WTO, the dispute settlement system was not initially overrun with Beijing's complaints or responses, as most parties concerned implicitly respected a latency period before plunging into trade disputes. Often presented as a passive actor in normative integration during the initial years of its WTO participation, China learned to act by observing the strategy of other Members while benefiting from the benevolent attitude of its main trading partners. Its participation as the third party in no less than 186 disputes is neither an anodyne detail nor a sign of passivity but rather proof that China was preparing to carefully seize new legal tools and all the laws at its disposal as a Member. China's WTO Accession Protocol was and remains unique in that it contains a certain number of obligations termed *"WTO-plus"* and rights dubbed *"WTO-minus"*. Like any other new WTO Member, China made a series of traditional commitments regarding market access and rules governing it. However, unlike other Members, China not only accepted extended commitments regarding market access, but also a certain number of specific rules that were subject to much criticism by high officials and trade experts in Beijing. Indeed, the Chinese Protocol imposes a more rigorous discipline than generally required in WTO agreements while the "WTO-minus" provisions allowed other WTO Members to take protectionist measures vis-à-vis Chinese exports deviating from the general discipline. Finally, China's accession Protocol bars the granting of special and differential treatment extended to developing countries. Evidently, China accepted all these special provisions, but as current disputes show, it is quite difficult now to apply them for both technical and political reasons.

---

[20] See Choukroune (2011, 2018).

[21] See the Chinese WTO Disputes at: https://www.wto.org/english/tratop_e/dispu_e/dispu_by_country_e.htm.

50   L. Choukroune

With 24 disputes as complainant, 32 as respondent, and 166 as the third party, India has also been an active user of the DSB.[22] New Delhi had to respond to its first complaint in 1948[23] and made its first one in the dispute settlement mechanism of GATT in 1952.[24] It took until the early 1990s for India to re-emerge as a fighter and target in anti-dumping, safeguard measures, or intellectual property. Among these, some complaints had major repercussions, such as that pertaining to shrimp products (DS58) made against the United States by India, Malaysia, Pakistan, and Thailand, which remains one of the most remarkable disputes in the history of international trade as it touched directly on linkages between trade discrimination and natural resource protection through the justify application of the exception provided in Article XX of GATT 94.[25] Another noteworthy dispute was India's complaint against the European Communities' generalized system of preferences in favour of some countries with which it had close relations (DS 246).[26] Finally, in a dispute over quantitative restrictions on the import of agricultural, textile, and industrial products (DS 90), India directly questioned the WTO's institutional balance. These disputes also contributed significantly to the development of WTO jurisprudence on issues of discrimination, a question at the heart of all Indian cases. Through its activism and consistent positions in favour of developing countries, India has contributed greatly to the enriching of WTO negotiations and enlarging the DSB's interpretative canvas.[27]

Recently, China and India have challenged anti-dumping and countervailing measures imposed by the EU or US. Already in 1998, New Delhi, in case DS 141 Anti-Dumping Duties on Imports of Cotton-type Bed Linen from India, questioned the legality of Council Regulation (EC) No 2398/97 of 28 November 1997 on imports of cotton-type bed linen from India. If it is not more rigorous and transparent in the determination of dumping and subsidies, the EU will certainly have to face more of these disputes, as exemplified by the case (DS405) of Anti-Dumping Measures on Certain Footwear from China, in which the DSB found in favour of China, and the recently introduced disputes by Indonesia (DS 480) on Anti-Dumping Measures on Biodiesel from Indonesia, and Pakistan (DS 486) on Countervailing Measures on Certain Polyethylene Terephthalate, which are yet to be concluded. In doing so, India and China have proven their abilities to use the system as it is and to their benefits.

As far as investment disputes are concerned, India and China are both relatively newcomers on the ISDS scene. According to the official data of the United Nations Conference for Trade and Development (UNCTAD), Chinese companies have filed

---

[22] See India WTO Dispute at: https://www.wto.org/english/tratop_e/dispu_e/dispu_by_country_e.htm.

[23] India—Tax Rebates on Export, GATT.CP.2/SR11, BISD II/12., 24 August 1948.

[24] Pakistan—Export Fees on Jute, GATT/L/41.

[25] DS 58 United States—*Import prohibition of certain shrimp and shrimp products*: http://www.wto.org/english/tratop_e/dispu_e/cases_e/ds58_e.htm.

[26] DS 246 European Communities—*Conditions for the granting of tariff preferences to developing countries*: http://www.wto.org/english/tratop_e/dispu_e/cases_e/ds246_e.htm.

[27] DS 90 *India—Quantitative Restrictions on Imports of Agricultural, Textile and Industrial Products*: http://www.wto.org/english/tratop_e/dispu_e/cases_e/ds90_e.htm.

six cases against a variety of States (Laos, Yemen, Greece, Belgium, Mongolia, Peru) and Beijing appeared four times as respondent (Japan, Germany, Korea, and Malaysia being the Home State of the investors). With a much greater presence of Chinese companies (including State owned), it is likely that China will take a larger role in Investor State Disputes Settlement system (ISDS). India's case is even more interesting as we could observe a recent and rather worrying surge in ISDS. India indeed appeared 25 times as a respondent with a massive increase from 2010 and the infamous *White Industries* case based on a rather liberal interpretation of the Most Favoured Nation (MFN) and the Fair and Equitable Treatment (FET), which led New Delhi to revise its investment policy and adopt a new Bilateral Investment Treaty Model in 2015 (see above).[28] Here again, it is likely that India will face new disputes in relation to its previous investor-friendly model, but also a number of regulatory policies, which have generated business instability.

In any case, the two players will be central and have already made a mark in the domain in questioning investment law standards of treatment and protection and questioning ISDS while fostering the development of local dispute settlement procedures. *In* and *out*, and in again, norms are integrated with the critical distance necessary to a beneficial usage for a sovereign State.[29]

3 International Labour and Human Rights: The Reluctant Internationalist

The internationalization although real and often profound has happened in more uneven and sometimes reluctant manner as far as labour and human rights are concerned. A few examples are however noteworthy of an inclination to use international law to push a national agenda for social reform. The most interesting one being Public Interest Litigation (PIL) related initiatives and cases.

It is indeed probably in Asia, and precisely in India, that PIL has achieved its most sophisticated, yet sometimes ambiguous variation.[30] As convincingly demonstrated at the time by Upendra Baxi in his 1985 article,[31] that is a few years after the end of

---

[28] See Choukroune and Rahul (2018).

[29] On standards, human rights and corporate social responsibility in Indian and Chinese IIAs, see Choukroune (2018, 2016).

[30] While relatively few publications directly refer to the PIL terminology when dealing with the US, a large number of articles and books have been released about Asia and India in particular. See generally, Baghwati (1984), Cunningham (1987), Sathe (2002), Rao (2004), Upadhyay (2007), Modhurima (2009), Razzaque (2004), Deva (2009), Singh (2010), Kosla (2010). For a general and recent overview: Yap and Lau (2010).

And more specifically on China: Gallagher (2006), Hualing Fu and Rihard Cullen, "The Development of public interest litigation in China", in Po Yen and Holning (eds.), *op.cit.* pp. 9–33, Webster (2011). Chen and Xu (2012).

[31] See Baxi (1985).

the 1975–76 Emergency period and at a time *"judicial democracy"* was revolutionizing Indian politics, the "extraordinary remedies" the Indian population was seeking out differed from the PIL general significance. They were indeed *"transcending the received notions of separation of powers and the inherited distinctions between adjudication and legislation on the one hand and administration and adjudication on the other"*. Not to mention that they brought *"a new kind of lawyering and a novel kind of judging"*.[32] Oriented towards the *"rural poor"* and not, as it has progressively been the case in the US—and in India itself—in the direction of "*civic participation in governmental decision making"* and eventually the representation of *"interests without groups"*,[33] the Indian incarnation of PIL was indeed first essentially social. This *"social action litigation"*[34] (SAL), as conceived by Uprenda Baxi, was *"primarily judge-led and even judge-induced"* and as such *"elated to juristic and judicial activism on the High Bench"*.[35] The Indian *"social action litigation"* trend was not deprived of populist rhetoric and judicial politics although putting forward humanist aspirations. But as demonstrated in the seminal decision *Kesavananda Bharati*,[36] these ambitions were originally framed by the division of powers and the inherent limitation of constitutional precedent:

> *these landmarks in the development of the law cannot be permitted to be transformed into weapons for defeating the hopes and aspirations of our teeming millions, half-clad, half-starved, half-educated. These hopes and aspirations representing the will of the people can only become articulate through the voice of their elected representatives. If they fail the people, the nation must face death and destruction. Then neither the Court nor the Constitution will save the country.*[37]

> *Whenever there is a public wrong or public injury caused by an act or omission of the State or a public authority which is contrary to the Constitution or the law, any member of the public acting bona fide and having sufficient interest can maintain an action for redressal of such wrong or public injury. (…).*

> *If public duties are to be enforced and social collective "diffused" rights and interests are to be protected, we have to utilize the initiative and zeal of public minded persons and*

---

[32] *Ibid.*, p. 108.

[33] *Ibid.*, p. 109.

[34] *Ibid.*, p. 108.

[35] *Ibid.*, p. 111.

[36] See *Kesavnanda Bharathi v. State of Kerala* (1973) 4 S.C.C. 225. *Kesavnanda Bharathi v. State of Kerala* (1973). This landmark decision constitutes the basis for the Indian Supreme Court to review parliamentary constitutional amendments. Dealing essentially with property right, this seminal case is key to Indian constitutional history as it elaborates on the "basis structure" doctrine: while fundamental rights can be amended, the Parliament cannot alter the "basis structure of the constitution". As showed by a recent book published by T.R. Andhyarujina, senior advocate and former Solicitor General, this case filed over a land issue by Swami Kesavananda Bharati Sripadagalavaru, the head of a Kerala math that challenged the State's attempt to impose restrictions on religious property, was settled in an overcharged political atmosphere. See Andhyarujina (2011). See as well, Austin (2003).

[37] See Justice Chandrachud in Kesavananda at 968 quoted by Upendra Baxi, *Supra* note …, p. 112.

3 Normative Internationalization Through Globalization: India …

organizations by *allowing them to move the court and act for a general or group interest; even though, they may not be directly injured in their own rights.*[38]

While the Indian SAL has now shifted from the poor to the middle class and so moved closer to the American PIL,[39] hence being at the centre of a controversy on *"judicial excessivism"* (see below), another original incarnation of public interest litigation is progressively appearing in China. Referring as well to general grievances litigated in relation to the complicated implementation of social and economic rights, the Chinese nascent approach of PIL however largely differs from the phenomenon analysed by Uprenda Baxi as well as today's Indian PIL for one essential reason: it is not judge-led nor it is judge-induced. In an authoritarian one-party State, the inexistence of a truly independent and professional Chinese judiciary could partly explain this key difference, but other Chinese specificities come into play. In the absence of a complete democratization movement and without the unanimous support of independent administrative and judicial institutions,[40] a number of elements have however permitted the emergence of a unique Chinese collective litigation movement that shows some similarities with PIL and, to some extent, finds its inspiration in its American or Asian predecessors. For the past 15 years indeed, Chinese legal scholars and China watchers are observing the birth, development, and logical limitations of a *rights-based and civil society-led* movement using the law as well as existing judicial (and non-judicial) avenues as powerful tools for social emancipation, hence furthering the basic legal regime offered by the Chinese Constitution and other legislative developments. Interestingly, this sinicization (中国化 *Zhōngguóhuà*) of PIL finds its roots and strength in the use of rights-based tools themselves powerfully reinforced by a language of rights largely disseminated by the media—including official channels—and ambiguously tolerated by a State that is both generating and limiting rights. While a number of rights are concerned by this grassroots-led movement, it is largely in the labour and the environment law fields that China is developing its most interesting and, as we will see, most debatable if not controversial variation of a PIL.[41] In this context, emerges a China-specific PIL I have called a *"Rights Interest Litigation"* or *RIL* that illustrates as well as questions the justiciability of

---

[38] See Justice Bhagwati's (1981), at 190–194. This case is often contemplated as the precursor of the Indian PIL. PIL writ petitions have been filed under article 226 (Power of High Courts to issue certain writs) or article 32 (remedies for enforcement of (fundamental) rights guaranteed by the Constitution) of the Indian Constitution.

[39] See Surya Deva, « Public Interest Litigation in India: A Quest to Achieve the Impossible», in Po Jen Yap and Holing Lau (eds.), *Supra* note …, p. 61.

[40] In their work on PIL in Asia, Po Jen Yap and Holing Lau identify three main engines for the development of PIL: "democratization, transnational migration of norms and ideals, judicial recognition of courts institutional role in shaping public law discourse within their jurisdiction". See Po Yen Yap and Holning Lau (eds.), *Public Interest Litigation in Asia, Supra* note …., p. 2.

[41] Environmental cases also provide an interesting basis for discussion, but have not always, as in other Asian countries such as India or even Hong Kong, involved the same innovative uses of law as labour law cases do. I will later refer to some of these cases in a comparative perspective.

socio-economic rights in an authoritarian regime, hence also interrogating the intentionality of China's legal reforms and the true interest of the Chinese leadership to challenge the current regime in establishing a genuine rule of law.[42,43, 44,45]

Interestingly, in a sort of parallel—although very distinctive—move, the Indian PIL lost some of its legitimacy and prestige as it has partly transformed into "populism and excessivism". So that the question of the intentionality of this judicial activism and its real impact on the realization of socio-economic rights is equally relevant in today's India.

Labour related cases are of particular comparative interest. In India, Labour PIL is essential to protect the rights of the most vulnerable workers from a particular period of time, that of a post-emergency country healing its wounds with more social justice. Taken seriously by handful of reformist judges, the sufferings of the disadvantaged Indian workers transformed into a fight for fundamental rights enforcement under the Constitution Article 32 petition. In this regard, the 1980s qualification of the Indian PIL by U. Baxi as SAL remains very relevant. From wages and equal pay issues (*Dhirendra Chamoli v. State of U.P*), to the right to form a trade union (*Damayanti v. Union of India),* the right to livelihood (*D.K. Yadav v. J.M.A. Industries)*, gender discrimination at work (*Mrs. Neera Mathur v Life Insurance Corporation of India*), sexual harassment (*Vishaka and Ors v State of Rajasthan), or* bonded labour and the precise issue of rehabilitation of bounded labourers *(Neeraja Chaudhary vs. State of Madhya Pradesh*), the Indian Supreme Court has dealt with the whole spectrum of labour rights violations, hence filling the gaps left by a quite basic and non-modernized legislation. But have these many attempts of mindful judges others would call zealous populists brought the social revolution expected? Probably not as showed by the poor realization of socio-economic rights in today's India in the context of what Partha Chatterjee has described as a *"political society"* only enabling the poorest to "expand their freedom by using means that are not available to them in civil society".[46] As in China indeed, beyond judicial activism, it is the question of the relationship between the governed and State, which is directly posed when analysing the real impact of socio-economic rights litigation on the effective implementation of the law and eventual realization of the rights theoretical hold by all.

In recent years, the ability of Chinese citizens to assert their rights in court has clearly expanded. As for environmental public interest litigation, the government's choice to support labour litigation is relatively easy to understand: the cases brought to court are often technical and do not directly question the government political choices. If ever they do, they are based on the rights enshrined in the amended

---

[42] See Choukroune (2013)., and Choukroune and Chloé (2013).

[43] Since February 2001, China is a party to the International Covenant on Economic, Social, and Cultural Rights and as such has been examined by the UN Committee reviewing the implementation of its obligations. See Choukroune (2005).

[44] As discussed below, a number of authors have interrogated the politics and practices of courts in authoritarian regimes hence providing a better view of the functions of the judiciary in non-democratic countries. See Ginsburg and Tamir (2008).

[45] See Choukroune (2016).

[46] See Chatterjee (2004).

Constitution and new labour laws and diffused by a language of rights the government itself promotes with the help of legal and judicial aid programs sponsored by local and international "NGOs" in cooperation with Chinese lawyers and with the support of Chinese leaders.[47,48] Oriented towards the working class and not the poorest strata of the society, this rights interest litigation (RIL) *à la chinoise* can also spill over its initial framework in fostering new legal developments hence participating in the protection of all citizens' rights. At the heart of this labour RIL, discrimination issues occupy a central place.

Can we however generalize this positive experience? In the absence of a genuine rule of law and independent judiciary, these collective victories as promising as they are, have not systematically transformed into more rights realization. So that the justiciability of rights legitimates a given regime more than it supports rights realization.

This impressionistic account of the two incomparable yet fascinating to compare Asian giants could only highlight some of the visible evolutions in the (non) realization of socio-economic rights at a time of frenetic globalization. As extremely encouraging and promising as the Indian and Chinese PIL/SAL/RIL were, they are now indeed by the inherent limitations of the current legal and judicial systems. As observed by Fu Hualing and Richard Cullen:

> The reliability of courts as a forum for PIL can no longer be taken for granted. Courts were a comparatively reliable forum for PIL in the 1990s. Under Xiao Yang's terms as Chief Justice, the courts were more receptive to challenging lawsuits and lawyers enjoyed some breathing space in the court room in advocating rights. Since 2003, unfortunately, more constraints (not least via the courts themselves) have been placed on legal activism and PIL. [49]

In India, on the other side, the recent evolutions of PIL also brings more confusion than clarity as evidenced by many observers and, for instance, PS Sathe:

> Judicial activism does not have its legitimacy because the other organs of the government have failed. That is only one reason for judicial activism bordering on excessivism. Even if other organs of the government function efficiently, there will be need for judicial activism for recognising and protecting the rights of powerless minorities.[50]

Beyond these general remarks, labour PIL appears as a paradoxical legal tool in both China and India. The Chinese and Indian Labour PIL are indeed fascinating illustrations of the ability to adapt and perpetuate a given system: while workers' rights are fostered at a micro level, these legal adaptations do not challenge a given order. A manifestation of justiciability such as the Chinese or Indian PIL can also reinforce the existing political system in providing the leaders with the necessary

---

[47] See Webster (2011).

[48] See as well, Simon (2013).

[49] *See* Fu Hualing and Richard Cullen, *supra* note …, at 28.

[50] See SP Sathe, *Judicial Activism in India: Transgressing Borders and Enforcing Limits*, supra note ….

The recent trends in an Indian PIL tempted by populist aspirations and private lobbies has been largely documented contemporary legal and socio-legal literature, see, for example, the excellent article of Surya Deva, "'Public Interest Litigation in India: A Critical Review", *Civil, supra note....*

time to delay complicated reforms, be it the real annihilation of caste, to paraphrase B.R. Ambedkar, the father of the Indian Constitution, or the advent of democracy in China.[51] As observed by Jessica Teets, China is at best pursuing a sort of "Consultative Authoritarianism" that is a system of consensus-based decision-making, which avoids contention.[52] In this context, the sinicization undertaken by a socialist harmonious society, which is reinventing China itself under the Party's watchful eye, is designed mainly to stall for time. Using law as a powerful tool to discipline[53] the society hence reacting to popular unrest, the socialist harmonious society adopts diversionary tactics allowing a troublesome political universal to be kept at bay. This, on the long run could be detrimental to the development and enforcement of labour rights as socio-economic and human rights.

However, these logical limitations and legitimate questions about the future and undesirable effects of the justiciability of economic and social rights in an authoritarian State should not hide other positive developments: the fact that socio-economic rights are increasingly taken seriously by the legislator and judge and, in parallel to this trend, the appropriation of these new rights by the Chinese and Indian population. Here again, China and India teach us a lesson in legal complexity. One that Marc Galanter already understood in his early social research on Indian law:

> (the papers in this collection) attempt to develop a view of Indian legal reality that steers between the 'classic" fallacy of treating India as a flawed pathological specimen of law and the 'romantic' fallacy of thinking that beneath Indian law's false 'foreign' surface lies a more authentic, ineffably Indian legal genius waiting to be released.[54]

While the Chinese and Indian incarnations of PIL may not directly contribute to a political reform, their pragmatic expansion of rights has already penetrated the minds of those who call for a rights-based change, which owes quite a lot to globalization.

4 Judicial Dynamism and Its Paradoxes

India's legal revolutions—PIL's development especially—have been supported by mindful lawyers and a handful of High Court and Supreme Court judges and the leading figures of Justices Iyer and Bhagwati. While the post-colonial legislator had tried to develop a robust set of norms suited to the political aspirations of the new Indian Republic in the form of an evolutionary constitutional project, this dynamic process has also been supported by a vibrant judiciary, which has had recourse to foreign and international laws as engines for social modernization. Not so long ago, however, the overwhelming majority of national courts shared a common reluctance to refer to foreign and international laws for these norms were envisaged as legally

---

[51] See Ambedkar (2016).

[52] See Teets (2013).

[53] On the law of China's harmonious society, see Choukroune (2012).

[54] See Galanter (1989).

inappropriate and politically hazardous. This situation has clearly evolved in the direction of a greater, if not systematic, use of foreign and international laws by the national judge.

In this context, the Indian Judiciary was free to have recourse to foreign and international laws as a rights implementation engine. The domains in which it intervened are very diverse and vary from boarder delimitation, to federalism, law of the sea, refugee law, or international trade and investment law including the impact and possible direct effect of the World Trade Organization (WTO) decisions in municipal law.[55] For instance, the case of WTO law is particularly interesting in that it reflects the dialogues of national and international courts on matters of incorporation. In the recent WTO Solar case indeed, India tried to win the legal battle in putting forward the very arguments of its own Supreme Court showing that a legislative act was not necessary to incorporate international norms, which were not affecting the rights of the citizens.[56] While not accepted by the WTO adjudicating body, this argument proves, once again, the keen reception and later re-exportation of international norms *in* and *by* India. As such, "judicial activism is not an aberration" but a "counter-majoritarian check on democracy".[57] Indeed, "the struggle for custody of the Constitution", as Granville Austin put it, required innovative interpretation and a non-traditional approach of the separation of powers. India's peaceful social revolution has yet to be completed, but the path taken by the Judge with the support of foreign and international laws, although often uncertain, still goes in the right direction, and often serves as a shield against government interference.[58]

Differently, in China, the evolutions towards a greater reliance on the law was essentially triggered by a nascent, yet dynamic and inventive civil society. In the two countries, mindful lawyers, and the media are playing a subtle game, sometimes against the State, but also often with its implicit support, to push forward difficult social reforms hence questioning the traditional conceptions of the relationship between the State and the society in countries which are not comparable to western democracies and so profoundly challenge traditional legal and political concepts. With or without democracy, social aspirations are not satisfied by an Indian or Chinese State itself unable or willing to implement the laws it has enacted, so the need to find alternative avenues for rights realization. The Chinese situation is particularly revealing of these new phenomena. Whether academics, professional lawyers, "barefoot lawyers", or self-taught lawyers such as "the representatives of the people" (*gongmin daili*), Chinese human rights defenders have significantly gained influence

---

[55] *See Haridas Exports v* (2002) available at: https://indiankanoon.org/doc/838587/; and *M/S. S & S. Enterprise vs Designated Authority & Ors*, on 22 February, 2005, available at: https://indiankanoon.org/doc/1868210/.

[56] *See* DS 456 *India—Certain Measures Relating to Solar Cells and Solar Modules,* Panel and Appellate Body Reports of 24 February 2016 and 16 September 2016 available at: https://www.wto.org/english/tratop_e/dispu_e/cases_e/ds456_e.htm/.

[57] See S.P. Sathe, *Judicial Activism in India, Transgressing Borders and Enforcing Limits, op.cit.*, p. 310.

[58] See Granville Austin, "The Supreme Court and the Struggle for Custody of the Constitution", *in Supreme but not Infallible, Essays in Honour of the Supreme Court of India, op.cit.*, pp. 1–15.

since the second half of the 1990s.[59] This has been supported and strengthened by the profound legal reform of the last 20 years, including the rehabilitation of the legal professions and their separation from the State apparatus. Banned between 1957 and 1977, lawyers were gradually allowed after the adoption of the 1978 Constitution and the new criminal rules of 1979, which restored the right to defence. However, lawyers remained "legal agents" of the State, a kind of special status given to officials whose activities were completely controlled by the administration. It was not until the adoption of the 1996 Law on Lawyers, that we could witness the emergence and development of private firms. At the heart of this new generation of lawyers, a number of specialized practitioners are defending the rights of migrant workers and their reputation has spread beyond the borders of China like Zhou Litai in Chongqing or Tong Lihua in Beijing. At the same time, encouraged by international donours programs and private foundations (Ford Foundation, American Bar Association, etc.), a number of "associations" of lawyers have been put in place as, for example, the Centre for the protection of the rights of disabled citizens of Wuhan University, launched at the initiative of Wang Exiang, or the Beijing Zhicheng Law Firm founded in 2008 by Tong Lihua. These "NGOs" echo other forms of organization that are especially developed to fill the void left by the social economic reforms. Emerged in the early 2000s, at the initiative of an urban elite close to the government—including in Beijing—to help social excluded category of urban public services and official unions, human rights NGOs representing countryside migrant workers have also experienced tremendous growth in recent years. They are now present throughout the Chinese territory, particularly in the southern province of Guangdong. Participating to the "harmonious society" without questioning the State's ambitions, these new organizations de facto help the Chinese State in performing some of its functions with the support of a governing elite legitimating civil society's initiatives as they participate to the State's objective of a "society governed by law". In this respect, Chinese media play a key role in diffusing the hopes and grievances of the workers at the national and international levels as exemplified by the 2010 Southern China strikes. The almost infinite capacity of Beijing to arbitrarily deploy its net of repression is intact and probably much stronger than before Xi Jinping's accession to power. It is clearly illustrated today with the ethnocide performed in Xinjiang against the Uyghurs or the silencing of the COVID19 whistleblowers. But the pockets of freedom for public participation are still conducive to a form of human rights realization as they make collective struggle more visible hence difficult to fully disregard for a governing elite concerned with its popular legitimacy. Is this eventually bringing more rights realization? As we have seen above, the greater justiciability of socio-economic rights does not necessarily equal their realization.

---

[59] See Zhang (2006), Gallagher (2005).

5 Conclusion: Globalization, Modernization, and Resistances to Democratization

How to transpose the European legal modernity project into other territories where law pre-existed but, as Max Weber believed, only on the basis of very distinct conceptions of norms and the role of institutions and the State. In this regard, can one even pose the question of legal modernity in India or China? Indeed, as exposed by Trubek from Weber's approach, it had long been accepted that:

> The European legal system was distinct in all () dimensions. Unlike the legal systems of other great civilizations, European legal organization was highly differentiated. The European State separated law from other aspects of political activity. Specialized professional or "status" groups of lawyers existed. Legal rules were consciously fashioned and rulemaking was relatively free of direct interference from religious influences and from other sources of traditional values. Concrete decisions were based on the application of universal rules, and decision making was not subject to constant political intervention.[60]

This rather idealized perception of European political modernity was put to the test of history in Europe itself by the ravages of Nazism, Fascism, and other Stalinist approaches of the law, which entertained a much less depoliticized and rational rapport with the norm, and finally "reincarnated" society, as Claude Lefort could put it, in the idea of the *One-People*.[61] As such, legal modernity is not a linear and irreversible construction. The temptation to challenge the modern is always present as the project is not completed but constantly in motion. If on the move then, legal modernity cannot be circumscribed to a given territory. It is polymorphous and, as the Indian and Chinese receptions have demonstrated, open to enrichment from other experiments, that of international law in particular.

Indian modern law has been defined against the backdrop of native norms and the various attempts by British scholars to rewrite this legacy as a "deliberate" and "adaptive re-creation", which culminated in the codification of an Anglo-Indian law supporting the Raj's ambitions.[62] This transformation has attracted a considerable amount of scholarship amongst which the work of Marc Galanter, for it is deeply grounded in a profound knowledge of Indian legal practices, remains remarkable. In analysing Indian legal modernity indeed, Galanter proves the death of Hindu, Muslim, or customary "traditional law" in its displacement by modern law and so the aborted restauration of "indigenous" practices as, today, the "*dharmasastra* component is almost completely obliterated".[63] There is no romantic fascination

---

[60] *See* D. Trubek, "Max Weber on Law and the Rise of Capitalism", *op.cit.*

[61] For an English language version of Claude Lefort's work, *see*, for example, Lefort (2007).

[62] See Galanter and Dhavan (1989).

[63] *Ibid. Dharmasastra,* in Hindu ancient scriptures, refers to the treatises on "dharma" (duties, rights, law and, in sum, a right way of living). They address, in poetic verses, the questions of duties, responsibilities, family, and the self in society. The term "dharma" is itself subject to many meanings and interpretations in different Indian religions (Hinduism, Buddhism, Sikhism). In Hinduism, it is often associated with the idea of righteousness and equated to "satya" (truth). *The Laws of Manu* is probably the most famous of these many *Dharmasastra*. First translated in 1794, it has influenced

for a glorious Indian past resting upon venerable ancient scriptures or an idealized village structure, but a blunt observation: modern law exists and is asserted as a distinct reality. There is indeed "an all-India legal system", which can be viewed as "an important unifying element" and goes hand in hand with an "all India legal culture" rationally carried forward by the legal profession. Hence, argues Galanter:

> The modern legal system provides both the personnel and the techniques for carrying on public business in a way that is nationally intelligible and free of dependence on particular religious or local authority. It thus provides one requisite for organizing Indian society into a modern nation state.[64]

Indian modern law is plural in its practice and so distinct in its nature.[65] In blending the reception of foreign law with the present reality of a domestic legacy, Indian law is not only globalized but truly distinctive.[66] Chinese law is also a blend of norms imported and sinicized through a strategic yet distantiated acculturation. Naturally, democracy is yet to be fully realized on the basis of a genuine equality of rights and opportunities in India and embraced in China. But even in China, which now seems to get back to the dark days of a neo-totalitarian regime, there are manifestations of democratic participations to the public sphere if not totally to political decisions, which remain even more so today than paradoxically 10 years ago in the hands of the one-State Party.

These tensions at the centre of which is globalization have shaped today's India and China's modern law through the many journeys of international norms internalized and, as in the case of trade and investment notably, although exported with the increasing presence of the two countries on the global scene. Jostled by globalization, as well as national resistances, domestic laws are indeed faced with an unprecedented epistemological revolution in which normative *hybridization* plays a central role. As in India and China, these legal journeys challenge modern Western conceptions of law while the new *metis* norms meet with other legal systems still invested by the West but on territories where globalization also happens without it, from the Silk Road to parts of Africa and Latin America. As such, traditional sources and actors of law are deeply questioned by a globalization of knowledge and practices that is not only exported from one legal order to another, but gradually de-territorialized and again re-territorialized by the former recipient of international law now turned exporters. There is, as such, a "Chinese" or an "Indian" international law which both inform the practice the two countries but also shape the conduct of world affairs.

---

many European thinkers including Nietzsche. Often mistranslated and poorly understood, it remains an essential text to approach the development of Indian norms. See, Doniger's (2000).

[64] *Ibid.*, p. 28.

[65] See Mendelsohn (2014).

[66] See Choukroune (2018).

References

Ambedkar, B.N. 2016. *Annihilation of Caste, Verso Books.* Critical edition, 416

Andhyarujina, T.R. 2011. *The Kesavananda Bharati Case: the Untold Story of Struggle for Supremacy by Supreme Court and Parliament, Universal Law Publishing*

Arnaud, A.-J. (1998) *Entre modernité et mondialisation. Cinq leçons d'histoire de la philosophie du droit et de l'État,* Paris: Librairie générale de droit et de jurisprudence (LGDJ)

Auby, Jean-Bernard. 2003. *La globalisation, le droit et l'État, Paris: Montchrestien, 2003 and Archives de philosophie du droit, La mondialisation entre illusion et utopie.* Paris: Dalloz

Austin, Granville. 2003. *Working a democratic constitution: a history of the Indian experience,* Oxford University Press, 2003

Baghwati, J. 1984. Judicial activism and public interest litigation. *Columbia Journal of Transnational Law* 23:561

Baxi, Upendra. 1985. Taking suffering seriously: social action litigation in the Supreme Court of India. *Third World Legal Studies* 4(1):107–132

Benvenisti, Eyal. 2008. Reclaiming democracy: the strategic uses of foreign and international law by national courts. *American Journal of International Law* 102: 241–274.

Berger, Axel. 2013. Investment rules in Chinese preferential trade and investment agreements, Discussion Paper/Deutsches Institut für Entwicklungspolitik

Chaisse, Julien, Leïla Choukroune and Sufian Jusoh (eds.). 2020–21. *Handbook in International Investment Law and Policy*, Springer

Chatterjee, Partha. 2004. *The Politics of the Governed*, 67. Columbia University Press

Chen, Feng and Xin Xu. 2012. Active judiciary: Judicial dismantling of workers collective action in China. *The China Journal*, N°67, 87–107

Choukroune, Leila. 2021. Corporate social responsibility and foreign direct investment, the indian investment treaty approach and beyond, In *Adjudicating Global Business in and with India International Commercial and Investment Disputes Settlement*, ed. Leïla Choukroune and Rahul Donde, Routledge

Choukroune, Leila. 2011. China's accession and participation to the WTO. In *China, Democracy and the Law*, ed. Mireille Delmas-Marty and Pierre-Etienne Will (eds.), Brill, 649–704

Choukroune, Leila. 2018. EU and developing Asia trade dispute settlement: assertive legalism for political autonomy. In *Handbook on EU Law Trade Policy*, ed. Sangeeta Khorana, Edward Elgar

Choukroune, Leila and Donde Rahul. 2018. *International Commercial and Investment Disputes in and with India, Transnational Dispute Management* (TDM), India Special (25 contributions). https://www.transnational-dispute-management.com/journal-browse-issues-toc.asp?key=77

Choukroune, Leila. 2018. CSR and Indian investment law. *Transnational Dispute Management (TDM), Special India.* Investment treaty arbitration and commercial arbitration in and with India (25 Contributions)

Choukroune, Leila. 2016. Non-investment concerns in India's international investment agreements, *Jindal Global Law Review* (Springer), Special issue on India's 2015 model bilateral investment treaty: issues and perspectives

Choukroune, Leïla. 2013. Socio-economic rights litigation and Chinese labour law reform, justiciability and authoritarianism. In *China's Influence on Non-Trade Concerns in International Economic Law*, ed. Paolo Farah, Ashgate Publishing

Choukroune, Leïla and Froissart Chloé. 2013. "Justiciabilité et négociation collective, la mise en oeuvre du droit du travail en Chine", *Le Mouvement Social*, accepted, forthcoming mai 2013

Choukroune, Leïla. 2005. Justiciability of economic, social, and cultural rights: the UN Committee on economic, social and cultural rights' review of China's first implementation of the international covenant on economic, social and cultural rights. *Columbia Journal of Asian Law* 19:1

Choukroune, Leïla. 2016. Rights interest litigation, socio-economic rights and Chinese labour law reform. In *China and non-trade issues*, ed. Paolo Farah, Ashgate

Choukroune, Leïla. 2012. "Harmonious Society" and the law: An epistemological break? How China's practice of international law is challenging legal theory. *German Law Journal*

Choukroune, Leïla. 2018. From without to within: Indian international law as modernizer. In *Indian Modernities: Exploring Ideas and Practices*, Springer

Choukroune, Leïla. 2016. Human Rights in international investment disputes: Global litigation as international law re-unifier. In *Judging the state in international trade and investment law*, ed. Leïla Choukroune, Springer

Cunningham, C.D. 1987. Public interest litigation in indian supreme court: a study in the light of the American Experience. *Journal of Indian Law Institute* 29:494

Delmas, Mireille. 2003. Global law: a triple challenge, trans. Naomi Norberg, Ardsley, NY: Transnational Publishers

Deva, Surya. 2009. Public interest litigation in India: a critical review. *Civil Justice Quarterly* 28(1):19–40

Galanter, Marc. 1989. *Law and Society in Modern India*, OUP, Delhi, p. 298

Galanter, Marc and Rajeev Dhavan. 1989. Rajeev Dhavan's Introduction to the Marc Galanter, *Law and Society in Modern India*, OUP, pp. xiii-xcixi

Gallagher, Mary. 2006. Mobilizing the law in China: informed disenchantment and the development of legal consciousness. *Law and Society Review* 40(4):783–816

Gallagher, M.E. 2005. Use the law as your weapon! institutional change and legal mobilization in China. In *Engaging the Law in China: State, Society and Possibilities for Justice*, ed. N.-J. Diamant, Stanley Lubman, K.J. and O. Brien, 54–83. Stanford, Stanford University Press

Ginsburg, Tom and Moustafa Tamir. 2008. *Rule By Law: The Politics of Courts in Authoritarian Regimes*, Cambridge University Press

Habermas, Jürgen. 2001. *The Post-National Constellation*, 216 Political Essays: MIT Press

Habermas, Jürgen. 2008. The constitutionalization of international law and the legitimation problems of a constitution for world society. *Constellations* 15(4):444–455

Hadley, Katle. 2013. Do China's BITs Matter? Assessing the effect of China's investment agreements on foreign investment flows, investor's rights and the rule of law. *Georgetown Journal of International Law* 45: 255–321

Haridas Exports v. All India Float Glass Manufacturers Association, 22 July, 2002

Justice Bhagwati's fascinating reasoning in *S.P. Gupta v. Union of India*, AIR 1982 SC 149: 1981, at 190–194

Kosla, Madhav. 2010. Making social rights conditional: Lessons from India. *International Journal of Constitutional Law* 8:739–765

Lefort, Claude. 2007. *Complications*. Communism and the Dilemmas of Democracy: Columbia University Press.

Leïla, Choukroune. 2014. Les BRICS et le droit international du commerce et de l'investissement, entre autonomie et intégration, In *Les dérèglements économiques internationaux: Crise du droit ou droit des crises*, ed. Habib Gherari, Paris, Pédone

Loquin, Éric and Catherine Kessedjian (eds.). 2000. *La mondialisation du droit*. Paris: Litec-Credimi

Mendelsohn, Olivier. 2014. How Indian is Indian Law? In *Law and social transformation in India,* OUP, pp. 47–80

Modhurima, Das Gupta. 2009. Courting development: The Supreme Court. VDM Verlag: Public interest litigation and socio-economic development in India

Morand, Charles-Philippe (ed.) 2001. *Le droit saisi par la mondialisation*. Brussels: Bruylant

Rajan, Prabhash. 2015. Most favoured nation provisions in India BIT, a case for reform. *Indian Journal of International Law*

Rao, Manta. 2004. *Public Interest Litigation in India: A Renaissance in Social Justice,* Eastern Book Co; 2nd edition

Razzaque, Jona (ed.). 2004. Public interest environment litigation in India, Pakistan, and Bangladesh, special issue of the comparative and environment law series, vol. 7, Kluwer Law

Sathe, S.P. 2002. *Judicial Activism in India*, OUP, New Delhi

Simon, Karla. 2013. Civil society in China, *The Legal Framework from ancient Times to the New reform Era*, OUP

Singh, Parmanand. 2010. Promises and perils of public interest litigation in India. *Journal of Indian Law Institute* 52:172–188

Slaughter, Anne-Marie. 2000. Judicial globalization. *Virginia Journal of International Law* 40 (1103): 1112–1123.

Sornarajah, M. 2010. India, China and Foreign Investment. In *China*, ed. M. Sornarajah and J. Wang, 132–166. India and the International Economic Order: Cambridge University Press, Cambridge

Teets, Jessica. 2013. Let many civil societies bloom: The rise of consultative authoritarianism in China. *The China Quarterly*, 213: 19-38

UNCTAD, 2021. *Investment Trends Monitor*, January 2021, https://unctad.org/webflyer/global-investment-trend-monitor-no-38

Upadhyay, Videh. 2007. Public interest litigation in India, concepts, cases and concerns, Lexis Nexis

Varella, Marcello Dias. 2014. *Internationalisation of Law, Globalisation, International Law and Complexity*, Springer

Webster, Timothy. 2011. Ambivalence and activism: employment discrimination in China. *Vanderbilt Journal of Transnational Law* 44:643–707

Webster, T. 2011. Ambivalence and activism: employment discrimination in China. *Vanderbilt Journal of Transnational Law* 44(643):643–709

Wendy Doniger's translation and presentation, *The Laws of Manu,* Penguin Classic, 2000

Yap, Po Jen and Holning Lau (eds.). 2010. *Public Interest Litigation in Asia*, Routledge Law in Asia

Zhang, Y. 2006. Law and labour in post-mao China, In *Debating Political Reform in China*, ed. S. Zhao, Armonk, Sharpe, 180–199

Chapter 4
Discontent Against Globalization: Reasons and Remedies

Abhijit Das

1 Introduction

It cannot be denied that over the past few years trade and globalization have increasingly been viewed with skepticism and suspicion in both, developed and developing countries. This was strikingly evident in the media reports during the US presidential elections during 2016-17, as well as during the debate on Brexit in the United Kingdom. Dissent and discontent against globalization, particularly in developing countries, is not a recent development. Although the backlash against globalization had already hit the streets in some of the developing countries way back in the early 1990s, this was derisively dismissed by many as a concern articulated mainly by fringe and radical left-oriented groups in the society. No doubt anti-globalization marches and street skirmishes that took place on the margins of meetings of G5/G8/G20, and reached their pinnacle during the Ministerial Conference of the World Trade Organization (WTO) held in Seattle in 1999, received intermittent visibility in the media. But these protests, along with the ephemeral media coverage, failed to leave even the trace of an imprint on international institutions that are the bedrock of globalization. It is only in the past few years when protests against globalization in the developed countries have gained more visibility and traction in the political discourse, that inter-governmental organizations are taking some cognizance of the discontentment against deeper trade and investment integration. Nevertheless, the response of these organizations fails to address the fundamental reasons behind the backlash against globalization. This needs to change if the benefits of globalization have to flow equitably among all nations, as well as to different groups within each country.

Before proceeding further, it is important to understand what is meant by globalization. Globalization has come to mean an unhindered flow of goods, services,

---

A. Das (✉)
Centre for WTO Studies, Indian Institute of Foreign Trade, New Delhi, India
e-mail: headwto@iift.edu

© The Author(s), under exclusive license to Springer Nature Singapore Pte Ltd. 2022   65
A. Palit (ed.), *Globalisation Impacts*, International Law and the Global South,
https://doi.org/10.1007/978-981-16-7185-2_4

and capital across borders. Logically, it should also include the free movement of persons across borders, but the developed countries have been resisting consideration of the free movement of persons on the ground that it involves immigration policy and security. In recent years, flow of data across borders is increasingly becoming an important component of globalization. While several international organizations are involved in providing rules and disciplines on certain aspects of globalization, this chapter is largely confined to discussing issues covered by the WTO.

This chapter seeks to answer four relevant questions. First, which issues have been highlighted in the protests against globalization? Second, using developments at the multilateral trading system embodied initially in the General Agreement on Tariffs and Trade (GATT) and subsequently the WTO as a case study, what could be some of the fundamental reasons for the backlash against globalization? Third, how have some of the international institutions that underpin globalization responded to the challenges emerging from the growing disenchantment with globalization? Fourth, what changes are required to address the challenges emerging from the protests against globalization?

The subsequent sections of the chapter are organized as follows. Section 2 describes some of the key episodes of protests against globalization, including with regard to trade-related issues at the GATT/WTO. This sets the context for identifying the main themes highlighted in these protests. Section 3 seeks to identify some of the key reasons for protests against globalization, many of which can be traced to the functioning of the WTO. Section 4 makes some recommendations for addressing the root causes of the discontent against globalization. Section 5 concludes the study.

2   Key Episodes of Protests Against Globalization: Identifying the Main Themes Raised in the Protests

Protests against globalization have manifested in different geographies and varied hues and shades. The protests have spanned continents and have highlighted a large number of issues. International institutions, including the WTO, International Monetary Fund (IMF), World Bank, G8, G20, etc., have been some of the targets of these protests. Starr (2005)[1] maps the emergence and consolidation of the anti-globalization movement during the 1980s to 2005. The following snippets from her book provide a rich tapestry of the protests against globalization:

- Coinciding with the implementation of the North American Free Trade Agreement (NAFTA), 1st January 1994 witnessed "what has probably been the most important single influence on the anti-globalization movement"—Zapatistas (an army of peasants and indigenous people), emerged from the mountain forests in the poorest state of Mexico, and took over several towns in Mexico. According to the Zapatistas, they "were against the great financial powers".

---

[1] Starr (2005).

4 Discontent Against Globalization: Reasons and Remedies

- In 1995, a general strike broke out in many Latin American countries largely in response to the problems of globalization. For the first time in Bolivia, Brazil, and Ecuador, these strikes witnessed alliances of peasants, indigenous people, and trade unions.
- In 1998, an organization called Peoples Global Action was formed for resisting globalization all over the world. This year also witnessed an "Intercontinental caravan of solidarity and resistance", involving 500 peasant farmers from India, who protested across Europe against globalization.
- In May 1998, a human chain of 70,000 protestors ringed the G8 meeting in Birmingham. Within a few days, 10,000 people, including a cycle and tractor caravan, protested against the Second Ministerial Conference of the WTO held in Geneva. In parallel, coordinated protests against the WTO were held simultaneously in 30 countries. This could be considered as the first global action day against globalization.
- In December 1998, the Association for the Taxation of Financial Transactions and Aid to Citizens was established to take democratic control of financial markets and their institutions.
- In June 1999, the second global carnival of resistance was held simultaneously in 43 countries at the time of the G8 summit held in Koln.
- The anti-globalization movement was much in prominence in the protests against the WTO Ministerial Conference held in Seattle in November 1999. These protests were held almost simultaneously in many cities including Seattle, Geneva, Paris, and Bangalore. The WTO building was occupied and festooned with banners protesting against international trade and globalization. Coordinated protests were also held against the World Bank. French farmers (along with their livestock) protested against the adverse impact of trade liberalization by eating regional products under the Eiffel Tower.
- In April 2000, a general strike was organized in Cochabamba in Bolivia to protest against the privatization of water supply.
- During 2000, there was a major mobilization in the US to coincide with the spring joint meeting of the IMF and the World Bank. In September 2000, large-scale protests were organized on the sidelines of the meeting of the World Economic Forum held in Melbourne.
- In January 2001, the World Social Forum was established to discuss alternatives to corporate-driven globalization. This has become the premier platform for civil society organizations world-over to "find solutions to the problems of our time".[2]

Apart from some of the protests against globalization highlighted in Starr (2005), it is also relevant to mention the following three important episodes relating to international trade in the anti-globalization movement:

- In what was perhaps the largest public display of opinion anywhere in the world against the Uruguay Round of multilateral trade negotiations at the GATT, about

---

[2] World Social Forum, available at https://fsm2016.org/en/sinformer/a-propos-du-forum-social-mondial/

half a million Indian farmers took part in a day-long procession and rally in Bangalore on 2 October 1993. They were protesting against the proposals in the Uruguay Round Draft Final Act texts that they claimed would have devastating effects on their livelihoods in general and on their control of seeds in particular.[3]

- One of the most significant protests against globalization took place in South Africa in March 2001, when AIDS activists, trade unions, and the African National Congress came together to protest the lawsuit against the South African government by 39 international pharmaceutical manufacturers attempting to block its plans to import cheaper anti-AIDS generic drugs. In parallel, in New York, over 200 demonstrators occupied the office of a prominent multinational pharmaceutical company that was allegedly at the forefront of the lawsuit against the South African government. The activists marched with banners that read: "Stop medical apartheid of AIDS: from Botswana to the Bronx" and posters "Drug company greed kills" and "Generic AIDS drugs save lives". These protests spawned a chain of events at the WTO, which sought to address issues related to patent laws, trade agreements, and access to affordable medicines.

- One of the most tragic protests against globalization took place during the Fifth Ministerial Conference of the WTO held in Cancun in September 2003, when Lee Kyung-Hae, a South Korean farmer, plunged a small Swiss Army knife into his chest. He was wearing a sign that read "WTO kills farmers". According to one press report, earlier in 2003, he had camped outside the WTO building in Geneva and refused food to demonstrate his belief that trade negotiations were killing farmers. The press report provides the following quotes from the close relatives of farmer Lee: "He had dedicated himself to organizing unions, influencing government policy and opposing trade liberalization". "He died to show the plight of Korean farmers—something he knew from personal experience".[4]

Subject to a few exceptions, as highlighted in the preceding paragraphs, most of the episodes of protests against globalization have generally raised issues of particular concern to the stakeholders in developing countries. It was only on rare occasions that any perceived adverse impact of globalization on economies of the developed countries was highlighted in the protests. However, in the past 3–4 years, the decibel against globalization has been raised by mainstream politicians in some of the developed countries. Further, in some developed countries, the impact of globalization appears to have even become a key issue in national elections. To illustrate, the finalization of the mega free trade agreement between 12 countries, popularly referred to as the Trans-Pacific Partnership Agreement (TPP), almost coincided with national elections in Canada in 2015. Not surprisingly, Canada's approach to the TPP became an important issue in the election. Thomas Mulcair, the leader of the New Democratic Party of Canada stated that he would not feel compelled to honor the provisions of the TPP if his party came to power.[5] In the United States, politicians across the political

---

[3] Khor (1993).

[4] Watts (2003).

[5] See, for example, Chase (2015).

4 Discontent Against Globalization: Reasons and Remedies

spectrum attacked the TPP, but for different reasons. Most of the candidates who ran in the 2016 presidential elections can be characterized as being "trade skeptics". Criticizing the TPP, Bernie Sanders was of the view that the USA needs "trade policies that promote the interests of American workers and not just the CEOs of corporations".[6] In his election campaign, Donald Trump characterized the TPP as a disaster and upon winning the elections, he directed the United States Trade Representative (USTR) to "withdraw the United States as a signatory to the Trans-Pacific Partnership (TPP), to permanently withdraw the United States from TPP negotiations, and to begin pursuing, wherever possible, bilateral trade negotiations to promote American industry, protect American workers, and raise American wages".[7]

It is relevant to ask the following question: what are some of the main themes raised in the protests against globalization? Given the vast sweep of globalization, it is not surprising that the anti-globalization movement has sought to highlight an extremely broad range of issues. These include the following—adverse impact of international trade on employment; privatization of basic services; opposition to "neoliberalism"[8] and biotech products; "construction of local alternatives to global capitalism"[9]; "critique on the cultural, social, political, and environmental impacts of economic globalization"[10]; "regulation of financial markets" and "cancellation of the debt of developing countries, fair trade, and the implementation of limits to free trade and capital flows".[11] A comprehensive discussion and analysis of all these issues are beyond the scope of this chapter. This chapter is confined to examining the underlying reasons for the protests against the perceived effects of binding rules in the area of international trade and investment. WTO, with its binding and legally enforceable rules governing international trade in goods and services, is the main international institution relevant for analyzing the effects of globalization, including the backlash against it. In addition, with the growing proliferation of free trade agreements in the past decade, some of the protests against globalization are also directed against deep trade and investment integration in these agreements. The next section seeks to identify some of the reasons for the protests against globalization, as represented by international trade and investment agreements.

---

[6] Source: http://learningenglish.voanews.com/content/trade-obama-trump-pacific-partnership-clinton-sanders/3032839.html.

[7] Presidential Memorandum Regarding Withdrawal of the United States from the Trans-Pacific Partnership Negotiations and Agreement, dated 23 January 2017. Available on website https://www.whitehouse.gov/the-press-office/2017/01/23/presidential-memorandum-regarding-withdrawal-united-states-trans-pacific.

[8] World Social Forum, available at https://fsm2016.org/en/sinformer/a-propos-du-forum-social-mondial/

[9] Starr, Amory. Global Revolt.

[10] International Forum on Globalisation, available at http://ifg.org/

[11] Association for the Taxation of financial Transactions and Aid to Citizens, available at https://www.attac.org/en/overview

3 Identifying the Main Reasons Behind the Protests Against International Trade and Investment Agreements

Over the past two decades, many developing countries and civil society organizations have been raising concerns about globalization. These concerns relate to the adverse impact of international trade on vulnerable sections of the economy in developing countries in general, and against the asymmetry in deep trade and investment agreements in particular. As most of the adverse economic impact of international trade in developing countries is a consequence of deeper systemic issues, it is more appropriate to focus attention on them, rather than examining the symptoms engendered by the root causes of dissent against globalization. These systemic concerns represent a long-simmering sense of injustice and unfairness in the institutional architecture of the multilateral trade regime, iniquities and imbalances in some of the existing multilateral trade rules, lack of transparency and inclusiveness in international trade negotiations, unbalanced progress in trade negotiations, the extreme reluctance of the developed countries to play by the rules of the game when the outcome starts going against their interests, the approach of "kicking away the ladder" adopted by the developed countries, etc. At the core of each of these reasons is a cluster of related questions—whose interests predominate the international trade regime, those of developing countries or the developed countries? Does the system serve the international community in a fair and balanced manner? Are the interests of those with a weaker voice taken into account sincerely and adequately? This section discusses some of the reasons underlying the protests against globalization, as represented by international trade and the rules governing it.

3.1 Pre-Dominance of a Power-Based System in the Multilateral Trading Regime

The multilateral trading regime, as enshrined in the rules of GATT/WTO, has often been depicted as a rules-based system. However, right from its inception with the establishment of the GATT in 1948, the multilateral trading system has been cast in the mold of the interest of the developed countries.[12] There have been many occasions when the developed countries have not hesitated to depart from the existent GATT rules if it did not serve their interest. Two examples are adequate to illustrate this power-based behavior of the developed countries. First, within a decade of coming into existence of the GATT, the United States obtained a waiver in 1955 to enable it to impose quantitative restrictions on imports of agricultural products, otherwise not permitted under provisions of Article XI:1 of GATT.[13] Following the

---

[12] Das (2003).

[13] GATT Document L/315, dated 28 January 1995. United States request, for waiver in connection with Sect. 22 of the Agriculture Adjustment Act.

4 Discontent Against Globalization: Reasons and Remedies

US example, some other GATT members also managed to keep their farm policies immune from legal challenges, either through waivers (Belgium and Luxembourg) or through special clauses in their protocol of accession (Switzerland).

Second, the action of some of the developed countries in the textiles and clothing sector provides a more blatant narrative of power-play. Although the rules of GATT explicitly prohibited countries from imposing quotas, for four and a half decades, some of the developed countries imposed a discriminatory and restrictive quota regime against imports of textiles and clothing products from efficient developing countries.[14] The quota regime in the textiles sector deviated considerably from the requirements of non-discrimination and avoidance of quantitative restrictions under the GATT.

Although both these actions—in agriculture and textiles—hurt the trade interest of many developing countries, they had little option, other than acquiescing to the GATT-inconsistent action of the developed countries. What accentuates this anti-development narrative is the fact that the developing countries had to pay a heavy price during the Uruguay Round of GATT negotiations for making the developed countries forego resorting to some of the GATT-inconsistent action in the sectors of agriculture and textiles and clothing. As a part of an iniquitous bargain, the developing countries had to agree to multilateral rules on intellectual property rights and services, in return for the developed countries removing trade measures that were ab initio inconsistent with GATT obligations.

3.2 Power-Based Negotiating Process in the Multilateral Trading Regime

During the initial round of multilateral trade negotiations at the GATT, developing countries were not required to offer concessions to other GATT contracting parties. However, starting with the Tokyo Round (1973–1979) and more extensively during the Uruguay Round (1986–1994), the developing countries were required to take on extremely onerous commitments. This was achieved through a combination of strategies and tactics, which essentially centered around power-based negotiations. First, the US resorted to "aggressive unilateralism"[15] and forced developing countries, such as Brazil and India, to fall in line with its wishes on negotiating at the GATT rules governing intellectual property rights, an issue that was strongly resisted by these countries.[16] Further in a display of raw "power-play", the US decided to close the Uruguay Round by forcing the developing countries to accept the obligations of *all* the Uruguay [17]Round agreements by subtly changing the meaning of a single undertaking. Although the negotiations on goods and services were initiated on separate

---

[14] Bagchi (2001).

[15] Bhagwati (1991).

[16] Shukla (2000).

[17] Steinberg (2002).

legal tracks, and the concept of a single undertaking was mentioned for goods, the Round was closed by extending the single undertaking to cover services as well.[18] The procedural fiction of consensus and the sovereign equality of states served as an external display to domestic audiences to help legitimize these outcomes.[19] In the face of blatant exercise of power-based negotiations by the developed world, it is little wonder that at the end of the Uruguay Round, the developing countries "agreed" to outcomes that were asymmetric, imbalanced, and iniquitous.

3.3 Asymmetries and Imbalances in WTO Agreements

The outcome of the Uruguay Round of multilateral trade negotiations consists of detailed agreements on trade in goods and services, along with rules for the protection of intellectual property rights. The substantive provisions of these agreements not only required the developing countries to take extremely onerous obligations but also contain rules that are marked with deficiencies and imbalances thereby adversely affecting the core interests of the developing countries. At a time when most commentators were extolling the virtues of the WTO for the developing countries, in an influential study Das (1998) provided a comprehensive analysis of the WTO agreements and identified almost 50 instances of deficiencies and imbalances in these agreements.[20] Some of the corrective actions suggested in this study inspired developing countries to make proposals at the WTO, which sought improvements in the WTO agreements.

The Agreement on Agriculture (AoA) provides a useful illustration of the asymmetries and imbalances in the WTO agreements. The AoA was an important outcome of the Uruguay Round of Multilateral Trade Negotiations, which introduced disciplines in three pillars—market access, domestic support, and export competition. The overall objective of the agriculture negotiations during the Uruguay Round was to move towards a *fair and market-oriented trading system* in agriculture. While the provisions contained in the AoA marked an important step in this direction, almost every substantive provision of the agreement is imbalanced against the interest of developing countries. The essential feature of the obligations contained in the AoA is that those countries (mainly developed countries) that were distorting global markets through high tariffs and non-tariff measures or distorting fair competition through high domestic support and export subsidies, acquired the right to continue with these trade-distorting measures. On the other hand, countries (mainly developing countries) that did not distort global trade and agricultural production through non-tariff barriers and subsidies lost the right to protect their farmers and promote their interests. This almost one-sided orientation of the AoA in favor of the developed countries

---

[18] Shukla (2000).

[19] Steinberg (2002).

[20] Das (1998).

4 Discontent Against Globalization: Reasons and Remedies

should not come as a surprise, because most of the substantial provisions in the agreement are based on a bilateral deal between the European Commission and the USA reached during the Uruguay Round. The developing countries had little, if any, say in the final contours of the AoA.

While the developing countries were constrained to accept onerous obligations during the Uruguay Round, the rules were further tilted against them as most of the special and differential treatment provisions in their favor were couched in non-mandatory language that is difficult to implement. Further, even where flexibilities exist in favor of the developing countries, as is the case with the Agreement on Trade-Related Intellectual Property Rights (TRIPS Agreement), an attempt was made by officers of the secretariat of a relevant inter-governmental organization in seminars and training programs to provide a more restrictive interpretation of the underlying provisions. If such attempts had succeeded, then many officers in developing countries would have been misled into interpreting the TRIPS Agreement in favor of the right holders and not fully appreciating the policy space available to governments in the area of intellectual property rights.[21] It is, therefore, not surprising that when the Doha Round of multilateral trade negotiations was launched by the WTO in 2001, issues of importance to the developing countries acquired center stage. However, as will be discussed in the next sub-section, the aspirations of the developing countries for a balanced and fair multilateral trading system were belied, yet again.

3.4 Promise of the Development Content in the Doha Round Not Fulfilled

The Doha Ministerial Declaration launching the Doha Round of trade negotiations contained strong language, raising hopes that problems of developing countries would be finally resolved by the WTO membership. Of particular relevance is paragraph 12 of the Doha Ministerial Declaration which states as follows: "We attach the utmost importance to the implementation-related issues and concerns raised by Members and are determined to find appropriate solutions to them".[22] In respect of negotiations on agriculture, it was agreed that "special and differential treatment for developing countries shall be an integral part of all elements of the negotiations". In respect of reductions in industrial tariffs, it was agreed that "the negotiations shall take fully into account the special needs and interests of developing and least-developed country participants". However, as the negotiations progressed, it became clear that the developed world had little inclination to deliver on the development promise, which was at the core of the Doha Round. A few illustrations are given below.

---

[21] Based on personal papers of Bhagirath Lal Das, a former ambassador of India to the GATT and a renowned trade expert, available with the author.

[22] WTO document WT/MIN(01)/DEC/1 dated 20 November 2001.

- In respect of most of the issues raised by the developing countries for addressing concerns related to the implementation of the WTO agreements, commonly referred to as Implementation Issues, there was little meaningful progress. Despite constructive engagement by the developing countries, meaningful outcomes could not be achieved, as the developed countries embroiled the issues in technical tangles.
- In respect of domestic support on Cotton (an issue of significance to some of the poorest countries in Africa), it was agreed that trade-distorting domestic subsidies for cotton production would be reduced more ambitiously than under whatever general formula is agreed and that it would be implemented over a shorter period than generally applicable. Countries also committed to giving priority to this issue in the negotiations. No concrete commitments were made on this issue.
- During the Hong Kong Ministerial Conference in 2005, it was agreed that the developed countries would provide duty-free quota-free market access to 97% of exports of the Least-Developed Countries.[23] This commitment has not yet been implemented by some of the developed countries.

While the developed countries failed to deliver on the development content of the Doha Round, the progress in other areas of the negotiations tilted towards the interest of the developed countries. This is discussed in the next sub-section.

3.5 Progress in Doha Round Negotiations: Survival of the Financially Fattest

In general, no country can be expected to adhere to its initial negotiating stand during trade negotiations or be expected to achieve all its objectives in WTO negotiations. The process of negotiations involves trade-offs and compromises, with countries conceding ground on certain issues to secure gains in other areas. However, it becomes a matter of concern if the trend in negotiations in respect of most of the elements in one area suggests outcomes that would be beneficial to developed countries and adverse to the interest of a large number of developing countries. Progress in negotiations on agriculture during the Doha Round illustrates this general malady that afflicts international trade negotiations, resulting in outcomes that are tilted against the interests of the developing countries.

Das and Sharma (2011) track the progress on almost 50 different elements in the negotiations on agriculture at the WTO during 2003–2010.[24] Their analysis highlights how many of the provisions which would have required liberalization of agriculture trade by the developed countries and could have reduced market distortions caused by their farm subsidies, progressively become less stringent over time. This was favorable to the developed countries. On the other hand, provisions that might

---

[23] WTO document WT/MIN(05)/DEC dated 22 December 2005.

[24] Das and Sharma (2011).

4 Discontent Against Globalization: Reasons and Remedies

have benefited developing countries were severely eroded and made more onerous. These two contrasting trends, one favoring the developed countries and the other going against the interests of many developing countries, suggest a significant lack of overall balance in agriculture negotiations. Such an imbalanced outcome could have serious implications for the continued relevance of the multilateral trading system, which is already perceived as being unresponsive to the genuine development aspirations of many developing countries. Other areas of negotiations under the Doha Round might likely contain similar imbalances.

3.6 Subtle (Mis)use of Research and Exaggerating Gains from Negotiations and Influencing Developing Countries

One of the most important reasons for the backlash against globalization is the subtle use of research to influence governments in developing countries to take positions that might not be entirely in line with their national interest. No doubt, objective, rigorous, and empirically sound research can be a useful tool for trade negotiators and policymakers to assess the likely impacts of different options in trade negotiations and policymaking. However, research becomes contentious, when it is not based on sound theoretical foundations, and yet is used with zeal to push one line in trade negotiations. At times, some experts have not hesitated in misinterpreting results of otherwise credible research to push their viewpoint. It is almost par for the course that while international trade negotiations are underway, research will emerge making highly exaggerated claims of gains from the negotiations. Many of the modeling exercises predicting the exaggerated gains are based on extremely questionable assumptions and appear to be brazen attempts at persuading the developing countries to conclude international trade negotiations, even if it may not be in their national interest. It is useful to consider a few specific illustrations from the context of GATT/WTO and also from mega-FTA negotiations.

First, during the Uruguay Round, many institutions including the GATT Secretariat, World Bank, and OECD made projections of welfare gains of the order of US $200 billion a year, with a large share of the gains being predicted to accrue to developing countries.[25] Part of the impetus for members to conclude the Uruguay Round was the promise of large welfare gains that had been projected by many researchers. These gains have not materialized. To compound the misery, UNDP's Human Development Report of 1997 had projected that least developed countries will be net losers from the round after full implementation of all the agreements. A large share of the net losers is among the poorest countries in the world, in particular sub-Saharan Africa, which has been estimated to have cost US$ 1.2 billion as a result of the round. Thus, a suspicion arises that the initial assessments of supposed gains for the developing countries from the Uruguay Round were a thinly veiled attempt

---

[25] Epstein (1995) as cited in Stiglitz and Charlton (2005), Free trade for all: How trade can promote development. Oxford University Press.

to induce them to make commitments that might have run counter to their perceived national interest and hasten the conclusion of the negotiations.

Second, while the Trade Facilitation Agreement was being negotiated at the WTO, the supposed global income gains from it were projected by the International Chamber of Commerce (2013) to be $1 trillion.[26] However, this projection is based on many questionable assumptions. Again, the supposed gains from trade liberalization do not appear to have a firm theoretical or empirical basis.[27]

Third, there have been instances when international institutions, including the World Bank, have put out research that had the potential to undermine the negotiating position of some of the developing countries. Unfortunately, some of the research was based on extremely questionable assumptions. In one of the most blatant attempts at advocacy masquerading as academic research, in 2006 the World Bank uploaded on its website a draft study by Maros Ivanic and Will Martin titled "Potential Implications of Agricultural Special Products for Poverty in Low-Income Countries". This study sought to discredit the negotiating approach of a group of developing countries at the WTO, commonly referred to as the G33, on the so-called "Special Products" (SP) for protecting the interests of millions of small farmers. Based on an econometric model, the draft paper had reached a rather alarmist conclusion. According to the draft paper, raising agricultural prices substantially through SPs "would create large increases in poverty—sufficient in some cases to undo decades of development progress—and push the already poor deeper into poverty". As the conclusion of the draft paper had implications for the negotiating position of many developing countries, the G33 undertook a detailed technical analysis of the paper. In its critique, the G33 pointed out that the World Bank paper was fundamentally flawed in its assumptions and methodology, ignored the reality of the prevailing agrarian structures in most developing countries, and misinterpreted the proposed operation and impact of SPs.[28] The G33 conveyed its technical reservations on the paper to the World Bank. Eventually, the draft paper was removed from the website of the World Bank.

In this context, it is useful and relevant to mention some of the findings of the evaluation of World Bank research between 1998 and 2005 carried out by a panel consisting of Abhijit Banerjee (MIT), Angus Deaton (Princeton, chair), Nora Lustig (UNDP), and Kenneth Rogoff (Harvard). The research on globalization by the World Bank attracted substantial criticism by the panel. The panel was critical of the way that this research was "used to proselytize on behalf of Bank policy, often without taking a balanced view of the evidence, and without expressing appropriate skepticism. Internal research that was favorable to Bank positions was given great prominence, and unfavorable research ignored".[29]

The fourth illustration of misuse of research is in the context of mega-FTA negotiations. Optimistic claims about one of the most influential deals—the Trans-Pacific Partnership Agreement (TPP)—are largely based on economic modeling projections

---

[26] International Chamber of Commerce (2013).

[27] Capaldo (2014).

[28] Raja (2007).

[29] Banerjee et al. (2006).

4 Discontent Against Globalization: Reasons and Remedies

in various studies by Petri et al. (2011),[30] Petri et al. (2012),[31] Petri et al. (2014).[32] Some of the signatory countries of the TPP have used the results of these studies to highlight the gains for their countries from the Agreement. This underscores the influence of these studies on the public policy of some countries participating in the TPP. However, as pointed out by Bertram and Simon (2014),[33] the gains from TPP as assessed in the studies by Petri et al., are based on *"certain assumptions that do not appear to have solid analytical foundations, nor have the assumptions been commonly used in previous modeling work"*. It is relevant to note that the changes in world GDP and exports in Petri et al. (2012)[34] are almost double the corresponding values in Petri et al. (2011).[35] This is mainly on account of different assumptions made in the two studies regarding trade costs, an important aspect that is generally ignored by experts and commentators who have used the results of these studies to argue for gains from deep trade and investment integration.

More controversial is the interpretation of the results of Petri et al. (2014).[36] According to the study, if India joins an expanded Free Trade Agreement of Asia Pacific (FTAAPX) comprising APEC members along with India, Cambodia, Laos, and Myanmar, its exports in 2025 would be higher than the baseline exports by $ 536 bn. Bergsten (2015)[37] misinterprets the estimates of Petri et al. (2014), and significantly overstates the gains for India from its membership of the FTAAPX. The study by Bergsten claims that "India could experience an export expansion of more than $500 bn. per year". Contrary to the claims of Bergstein (2015), it should be clarified that $ 536 bn. does not represent the amount of *annual increase* in India's exports in 2025. Instead, it represents the likely increase in exports of India by 2025 if it joins the FTAAPX, above the baseline projection of exports in the absence of TPP and FTAAPX. While this figure of annual export gains was widely cited by commentators and analysts to argue for India joining the TPP, it should be noted that this claim is based on an elementary mistake resulting in misunderstanding the modeling results.

The examples discussed above suggest that many academicians and experts appear to be functioning as an epistemological community, whereby the supposed gains for developing countries from trade liberalization have become the predominant mantra while being soft on the protectionist policies of the developed countries. However, as discussed in the next sub-section, a few exceptions to this trend exist.

---

[30] Petri et al. (2011).

[31] Petri et al. (2012).

[32] Petri et al. (2014).

[33] Bertram and Simon (2014).

[34] Petri et al. (2012).

[35] Petri et al. (2011).

[36] Petri et al. (2014).

[37] Bergsten (2015).

3.7 Kicking Away the Ladder

It is a stark reality that most of the advanced industrial countries—including the United States and Japan—have built their economies by selectively protecting some of their industries until they were strong enough to compete with foreign firms. Based on a comprehensive and incisive analysis of the development strategies followed by countries that are developed today, Chang (2002) identifies some of the policy instruments used by these countries to nurture and thereafter strengthen the financial muscle of their domestic producers.[38] However, after their domestic producers acquired financial heft, the developed countries have prohibited through WTO agreements, or are seeking to impose prohibitions through other international trade agreements, developing countries from implementing similar measures.

According to Chang (2002), some of the policy instruments that were used by the developed countries to initially nurture their domestic producers but subsequently prohibited or restricted for use by the developing countries, include the following: not protecting the intellectual property of foreigners, granting export subsidies, protecting domestic producers behind high tariff walls, providing assured market through government procurement, mandating the producer to purchase its raw materials and other inputs from domestic sources, granting subsidies contingent on local sourcing of inputs and stipulating a minimum threshold of production to be exported. Chang notes that for over one century (1816–1945), the USA had one of the highest average tariffs on manufacturing imports in the world. He further observes that—"it was only after the Second World War that the USA—with its industrial supremacy unchallenged—finally liberalized its trade and started championing the cause of free trade". Relying on Bairoch (1993),[39] Chang is of the view that "Britain's technological lead that enabled this shift to a free trade regime had been achieved behind high and long-lasting tariff barriers". This phenomenon of "kicking away the ladder" can be considered to have significantly contributed to the negative perception about globalization and trade agreements.

3.8 Hypocrisy in the Stance of Some of the Developed Countries

Developed countries have not hesitated in challenging measures of developing countries under the dispute settlement mechanism of the WTO, but ignore the fact that in some cases they are implementing similar measures within their own country. To illustrate, the US successfully challenged India's Jawaharlal Nehru National Solar Mission (JNNSM). The JNNSM mandated that solar power developers purchase

---

[38] Chang (2002).
[39] Bairoch (1993).

4 Discontent Against Globalization: Reasons and Remedies

or use solar cells or modules of Indian origin to enter into power purchase agreements under Phase I or Phase II of the scheme. The panel/Appellate Body upheld the claims of the US that India had violated its WTO obligations by mandating domestic content requirements in some aspects of JNNSM. After successfully challenging India's localization requirements under the JNNSM, Michael Froman, the US Trade Representative, stated that the dispute should send out a message to other countries considering discriminatory localization policies.[40] If only he were to turn his gaze to some of the states in the USA, he would find a slew of such policies, some of which were subsequently successfully challenged by India.[41]

The statement of the US at the plenary session of the 11th Ministerial Conference of the WTO held in Buenos Aires in December 2017 provides an example of blatant hypocrisy in the approach of the developed countries to international trade rules. Referring to the larger developing countries, the US launched a withering attack on the role of development at the WTO. The US found it troubling that "so many Members appear to believe that they would be better off with exemptions to the rules".[42] Ironically, during the inconclusive Doha negotiations, it was the US that had secured a slew of exemptions from the application of future trade rules in agriculture. Even earlier, starting from the early years of GATT, the US and other developed countries had secured exemptions from non-discriminatory trade obligations to promote their protectionist agenda in the agriculture and textiles sectors for nearly five decades. These are good examples of special and differential treatment for the developed world, something that the developed countries may not want to be reminded about.

3.9 One-Sided Discourse on International Trade and WTO Negotiations

The role played by the international media in reporting developments related to international trade and WTO negotiations is another contentious issue for many developing countries. It is extremely rare to find articles and news reports in the mainstream media, which provide the perspective of some of the developing countries. On the other hand, the international media gives rather extensive coverage to the point of view articulated by the developed countries. The reality, as perceived by some of the developing countries, often gets lost in this lop-sided battle of perception; thereby further tilting the playing field against these countries. Two specific examples can be cited to illustrate how the mainstream media ignored the reality at the negotiating table, and instead projected an imbalanced and one-sided perspective that promoted the interests of the developed countries.

---

[40] Press Release of USTR (2016).

[41] WTO document WT/DS510/R dated 27 June, 2019.

[42] Opening Plenary Statement of USTR Robert Lighthizer at the WTO Ministerial Conference. Available at https://ustr.gov/about-us/policy-offices/press-office/press-releases/2017/december/opening-plenary-statement-ustr.

When the fifth Ministerial Conference of the WTO held in 2003 in Cancun collapsed, much of the blame for the failure of the meeting was put at the door of the developing countries. Soon after the collapse of this meeting, in an article in the Financial Times (London), Robert Zoellick, the USTR at that time, excoriated the developing countries for their reluctance to move in the negotiations and branded many of them as "won't do countries". Of course, he portrayed the developed countries as "can-do countries" who were willing to advance the negotiations.[43] Subsequently, this characterization of "can do" and "won't do" countries almost became the leitmotif in media reports on WTO negotiations. Not only was this characterization by the USTR unfair and inaccurate, but it was also an attempt by the USA to deflect attention from its role in triggering the collapse of the ministerial meeting. Drawing upon the recollection of Arancha Gonzalez who was Pascal Lamy's spokeswoman when the Cancun meeting failed, Blustein (2009) hints that in 2003 the US allowed the Cancun Ministerial Conference of the WTO to collapse on the so-called Singapore Issues. By avoiding a discussion, and hence a breakdown of this important meeting, on cotton subsidies, the EU officials suspected that the US prevented being blamed for the failure of the Cancun meeting.[44] The narrative in the mainstream media about the collapse of the Cancun meeting was a one-sided depiction based on the interests of the USA.

The illustration discussed above is not an isolated case. History got repeated in the media reports on the developments during the tenth Ministerial Conference of the WTO held in Nairobi in 2015. At this crucial meeting, the WTO membership failed to endorse concluding the Doha Round based on the Doha mandates. As a result, the United States freed itself "from the strictures of Doha", an objective strongly advocated by the US (see, for example, the statement by Michael Froman, USTR, at the plenary session of the Nairobi Ministerial Meeting of the WTO). While it was the developed countries, which dug in their heels and refused to move further on the negotiations, the media reports yet again blamed some of the developing countries for the predicament.

3.10 Lack of Transparency in the Conduct of WTO Ministerial Conferences

The Ministerial Conference of the WTO, held once in 2 years, is the highest decision-making body of this inter-governmental organization. Its role has acquired additional salience in the context of the Doha Round of multilateral trade negotiations. To inspire confidence in the developing countries, these meetings must be organized transparently and inclusively. Further, to enhance the feeling of ownership of the outcomes of the ministerial conferences, each WTO member must be provided adequate opportunity to have a say in the final decisions. However, the stark reality is that the WTO

---

[43] Zoellick (2003).
[44] Blustein (2009).

ministerial conferences are marked by non-transparency and lack of inclusiveness. Most of the developing countries are excluded from the key decision-making process. To compound the woes for developing countries, the final text of the ministerial declaration is foisted on them almost at the last minute, with virtually no time being given to them to examine the implications of the outcome. Das (2003) provides a detailed account of the lack of transparency in the conduct of some of the ministerial conferences of the WTO, which has caused considerable resentment and disappointment among a large number of developing countries.[45] As almost identical tactics have been used in successive ministerial conferences to exclude most of the developing countries from effective and meaningful participation in the outcomes, it demonstrates the utter helplessness of the developing countries to reverse this sad trend. It is, therefore, not surprising that most of the governments of developing countries and their stakeholders resent globalization as represented by international trade negotiations and meetings of inter-governmental organizations such as the WTO.

4 What Can Be Done to Address the Anti-Globalization Sentiment in Some Developing Countries

In the previous section, 10 root causes of the protests in some developing countries against international trade agreements and globalization have been identified. While it is not sufficient to identify the maladies afflicting the existing institutional architecture of global trade governance, prescribing remedies that would be balanced, practical, effective, and acceptable to most countries is an extremely difficult task. This section attempts to provide some solutions to address the underlying root causes. The suggestions require action at both the international and national levels.

4.1 Taking the First Step by Recognizing the True Nature of the Problem

It is a cliche to say that admitting that a problem exists is the first step towards its solution. Like most cliches, this rings true for addressing the protests against international trade and globalization. It is particularly relevant to emphasize this point, as the international institutions and inter-governmental organizations remain in a denial mode about the true origins of the problem. Instead, the focus of international institutions such as the G20 and WTO secretariat does not even touch the fringe of the problem. To illustrate, in the context of rising protectionism in the sphere of trade and investment, the G20 leaders emphasized that "that the benefits of trade and open markets must be communicated to the wider public more effectively".[46] The attempt

---

[45] Das (2003).

[46] G20 Leaders' Communique: Hangzhou Summit, 5 September, 2016.

appears to be to reduce the problem to merely one of the wrong perceptions about trade.

The response of the WTO secretariat also misses the target. To quote Roberto Azevedo, the then Director-General of the WTO, "We need to correct *misperceptions* about trade in a credible way. Trade plays a relatively minor role in job displacement. The evidence shows that trade is a generator of high-quality jobs and sustained economic growth. But, of course, this is no comfort to those who have lost their jobs. We need to acknowledge that trade can cause dislocation and can create uncertainties in some sectors and communities. We need to respond in a targeted and credible manner—including by providing better education, better training and skills development, and adjustment support to the unemployed".[47] Again, not a word about deficiencies and imbalances in the existing agreements, or any reference to the non-transparent manner of organizing WTO ministerial conferences. Unless the international institutions and inter-governmental organizations involved in international trade and globalization acknowledge the true nature of the problem, any attempt at finding solutions will be merely cosmetic and without any credibility.

4.2 Increased Transparency in the Conduct of WTO Ministerial Conferences

As discussed in the previous section, the power-play and lack of transparency during WTO Ministerial Conferences have been extremely sore points for most developing countries. Some of them had jointly submitted a proposal in 2002 for enhancing the transparency and inclusiveness in the conduct of these meetings.[48] The proposal contains a large number of procedural and substantive suggestions. Concrete action by the WTO membership, particularly the developed countries, on the suggestions could help remove an important irritant for the developing countries and make the outcomes of the WTO more acceptable to them.

4.3 According to Formal Recognition to "Representative Negotiators Group"

International trade negotiations have to be managed to keep the following two broad constraints in view: first, as direct negotiations among more than a hundred countries

---

[47] WTO 2016 News Items. DG Azevêdo calls on G20 leaders to make the credible case for trade. Available on https://www.wto.org/english/news_e/news16_e/dgra_05sep16_e.htm.

[48] Preparatory process in Geneva and negotiating procedure at the Ministerial Conferences. Communication from Cuba, Dominican Republic, Egypt, Honduras, India, Indonesia, Jamaica, Kenya, Malaysia, Mauritius, Pakistan, Sri Lanka, Tanzania, Uganda, and Zimbabwe. WTO document WT/GC/W/471 dated 24 April, 2002.

4 Discontent Against Globalization: Reasons and Remedies 83

may not be practical, negotiations need to be held in small groups; and second, any country with a deep interest in an issue, but excluded from the small group discussions, would understandably feel aggrieved. Das (2003) makes a useful suggestion for creating a formal representative negotiators group.[49] According to the suggestion of the author, the representative negotiators' group would comprise a small group of negotiators, each of whom would negotiate on behalf of a different group of countries. A group of countries with a broad common interest could select the representative negotiator, who would negotiate on their behalf. Countries would have the flexibility to shift from one group to another if they do not find their interests being adequately promoted by their group. Small countries, which do not normally get an opportunity to participate in WTO negotiations, would get adequate opportunity to influence the course of international trade negotiations through their representative negotiator. Developing countries will also feel more empowered to resist the unfair and unjust demands of the developed countries in the representative negotiators' group. This negotiating structure will also make it more difficult for the developed countries to target specific developing countries during the concluding stages of negotiations—a phenomenon that was largely visible during the Uruguay Round.

4.4 Negotiating Through Coalitions

The success of negotiating through coalitions has been particularly evident in agriculture negotiations in the Doha Round. As mentioned earlier, the AoA that emerged after the Uruguay Round was based substantially on the bilateral understanding between the US and the EC, commonly referred to as the Blair House Accord. When the USA and the EU made a joint proposal on agriculture in August 2003,[50] it appeared that the history of the Uruguay Round would be repeated yet again, but in the Doha Round. However, in contrast to the response of developing countries during the Uruguay Round, some developing banded together in August 2003 and made a counter-proposal. The counter-proposal gathered considerable support from many other developing countries, resulting in the creation of G20. This coalition, led by countries such as Argentina, Brazil, China, and India, dramatically changed the dynamics of agriculture negotiations after August 2003. In parallel, another group of countries, led by Indonesia, India, and the Philippines, created G33 for focusing on issues of food security, livelihood, and rural development. It would not be an exaggeration to state that during September 2003–2008, the central dynamics in agriculture negotiations were dominated by the two coalitions—G20 and G33. While the eventual achievement of the two coalitions in terms of negotiated outcomes may be modest, their real success lay in preventing the US and the EU from foisting yet again an imbalanced agreement on the developing countries. This holds an important lesson for the developing countries—some success in trade negotiations can be

---

[49] Das (2003).
[50] WTO document JOB(03)/157.

garnered by forming coalitions. This lesson needs to be implemented by the developing countries, even if it might require them to make some mutual adjustment in their interests.

4.5 Enhancing the Role and Capacity of Inter-Governmental Organizations and Other International Institutions Working for the Interest of Developing Countries

Most developing countries lack adequate technical capacity, from the perspective of both human resources and institutional, to undertake an in-depth analysis of the effects of international trade agreements and globalization. They also lack the capacity to fully assess and evaluate the implications of various negotiating proposals for their countries. It is, therefore, not surprising that many developing countries are unable to distinguish between empirically sound research undertaken in the context of trade negotiations and simple advocacy disguised as econometric modeling. Further, some developing countries do not even have the resources for drafting negotiating proposals. Given these gaps in technical capacity, developing countries find it extremely difficult to adequately protect and promote their interests in international trade negotiations, or to participate fully and effectively in the regular work program of institutions such as the WTO. This calls for strengthening the capacity of existing inter-governmental organizations and other international institutions working for the interest of developing countries.

During the Uruguay Round of multilateral trade negotiations under the GATT, UNCTAD played a pivotal role in undertaking research and strengthening the capacity of developing countries to participate in these negotiations. However, during the Doha Round, UNCTAD appeared to have become a bit dormant in providing technical support to developing countries. To some extent, this gap was bridged by the South Centre, a Geneva-based inter-governmental organization. However, despite the active involvement of the extremely dynamic and dedicated staff of the South Centre, this organization is severely constrained by inadequate financial resources. Gradually, technical support to developing countries in the area of international trade, particularly international trade negotiations appears to be fading. If this trend is not decisively reversed, then many developing countries, particularly the smaller countries, run the risk of being further marginalized in the international trading regime. Some thought needs to be given to enhancing the financial resources of the South Centre. Perhaps larger developing countries, including Argentina, Brazil, China, India, Indonesia, Malaysia, etc., could take some initiative in this direction.

5 Conclusion

According to Joseph Stiglitz, the Nobel Prize-winning economist, "globalization itself is neither good nor bad. It has the *power* to do enormous good, and for the countries of East Asia, which have embraced globalization *under their terms,* at their own pace, it has been an enormous benefit, despite the setback of the 1997 crisis. But in much of the world, it has not brought comparable benefits. For many, it seems closer to an unmitigated disaster".[51] This seems to capture what is wrong with globalization and why it faces protests in developing countries. If the root causes of the backlash against globalization, as identified in this chapter are not adequately addressed, an already fraying multilateral trading regime will fall apart sooner, rather than later. This would do no good, even to the developed countries. Wisdom lies in reforming the existing international institutions and creating an architecture of global economic governance, which is more responsive to the needs of the developing countries.

References

Bagchi, Sanjoy. 2001. *International trade policy in textiles: Fifty years of protectionism.* Geneva: International Textiles and Clothing Bureau

Bairoch, P. 1993. *Economics and world history- myths and paradoxes.* Wheatsheaf, Brighton

Banerjee, Abhijit, Angus Deaton, Nora Lusting and Ken Rogoff. 2006. An evaluation of World Bank research, 1998–2005

Bergsten, Fred C. 2015. India's rise: A strategy for trade-led growth. *PIIE Briefing* 15–4

Bertram, G., and Simon Terry. 2014. Economic gains and costs from the TPP. *Sustainability Council of New Zealand*

Bhagwati, Jagdish. 1991. *The world trading system at risk.* New York: Harvester Wheatsheaf

Blustein, Paul. 2009. *Misadventures of the most favoured nations.* Public Affairs, 155

Capaldo, Jeronim. 2014. *Trade Hallucination: Risks of trade facilitation and suggestions for implementation.* Global Development and Environment Institute, Tufts University, USA. Working Paper No. 14–02

Chang, Ha-Joon. 2002. *Kicking away the ladder: Development strategy in historical perspective.* London: Anthem Press.

Chase, Steven. 2015. "NDP government would not adhere to a TPP deal, Mulcair says in letter", The Globe and Mail. http://www.theglobeandmail.com/news/politics/ndp-government-would-not-adhere-to-a-tpp-deal-mulcair-says-in-letter/article26631467/

Das, Abhijit, and S.K. Sharma. 2011. Evolution of WTO Agriculture modalities: Survival of the financially fattest. Occasional paper no 1, Centre for WTO Studies, New Delhi

Das, Bhagirath L. 1998. *The WTO Agreements: Deficiencies, imbalances and required changes.* London: Zed Books.

Das, Bhagirath Lal, 2003. The WTO and the multilateral Trading system: Past, present and future. Third World Network, Penang

Interntional Chamber of Commerce, 2013. Payoff from the World Trade agenda 2013, by Hufbauer, Gary Clyde, and Jeffrey Schott, Peterson Institute for International Economics

Khor, Martin. 1993. Indian farmers rally against GATT, bio-patents. http://www.chasque.net/frontpage/suns/trade/areas/intellec/10040093.htm

---

[51] Stiglitz (2003).

Petri, A. Peter., Michael G. Plummer, and Fan Zhai. 2012. *The Trans-Pacific Partnership and Asia-Pacific Integration: A Quantitative Assessment*. USA: Peterson Institute for International Economics

Petri, A. Peter, Michael G. Plummer and Fan Zhai. 2014. The effects of a China-US free trade and investment agreement. Social Science Research Network

Petri, A. Peter, Michael G. Plummer and Fan Zhai. 2011. The Trans-Pacific partnership and the Asia-Pacific integration: A quantitative assessment. Economic Series No. 119, East- West Centre, Working Paper

Press Release of USTR. 2016. United States prevails in WTO dispute challenging India's discrimination against U.S. solar exports. https://ustr.gov/about-us/policy-offices/press-office/press-releases/2016/february/united-states-prevails-wto-dispute

Raja, Kanaga. 2007. G33 criticizes World Bank paper on Special Products. Published in SUNS #6170 dated 17 January 2007, Geneva

Shukla, SP. 2000. From GATT to WTO and beyond. United Nations University World Institute for development economics research working papers no. 195 (August 2000), Helsinki

Starr, Amory. 2005. *Global revolt: A guide to the movements against globalization*. London: Zed Books.

Steinberg, Richard H. 2002. In the shadow of law or power? Consensus-based bargaining and outcomes in the GATT/WTO. International Organization, Vol. 56, No. 2 (Spring, 2002). pp. 339–374

Stiglitz, Joseph E. 2003. *Globalization and Its Discontents*. W.W: Norton

Stiglitz, Joseph E., and Charlton, A. (2005). *Free trade for all: How trade can promote development*. Oxford University Press

Watts, Jonathan. 2003. Field of tears. The Guardian. https://www.theguardian.com/world/2003/sep/16/northkorea.wto

Zoellick, Robert. 2003. America will not wait for the won't-do countries. Financial Times (London). https://ustr.gov/archive/Document_Library/Op-eds/2003/America_will_not_wait_for_the_won't-do_countries_printer.html

Chapter 5
China and the Impact of Economic Globalization: A Complex Tale of Gains and Losses Viewed Through the Lenses of FDI

Jean-Marc F. Blanchard

1 Introduction

Economic globalization (EG), as well as the upsides and downsides associated with it, have been a big topic for a long time[1]. However, it was not until the 1999 infamous "Battle for Seattle" protests which were directed against targets such as EG, multinational corporations (MNCs), and the World Trade Organization (WTO) that EG seemed to become a *mass* popular issue around the world. Donald Trump's victory in the 2016 presidential election in the United States (US) as well as "Brexit," the successful vote to withdraw the United Kingdom from the European Union (EU), which many argue were votes against EG, brought to the fore yet again the implications of EG, the issue of helping those that could not profit from EG or, worse, were harmed by it, and whether or not EG would continue to advance, stagnate, or retreat.

China started on the road to meaningful EG in the late 1970s, dramatically intensifying its participation in the run-up to and after its 2001 accession to the WTO. As one of the biggest participants in EG and, per many, a big winner from it, China seems *prima facie* a powerful illustration of the gains derivable from participation in EG.[2] It also provides an example, some would argue, of how countries might use vigorous state action to extract the benefits of EG while ameliorating its costs.[3]

---

[1] Unless otherwise noted, all figures herein are given in US dollars (USD).
[2] Liang (2007): 125–149; Bremmer (2018); Wang (2019): 215–220.
[3] Rodrik (2012).

This is a substantially revised version of a paper presented at the ISAS Workshop "Revisiting Globalization," National University of Singapore, Singapore in October 2017. I thank the editor and workshop participants for their useful feedback.

J.-M. F. Blanchard (✉)
Mr. and Mrs. S.H. Wong Center for the Study of Multinational Corporations, PO Box 579, Los Gatos, CA 95031-0579, USA
e-mail: executive_director@mnccenter.org

© The Author(s), under exclusive license to Springer Nature Singapore Pte Ltd. 2022
A. Palit (ed.), *Globalisation Impacts*, International Law and the Global South,
https://doi.org/10.1007/978-981-16-7185-2_5

Moreover, since 2017 or so, China seems to have become a champion of EG through its strong rhetoric support of openness and inclusiveness and EG institutions like the WTO and concrete measures such as its Belt and Road Initiative (BRI), described below.[4] The story about China's embrace of EG, its increasing EG in multiple realms, and the gains it has obtained from it has been oft-told, but the conventional narrative omits many important elements including the *internal* downsides associated with its involvement in it and the negative externalities tied to its method of managing it.

The aforementioned multiple realms of China's EG include international trade, inward FDI (IFDI), outward FDI (OFDI), one or more sovereign wealth funds (SWF), business-related science and technological exchange, special economic zones (SEZs), the consumption and production/distribution of cultural goods, and the promulgation of international technical and economic governance standards, and engagement with as well as the creation of international economic institutions (IEIs). Since it is not possible to cover all of these areas well in a single chapter, this chapter focuses specifically on IFDI and OFDI. They represent very important areas of China's EG; are areas where the narrative has insufficiently covered EG's downsides for China as well as downsides associated with China's management, and constitute areas, unlike, e.g., China's SWFs, where the available information allows for a cost–benefit analysis. The chapter notes that China has profited from IFDI in ways such as job and tax revenue creation, boosting its operational knowledge, and accessing global markets. It further reports that OFDI has brought China benefits such as access to markets, securing natural resources, and obtaining brands. It also demonstrates, though, that IFDI and OFDI have downsides for China. Furthermore, it shows that China's ways of managing IFDI and OFDI have resulted in several problems/distortions.

My analysis has three broad policy implications. First, the China case confirms that participating in EG can yield many economic benefits and thus countries should be very cautious about shunning involvement in EG. Second, it suggests government management of EG can be advantageous, though the "devil is in the details." Third, policymakers need to think carefully about the "Chinese Model" of engagement because it and Beijing's management of it have shortcomings. As far as theory is concerned, this analysis calls into question simple assessments that assume engagement with EG automatically provides benefits. Furthermore, it suggests there are problems with theories advocating unqualified state-led development/management of EG. Finally, it shows the value of separately analyzing different facets of EG like trade, investment, currency, and so on.

The next (second) section supplies a brief overview of China's EG post-1978. The third details the contemporary features of China's EGs in areas like trade and bilateral investment treaties (BITs). The fourth delves into China and IFDI, reviewing its patterns and drivers, Beijing's management of it, and the costs and benefits of China's IFDI given how Beijing has controlled it. The fifth part looks at China and OFDI. It discusses its patterns and drivers, Beijing's involvement in it, and the upsides and downsides associated with China's management. The final section provides some

---

[4] For discussion, Lechmacher (2016); Elizabeth Economy (2017); Goh and Chen (2017).

5 China and the Impact of Economic Globalization … 89

summary remarks, reflects on this paper's policy and theoretical implications, and offers some concluding remarks.

1.1 China's Economic Globalization Post-1978

China was engaged with the international economic order before 1978, though its interactions were highly limited. In 1978, for various domestic and international economic and political reasons, it launched its reform and open-door policy that put it on the path to rejoining global trade, financial, and investment systems. In tandem with this, China began to participate in IEIs like the World Bank and International Monetary Fund (IMF), adjust its currency from a tool to encourage imports to a device to promote exports, create SEZs, expand the space for a greater range of actors (state and non-state, central and sub-national) to involve themselves in EG, and to draw MNCs into China by reducing or eliminating entry and operating barriers and offering economic incentives such as lower tax rates, preferential tariffs on inputs used in exports, and current account convertibility.[5]

In the 1990s, China underwent two major waves of EG. The first came in the wake of the government's crackdown on the 1989 Tiananmen Protests, which spurred a tremendous slowdown in domestic economic growth, isolated Beijing internationally, and paralyzed foreign investment flows into China, while the second began in the period leading to China's accession to the WTO. The first wave entailed the creation of new kinds of SEZs and the spread of SEZs geographically, the opening of new sectors to foreign investors, reductions in subsidies, more initiatives to protect intellectual property rights (IPR), and the Chinese government's further withdrawal from direct management of the economy.[6] The second wave consisted of China intensifying, especially with the US, its negotiations to become a member of the WTO and, in part to lay the groundwork for WTO membership, undertaking some massive economic restructurings in the agricultural, industrial, and other sectors. China also gave foreign investors more freedom in terms of market access and ownership rights.[7]

In 2001, China became a member of the WTO. As part of this, China accepted a tremendous number of obligations. It accepted the core principles of the WTO—e.g., most favored nation (MFN), national treatment, and transparency, massively reduced or eliminated tariffs, committed to widening opportunities for foreign investors in areas such as banking, insurance, legal and professional services, payment services,

---

[5] Pearson (1999), esp. 167–175; Naughton (2007), chaps. 16–17; Branstetter and Lardy (2008): 634–641.

[6] Pearson, "China's Integration into the International Trade and Investment Regime," 169–181; Naughton, *The Chinese Economy*, esp. 409–410; and Branstetter and Lardy, "China's Embrace of Globalization," 642–644.

[7] Lardy (2002): 29–62; Zweig (2001): 231–247; and Branstetter and Lardy, "China's Embrace of Globalization," 645.

and shipping/delivery services.[8] On top of this, it accepted WTO accords like the Technical Barriers to Trade (TBT) agreement, the Trade-Related Investment Measures (TRIMS) agreement, the Trade-Related Aspects of Intellectual Property (TRIPs) agreement, the Sanitary and Phytosanitary (SPS) agreement, and the Agreement on Subsidies and Countervailing Measures (SCM Agreement), all which had important implications for the way China dealt with imports, MNCs, and trade disputes.[9] Many of China's "concessions" (e.g., its commitment to open its financial and sectors) were qualified/limited or allowed for multi-year implementation timeframes.[10]

In 2013, Beijing ostensibly moved to intensify China's engagement with the global economic system when it announced the birth of the Shanghai Free Trade Zone (SFTZ). Among other major advancements, the SFTZ was supposed to feature innovations such as a "negative list" for IFDI, less government interference in business establishment and operations, simpler and faster customs procedures, an opening of the service sector to IFDI in areas like education and health care, interest rate liberalization, and a fully convertible currency.[11] There was some progress on the first three fronts, but little or no progress on the last three for various political and economic reasons. It is highly debatable that the SFTZ model, which was extended to other places in China, made a meaningful contribution to China's EG (e.g., trade, IFDI, or currency internationalization) given the limited reforms that took place and the nature of their implementation. To illustrate, China adopted a system for currency convertibility that essentially allowed limited convertibility only *within* the SFTZ, developed a negative list that was too long and restricted the juiciest investment sectors, and imposed limits on foreign investors in the service sector that essentially confined them to the SFTZ.[12]

2013 also witnessed the birth of China's BRI, which entails a land-based scheme called the Silk Road Economic Belt (SREB) and a maritime-based plan labeled the Maritime Silk Road Initiative (MSRI). There are many facets to the BRI, but one of the most visible is the construction of massive amounts of infrastructure. These airports, ports, power generation and distribution facilities, railways, roads, and telecommunication networks are supposed to interconnect provinces and cities within China and localities and sub-regions throughout Southeast Asia, South Asia, the Middle East, Central Asia, Eastern Europe, and Western Europe. In theory, these connections will boost China's EG by opening new export markets or enlarging existing ones for Chinese goods, enhancing flows of resources to China, and providing new opportunities for Chinese companies to invest, provide services, and operate projects. Of note, the BRI is not just about hard infrastructure, it also encompasses trade agreements, customs clearance accords, and dispute settlement agreements, all

---

[8] Lardy, *Integrating China into the Global Economy*: 63–105; Breslin (2003): 213–229; Blanchard (2013): 263–286.

[9] For discussion, see, e.g., Blanchard (2013): 43–68; Paradise (2013): 312–332.

[10] Don Harpaz (2013): 69–102.

[11] Shen and Vanhullebusch (2015): 321–352.

[12] On some of these issues, see Ibid.

of which presumptively will lay the foundation for greater Chinese EG.[13] It must be pointed out that existing studies make quite clear that it cannot be assumed all the aforementioned infrastructure will be built, will deliver the promised economic benefits, or will deliver true Chinese EG versus a closed economic system.[14]

1.2 China's Contemporary Involvement in the Global Economic System

Undoubtedly, the best-known facet of China's post-1978 EG is its involvement in the global trade system. China also has been a major recipient of IFDI, though for a long time this was true only when compared to other developing countries. Furthermore, China recently has become a major sender of OFDI, investing amounts comparable to other major developed economies. On a related note, China is a player in the world of SWFs with its marquee SWF the China Investment Corporation (CIC) constituting the 2nd biggest SWF in the world.[15] Yet another component to China's involvement in the international economic sphere has been growth in the usage of the yuan (renminbi/RMB). Aside from this, China has embraced certain EG legal institutions such as BITs. Given this chapter later devotes extensive attention to IFDI and OFDI, this section gives a very brief overview of China's trade globalization (which is covered in other chapters) and BITs to paint a richer portrait of China's EG. BITs, of course, also have a close relationship with both IFDI and OFDI.

In 1990, mainland China exported FOB $62.76 billion. By 2002, the year after China joined the WTO, its exports had exploded to $325.75 billion, making it the world's 4th largest exporter after the US, Germany, and Japan. Three short years later, China's exports had rocketed to $762.22 billion, with China becoming a larger exporter than Japan. By 2007, Chinese exports had surpassed the US's (China became the world's largest trading nation in 2011). In 2010, 2015, and 2019, China's exports totaled, respectively, $1.59 trillion, $2.28 trillion, and $2.50 trillion. In 2019, its major export destinations were, in order of value, the US ($418.54 billion), the EU ($365.88 billion), Hong Kong ($279.62 billion), Japan ($143.22 billion), and Korea ($110.98 billion).[16] Turning to imports, in 1990, mainland China imported CIF $53.81 billion. In 2002, its imports had surged to $295.44 billion. By 2005, they exploded to $660.20 billion. In 2010, they jumped to $1.39 trillion. Five years later, they reached $1.60 trillion. In 2019, they hit $2.07 trillion. China drew the largest amount of its imports

---

[13] For background, see Wang (2016): 455–463; Blanchard and Flint (2017): 223–245; Blanchard (2017): 251–253.

[14] Blanchard (2018): 329–343; Blanchard (2020): 159–174; Blanchard (2021).

[15] On China's SWF, see Blanchard (2014): 155–175.

[16] International Monetary Fund (IMF), "Direction of Trade Statistics (DOTS): Tables-Exports to and Imports from Counterpart Countries," https://data.imf.org/regular.aspx?key=61013712.

from, excluding Taiwan, the EU ($252.70 billion), Korea ($173.55 billion), Japan ($171.52 billion), the US ($123.24 billion), and Australia ($119.61 billion).[17]

Another feature of China's EG has been its participation in the international investment regime. As there is no global regime for investment, countries frequently use BITs to set rules that protect foreign investors and create mechanisms for dealing with disputes. China signed its first BIT in 1982 and since that time has become the world's second-largest user of BITs after Germany. Initially, China signed most of its BITs with developed countries, offering no or conditional protections (which varied by country and year) such as national treatment, MFN status, full protection and security, no restrictions on profit remittances, and even international arbitration. Over time, as it became more familiar with BITs and sought to become a more attractive destination for IFDI it came to accept not only more standard protections, but also unrestricted protections regarding MFN, national treatment, and international arbitration. Additionally, China's increasing OFDI and the growth of its OFDI to the developing world not surprisingly led China to turn its attention to concluding BITs with developing countries.[18] In the aggregate, China's usage of BITs both fueled its EG and the spread of a global EG institution.

1.3 IFDI as a Facet of China's EG

As alluded to above, integral to China's reform and opening in the late 1970s was an effort to reduce and eliminate barriers to IFDI. Early on, the entry of foreign MNCs was seen as a pathway to achieve goals such as increasing exports, acquiring higher technology foreign equipment, and creating jobs. These motives have remained salient up to the present. Nevertheless, China currently does not prioritize leveraging IFDI to increase exports, generate jobs, and produce tax revenues. Instead, it seeks to obtain knowledge and IP that will reduce its dependence on foreign knowledge and IP, help it dominate so-called 21st-century sectors like alternative energy, artificial intelligence, and the internet-of-things, and enable it to move up the value-added chain so that it captures a larger portion of the value-added pie.[19] Regardless of its specific goals, the Chinese government has embraced a similar set of tools to maximize the value it derives from IFDI, which many observers feel has brought China great gains. This section gives some background information on China's contemporary IFDI situation, discusses its benefits and costs for China, and looks at China's management of IFDI and the advantages and disadvantages of China's strategy.

In the late 1990s, in no small measure due to China's forthcoming accession to the WTO, IFDI into China began to rise steadily. By 2002, the year after China's WTO accession, annual FDI had reached $52.74 billion. By 2005, it had soared to $72.40 billion. Five years later, it totaled $114.73 billion. In 2015, it hit $135.58

---

[17] Ibid.

[18] Berger (2019): 151–168.

[19] Nicolas (2008).

5 China and the Impact of Economic Globalization …   93

billion. As of 2019, annual flows increased to $141.23 billion with China's total stock of IFDI reaching $1.77 trillion that year. This compares to a total stock of $1.22 trillion in 2015 and a total stock of $586.88 billion in 2010.[20] Previously, the bulk of IFDI flowing into China went into manufacturing (e.g., electronics and communication equipment), above all, real estate, services (e.g., hotels), and transport, as foreign companies sought to exploit China's low-cost manufacturing base.[21] Of late, a significant amount of FDI has flowed into sectors like finance, real estate, retail, R&D, and transport as foreign businesses seek to profit from the China market, exploit government incentives for R&D and China's S&T talent pool, and adjust to Beijing's quest to make the economy more service/consumption-oriented.[22] In line with historical patterns, China's IFDI continues to be heavily concentrated geographically despite Beijing's repeated initiatives to shift it from China's coastal or eastern regions to its interior and western regions. Indeed, coastal/eastern regions regularly garner two-thirds or more of China's annual IFDI.[23]

Many factors are influencing the scale and patterns of Chinese IFDI. These differ by home country, time period, industrial sector, firm, and other variables. This said, there is no doubt many foreign investors were attracted to China in the early decades of its EG due to the fact it offered multiple locational advantages such as a low-cost production venue, good infrastructure, flexible supplier networks, proximity to the big Asia Pacific Region (APR) market, and numerous incentives for investment ranging from reduced taxes to low cost or free land to flexible labor conditions. Later the motives for firms to invest in China evolved, again with many variations. Regardless, many investors came to value China less as a place to produce goods for export and more as a market for their goods and services.[24] In addition, companies invested in China to locate closer to other businesses from their same home country or sector to supply parts and services.[25] A classic example of this is Japanese banks, insurance, and parts suppliers establishing a presence in China so that they could readily service Japanese automobile, electronics, and other firms that entered China to produce products for the domestic market as well as to export. Aside from the above, China's rising S&T capabilities/large pool of scientific talent and government R&D incentives have meant China has become more attractive as a place to locate such activities.[26] Finally, more and more companies are locating regional headquarters in

---

[20] United Nations Conference on Trade and Development (UNCTAD), *World Investment Report*, http://unctad.org/en/Pages/DIAE/World%20Investment%20Report/Annex-Tables.aspx.

[21] Prasad and Shang-Jin Wei (2005): 7, 42; Long (2005): 317–320; Davies (2012): 63–64.

[22] Davies (2013): 13–14; Blanchard (2017), 17; Zheng (2019): 63–65.

[23] Davies, "China Investment Policy," 13; Liang (2015): 1519–1530; and Zheng, "Foreign Direct Investment in China," 64–66.

[24] Buckley and Meng (2005): 111–131; Davies, "Inward Foreign Direct Investment in China and its Policy Context," 72–73; and Zheng, "Foreign Direct Investment in China," 71–72.

[25] He (2002): 1029–1036.

[26] Prater and Jiang (2008): 211–233; Marro (2015); Holmes Jr. et al. (2016): 594–613.

China. Factors include China's economic prominence, central location in the APR, and government incentives.[27]

It is incontrovertible that a huge number of benefits have flowed to China from opening its doors to foreign investors. In the early decades, Chinese leaders were particularly excited about the fact foreign investors could help the country boost its exports and, relatedly, foreign exchange earnings.[28] Increased IFDI also created jobs to help absorb the massive number of workers that China had to employ in the wake of the economically disastrous Cultural Revolution and the early stages of state-owned enterprise (SOE) reform, which saw an end to guaranteed employment for many. Needless to say, the ability of foreign MNCs to create jobs remained important in later periods, too.[29] Of note, foreign investment often meant higher wages.[30] It also meant better opportunities for female workers.[31] Aside from the economic and industrial growth that they spurred through their activities, foreign companies investing in China facilitated growth by bringing technology and knowledge. While, in the early decades, they did not routinely transfer IP to China, they still brought more advanced machinery and production lines, managerial knowledge, marketing expertise including insights about regional and global markets, and technical assistance. Not to be neglected was the added dynamism foreign firms brought to China by injecting more competition into the system which, in turn, forced Chinese firms to become more efficient. Finally, foreign businesses were a source of additional tax revenues.[32] This was less important for China's national government, though, than sub-national actors like cities.

China's pursuit of EG through the embrace of IFDI had/has various externalities. One is that given the propensity of foreign investors to locate in the "best" provinces and cities to satiate their sundry needs (and China's efforts to confine them), the growth of IFDI exacerbated the economic divides that exist between China's coastal and interior regions. Another is that it led, for some time, to the dominance of foreign brands and companies in many economic sectors such as automobiles, consumer goods, construction equipment, fast food, and lower-end manufactured products as well as exporting. This, in turn, pigeonholed Chinese firms in low value-added production activities, hurt their profit margins, and hindered their ability to upgrade.[33] China's transformation into the factory of the world has increased China's dependence on or exposure to foreign supply chains (which powered its export activities), markets, and natural resources and technologies, which has become more

---

[27] "Over 500 Multinational Set Up Regional Headquarters in Shanghai," *China Daily*, December 8, 2016, http://www.chinadaily.com.cn/business/2016-12/08/content_27609335.htm.

[28] Long, "China's Policies on FDI," 321–322.

[29] Enright (2017): 31–58.

[30] Chen et al. (2017).

[31] Yu et al. (2019): 3404–3429.

[32] Long, "China's Policies on FDI: Review and Evaluation," 327–331; Wang and Wang (2015): 325–338; and Fan et al. (2019): 1675–1682.

[33] Yue (2012).

5 China and the Impact of Economic Globalization … 95

worrisome to Beijing over time.[34] Early on, another externality/dependency flowing from China's embrace of IFDI, though more closely tied to China's preference for export-driven growth and its related support for IFDI that involved exporting, was China's need to accumulate massive currency reserves to support a currency value that facilitated exports. This policy has created many problems for China.

Beijing has closely managed IFDI since 1978. The reasons for this are manifold, but two major ones are the desire to ensure IFDI served China's goals and to limit negative externalities such as losing control over the vital banking sector, environmental pollution, or "spiritual pollution." Regardless, China's management of IFDI has consisted of several enduring components of which a few are discussed below. One prominent one has been the closure or restricted opening of critical sectors such as aviation, energy, insurance, shipping, and telecommunications. In terms of limiting openings, China has used capital requirements, licensing rules, ownership stake caps, joint venture (JV) requirements, and branching limits to control the entry of foreign companies into various sectors and the breadth and depth of their operations in those sectors. Another technique China has used to squeeze more out of FDI is explicit (pre-TRIMs) and implicit pressure on foreign businesses to transfer technology. Pressure has taken forms like Beijing granting market access or favorable treatment after foreign companies have transferred technology, "encouraging" foreign businesses to set up R&D centers in China, and leveraging anti-monopoly cases to extract technology-sharing concessions from foreign businesses.[35] Although the situation appears to be improving, China's historically lax protection of the theft of foreign patents, copyrights, and trade secrets has been another way it has extracted greater benefits from IFDI.[36] On the domestic front, Beijing has used cheap credit, tax rebates, export rebates, government-sponsored research programs, subsidies, and reduced-cost inputs (e.g., energy) to create a playing field that inoculates and empowers Chinese firms against foreign competitors.[37]

Beijing's methods have delivered multiple gains. For example, they have encouraged foreign companies to enter into partnerships they would not otherwise have joined or to locate in regions where they would not otherwise have invested because of their desire to meet Chinese requirements or gain the goodwill of Chinese policymakers. Likewise, foreign businesses have transferred technology and set up dozens of R&D centers. But China's policies have not been an unvarnished success. Some believe, for instance, that China's JV requirements have, in some sectors, made Chinese firms overly dependent on foreign technology and removed the incentives for innovation and greater competitiveness.[38] As well, while foreign investors have transferred technology, they have held back on sharing the best technology or have

---

[34] Friedberg (2018): 7–40.

[35] Carbaugh and Wassell (2019): 306–319.

[36] Brander et al. (2017): 908–921.

[37] European Chamber of Commerce in China (2009), esp. 6–17; Haley and Haley (2013); Wu et al. (2020): 42–59.

[38] Howell (2018): 1448–1462.

spent resources protecting IP that might be put to more productive uses.[39] Another fallout of Chinese policies is that European and US businesses have become increasingly discontent with China to the extent that were it not for the continuing allure of the China market many might shift their investment elsewhere.[40] Yet another potential problem flowing China's measures for controlling IFDI is that it promotes corruption as foreign firms use bribes, gifts, and other methods to gain access to markets, supplies, and favorable treatment from well-placed Chinese officials. With respect to China's support for domestic firms, it has produced overcapacity, lower productivity and profits, ill-conceived investments, excessive debts, and frictions with China's trade partners.[41]

1.4 OFDI as a Component of China's EG

For a long time, business people, policymakers, and scholars paid relatively little attention to the topic of COFDI. This was quite understandable given the low volume of COFDI. Surging COFDI around the mid-2000s, however, exploding COFDI in the natural resource sector (which spurred worries about a great resource grab), and Lenovo's acquisition of iconic assets like IBMs "Think Pad" PC Division in 2005 quickly ended this inattention. This section focuses on COFDI as a dimension of China's EG. It first gives a snapshot of some of the contemporary features of COFDI. It then discusses some of the economic and business drivers of OFDI. Next, it looks at the Chinese government's efforts to direct/shape COFDI. Following this, it looks at the benefits China has derived from COFDI. Finally, it contemplates the negative externalities flowing from Beijing's management of COFDI.

Statistical data from the United Nations Conference on Trade and Development (UNCTAD) reveals that COFDI rose to a new level between the 1990s and the mid-2000s when the annual average jumped from the low two to the high three billion. It is in the 2nd half of the 2000s, though, that it soared, with annual flows hitting $12.26 billion in 2005 and $68.81 billion by 2010. Moreover, in 2013, it topped $100 billion for the first time, reaching $127.56 billion two years later. In 2019, China's annual OFDI was $117.12 billion. As one might expect in tandem with rising annual flows, total COFDI stocks have been experiencing dramatic increases. They totaled $27.77 billion in 2000, $57.21 billion in 2005, $317.21 billion in 2010, more than $1 trillion in 2015, and $2.10 trillion in 2019.[42] It is relatively difficult to assess where COFDI is flowing because of the large amount that goes to tax havens, the round-tripping issue,

---

[39] Keupp et al. (2009): 211–224.

[40] See, e.g., "EU Chamber Warns China: Open Economy Faster or Risk Backlash (2017).

[41] See, e.g., European Chamber of Commerce in China, "Overcapacity in China," 38–40; Barwick et al. (2019); Howell (2020): 1025–1046.

[42] Blanchard (2019): 78–82; and UNCTAD, *World Investment Report*, http://unctad.org/en/Pages/DIAE/World%20Investment%20Report/Annex-Tables.aspx.

and the first-destination problem.[43] To surmount these data compilation problems, many use the American Enterprise Institute (AEI)/The Heritage Foundation "China Global Investment Tracker." Based on CGIT figures, even though billions of dollars of COFDI flowed to developing countries, the bulk of COFDI between 2005 and 2015 went to developed countries such as Australia, France, Singapore, Switzerland, United Kingdom, and the US.[44] Turning to COFDI's sectoral destination, there is, not surprisingly, a very strong resource orientation to COFDI during this same period, with large amounts also going into services, transport, and infrastructure.[45]

The drivers of the volumes and distribution of COFDI are many and varied and it is hard to point to any single decisive factor beyond China's massive accumulation of foreign currency which has provided multiple impetuses for COFDI. Relevant macro- or national-level variables include the imbalance between China's natural resource production and consumption, intense competitive pressures within China, and the changing consumption patterns of Chinese consumers.[46] Salient firm-level factors include companies' desires to access new markets, acquire brands and IP, exploit their low-cost production abilities, diversify into areas fitting China's new economic model focused on consumption, leisure, and services, and serve other Chinese firms (a motive for Chinese banks). Not surprisingly, resource investing remains quite salient.[47] Concrete recent examples of deals shaped by firm-level variables like those just enumerated are China National Chemical Corporation (ChemChina)'s purchase of an almost $8 billion stake in Pirelli (Italy) in 2015, Tencent's massive investment in Supercell (Finland) in 2016, COSCO Holdings large stake in the port of Piraeus (Greece) in 2016, ChemChina's eye-catching $43 billion deal to buy Syngenta (Switzerland) that closed in 2017, and State Grid's multiple billion-dollar-plus investments in power generation and distribution assets in Brazil.

Not to be neglected in any serious discussion of COFDI is Beijing's role in its growth and patterns. In many cases, its contribution has involved nothing more than supportive, rhetorical statements or the elimination of laws/regulations that inhibited COFDI. Still, given its domineering role in the economy, especially, in the case of SOEs, a government statement that something is not prohibited or, better yet, encouraged can be a powerful spur to action as we see with the aforementioned BRI. In any event, China's support goes far beyond words. On the policy front, its efforts to boost OFDI have encompassed easier processes for accessing foreign exchange, increasing investment threshold amounts for regulatory approval, and the decentralization of approval to the sub-national level. China also provides loans, trade financing, and commercial and political risk insurance to enable COFDI. On a

---

[43] The "round tripping" issue refers to money that flows out of China only to be returned to China to exploit incentives for "foreign" investment. The "first-destination" issue relates to the fact that money "invested" out of China may end up in an investment destination other than the locale where it initially flowed.

[44] Blanchard, "Chinese Outward Foreign Direct Investment (COFDI)," 80–82.

[45] Ibid.

[46] An article focusing on such determinants is William X. Wei and Ilan Alon (2010).

[47] Blanchard, "Chinese Outward Foreign Direct Investment (COFDI)," 78–82.

related note, Chinese loans often require host countries to use Chinese suppliers and contractors, which can encourage COFDI. Beyond the above, government backing encompasses research on investment locales, training programs, and support for quasi-formal business groupings in host countries.[48] Aside from the BITs which were discussed above, China's diplomatic activities, directly and indirectly, contribute to COFDI by molding the host country environment in a fashion favorable for it.[49] Similarly, the political importance of China to countries like Cambodia, Pakistan, and Venezuela and/or their leaders creates an environment where these countries are disposed to act favorably toward Chinese firms.

EG on the OFDI front has, on the surface, brought many gains to China. Investments in resource-rich countries such as Angola, Australia, Canada, Nigeria, and Peru have given Chinese companies stakes in foodstuffs, copper, natural gas, oil, and timber.[50] Deals with or investments in American and European firms such as Amer Sports, General Electric, IBM, Kuka, Linxens, and Volvo have allowed public and private Chinese firms opportunities to lock up well-known brands, design facilities, and IP.[51] Investments in infrastructure projects in Africa, South Asia, and Southeast Asia have given Chinese companies a toehold to sell goods and services.[52] COFDI into Malaysia gives Chinese entities the ability to jump tariff walls and profit from regional integration schemes like the Association of Southeast Asian Nations (ASEAN) economic community.[53]

Despite these positive outcomes, Beijing's management of COFDI has costs, one of which is that SOEs dominate COFDI, which, in turn, has its own set of downsides. First, most SOEs are not paragons of efficiency or good CSR practices, which means, in the former case, that they often perform poorly on metrics like return on investment (ROI) or return on equity (ROE) and, in the latter case, that they create a tough operating environment for themselves and other Chinese firms.[54] Second, SOEs generally easy access to capital, and a lack of oversight has encouraged them, on occasion, to overbid for assets.[55] Third, SOEs have a higher tolerance for risky investment destinations given their implicit government backing and the reticence of many host governments and populations to act against them.[56] Fourth, as shown by sundry episodes in Europe and the US, the outsized role of SOEs makes host

---

[48] Ibid., 78–83.

[49] Zhang et al. (2014): 216–235.

[50] A useful study on Chinese resource investments in energy is Lai et al. (2015): 77–95.

[51] Meunier (2014): 283–302; Yang and Ping Deng (2017): 263–280; Top 10 Largest Overseas M&A Cases for Chinese Firms (2019).

[52] For rich discussion of BRI investments in these regions, see the chapters in Jean-Marc F. Blanchard (2018); Jean-Marc F. Blanchard (2019); and Blanchard, ed., *China's Maritime Silk Road, Africa, and the Middle East*.

[53] See, e.g., Ho Wah Foon (2016).

[54] On the low efficiency of Chinese SOE outward investors, see Guo and Clougherty (2015): 141–159. On issues associated with the CSR practices of Chinese firms, see May Tan-Mullins (2020): 207–220.

[55] Guo et al. (2016): 614–631.

[56] Daniel O'Neill (2014): 173–205.

countries suspicious of the extent to which Chinese businesses are driven by business and economic versus political considerations and thus reluctant to accept Chinese investment.[57] A fifth cost is that private firms often do not get government support for their OFDI activities and thus are forced to resort to more convoluted or costly OFDI methods. A sixth is that Beijing's close management of COFDI can increase the volatility of COFDI as was seen with the government's crackdown in 2016 and 2017 on COFDI in the name of protecting foreign currency reserves and preventing so-called "irrational" investment. This volatility has, in the past, made prospective investment targets shun Chinese buyers.[58]

2 Conclusion

One of the aims of this volume is to consider the diverse impacts of EG. This chapter attempts to contribute to this objective by using the China case as a way to illuminate the gains that flow from much-maligned EG as well as identify some of the steps that countries can take to increase the benefits and minimize the costs associated with EG. It began by summarizing the growth of China's participation in the international economic system and detailing some of the features of China's contemporary EG. Subsequently, to permit a more focused analysis, it delved extensively into the positive and negative outcomes associated specifically with China's IFDI and OFDI. It also discussed Beijing's style of managing these two flows and enumerated some of the positive and negative externalities associated with China's efforts to control them.

This chapter shows China has benefitted tremendously from participating in EG in the form of welcoming IFDI and increasing its OFDI. However, different from many other treatments, it does not see China's engagement with EG and China's management of this engagement solely in a positive light. On the positive side, welcoming IFDI brought China, among other things, foreign exchange, jobs, and competitive dynamism. For its part, increasing OFDI improved *inter alia* China's resource situation opened new markets, and brought in foreign brands. Market forces generated some of these gains, but it seems the case that Beijing helped to broaden and/or increase them through its active management. Examples include protecting domestic firms, encouraging greater technology transfer, and ensuring support for greater OFDI. On the negative side, embracing huge amounts of IFDI fueled regional inequalities, increased Chinese dependence on the outside world, and encouraged problematic currency policies. With respect to OFDI, Beijing's close involvement led to problems of capital flight, wasted money, and so on. Turning to China's management of IFDI and OFDI, this chapter noted that problems linked to its management policies include, to illustrate, poor economic relations with partner

---

[57] Blanchard, "Chinese Outward Foreign Direct Investment (COFDI)," 83–84.

[58] Sidders and Chan (2017).

countries, making its firms dependent on their JV partners or foreign technologies, and distortions in the relative weight given to SOEs in COFDI.

There are at least three general policy implications to my analysis. First, EG can help participating countries obtain many gains and thus decision-makers should be very cautious about shunning it. Second, government management of EG can be beneficial, though policymakers need to think long and hard about the specifics. Third, policymakers need to view the Chinese "model" of engagement with EG critically, with full recognition that while it has much appeal it also has various limitations. Relatedly, it needs to be appreciated that China's management of EG generates diverse negative externalities. As far as theory is concerned, this analysis challenges simple analyses which assume EG automatically brings benefits. Furthermore, it raises questions about theories of state-led development/management of EG that take for granted such paths only have advantages.

There are several limitations to this analysis. First, it concentrates on IFDI and OFDI. For a fuller understanding of China's experience with and management of EG, it also is critical to delve thoroughly into other EG realms such as trade. Second, even focused treatments of IFDI or OFDI can be very general. In some instances, it may be desirable to analyze EG and EG management strategies regarding specific sectors like automobiles, banking, or power/utilities to unpack what is transpiring. Third, this analysis is limited to EG's costs and benefits for China alone. Yet China's plunge into EG certainly has had ramifications for its neighbors, other developing countries, and rich nations in terms of investment and trade diversion, deindustrialization, and job creation/losses. The point is not that China's participation in EG is uniformly bad for others.[59] Instead, it is that when thinking about the lessons of China for realizing better EG there are both country-specific as well as system-wide issues that need to be taken into account.

The pressures on EG these days are many. They come from global economic conditions, popular angst about the costs of EG, and anti-globalization and anti-MNC activists. For those that believe EG has promise, the case of China seems to stand out as a shining example to counter the critics. It further seems to be a case worth understanding given China's strong public support of EG and the potential for China to become a future leader of EG given its economic might and initiatives coupled with Washington's seeming withdrawal from leadership. This chapter indicates China indeed has much to offer, but we must be careful in the lessons we draw from the China case lest we take the wrong actions, damaging EG even further, and sit on our hands in hopes of Chinese leadership when alternative courses of action need to be pursued to sustain and advance EG.

---

[59] See, e.g., Eichengreen and Tong (2007): 153–172; Feenstra and Sasahara (2018): 1053–1083; Jenkins (2019).

References

Barwick, Panle Jia, Myrto Kalouptsidi, and Nahim Bin Zahur. 2019. China's industrial policy: An empirical evaluation. *NBER Working Papers*, no. 26075, September. https://www.nber.org/papers/w26075.

Berger, Axel. 2019. The political economy of Chinese investment treaties. In *Handbook on the International Political Economy of China,* ed. Ka Zeng, 151–168. Cheltenham: Elgar.

Blanchard, Jean-Marc F. 2013. The dynamics of China's accession to the WTO: Counting sense, coalitions, and constructs. *Asian Journal of Social Science* 41 (3–4), December: 263–286.

Blanchard, Jean-Marc F. 2013. China, foreign investors, and TRIMS: Bulking up, but not fully compliant. In *China and Global Trade Governance*, eds. Ka Zeng and Wei Liang, 43–68. London: Routledge.

Blanchard, Jean-Marc F. 2014. The China investment corporation: power, wealth, or something else. *China: An International Journal* 12(3), December: 155–175.

Blanchard, Jean-Marc F. 2017. Probing China's twenty-first century maritime silk road initiative (MSRI): An examination of MSRI narratives. *Geopolitics* 22 (2): 246–268.

Blanchard, Jean-Marc F. 2017. Global FDI Trends. In *The Russian economy and foreign direct investment*, ed. Kari Liuhto, Sergei Styrin, and Jean-Marc F. Blanchard, 7–24. London: Routledge.

Blanchard, Jean-Marc F., ed. 2018. *China's Maritime Silk Road and South Asia.* Singapore: Palgrave MacMillan.

Blanchard, Jean-Marc F. 2018. China's Maritime Silk Road Initiative (MSRI) and Southeast Asia: A Chinese 'Pond' Not 'Lake' in the works. *Journal of Contemporary China* 27 (111): 329–343.

Blanchard, Jean-Marc F., ed. 2019. *China's Maritime Silk Road and Southeast Asia.* Singapore: Palgrave MacMillan.

Blanchard, Jean-Marc F. 2019. Chinese Outward Foreign Direct Investment (COFDI): A primer and assessment of the state of COFDI Research," In *Handbook on the International Political Economy of China*, ed. Ka Zeng, 76–95. Cheltenham: Elgar.

Blanchard, Jean-Marc F. 2020. Problematic prognostications about China's Maritime Silk Road Initiative (MSRI): Lessons from Africa and the Middle East. *Journal of Contemporary China* 29 (122): 159–174.

Blanchard, Jean-Marc F., ed. 2021. *China's Maritime Silk Road, Africa, and the Middle East.* Singapore: Palgrave MacMillan.

Blanchard, Jean-Marc F., and Colin Flint. 2017. The geopolitics of China's Maritime silk road initiative. *Geopolitics* 22 (2): 223–245.

Brander, James A., Victor Cui, and Ilan Vertinsky. 2017. China and intellectual property rights: A challenge to the rule of law. *Journal of International Business Studies* 48 (76): 908–921 September.

Branstetter, Lee, and Nicholas Lardy. 2008. China's embrace of globalization. In *China's great economic transformation*, ed. Loren Brandt and Thomas G. Rawski, 633–682. Cambridge: Cambridge University Press.

Bremmer, Ian. 2018. China is globalization's greatest success story. *Asia Society*, April 23. https://asiasociety.org/blog/asia/china-globalizations-greatest-success-story-can-good-times-last.

Breslin, Shaun. 2003. Reforming China's embedded socialist compromise: China and the WTO. *Global Change, Peace, & Security* 15 (3): 213–229.

Buckley, Peter J., and Chen Meng. 2005. The Strategy of foreign-invested manufacturing enterprises in China: Export-orientated and market-orientated FDI revisited. *Journal of Chinese Economic and Business Studies* 3 (2): 111–131.

Carbaugh, Bob, and Chad Wassell. 2019. Forced technology transfer and China. *Economic Affairs* 39 (3): 306–319.

Chen, Cen, Hongmei Zhao, and Yunbo Zhou. 2017. Foreign direct investment and wage inequality: Evidence from the People's Republic of China. *ADB Institute Working Paper* no. 734 (May 2017). https://www.adb.org/publications/foreign-direct-investment-and-wage-inequality-evidence-prc.

Davies, Ken. 2012. Inward foreign direct investment in China and its policy context. *China: An International Journal* 10(1) (2012): 102–115.

Davies, Ken. 2013. China investment policy: An update. *OECD Working Papers on International Investment*, January. https://www.oecd.org/china/WP-2013_1.pdf.

Economy, Elizabeth. 2017. Beijing is no champion of globalization. *Foreign Affairs*, January 22. https://www.foreignaffairs.com/articles/china/2017-01-22/beijing-no-champion-globalization.

Eichengreen, Barry, and Hui Tong. 2007. Is China's FDI coming at the expense of other countries? *Journal of the Japanese and International Economies* 21 (2): 153–172 June.

Enright, Michael J. 2017. *Developing China*. London: Routledge.

EU Chamber Warns China: Open Economy Faster or Risk Backlash. *The New York Times*, September 19, 2017. https://www.nytimes.com/aponline/2017/09/18/world/asia/ap-as-china-foreign-business.html.

European Chamber of Commerce in China, "Overcapacity in China: Causes, Impacts, and Recommendations," 2009. https://www.europeanchamber.com.cn/en/publications-archive/27/Overcapacity_in_China_Causes_Impacts_and_Recommendations.

Fan, Hongzhong, Shi He, and Yum K. Kwan. 2019. Foreign direct investment and productivity spillovers: Is China different? *Applied Economics Letters* 26 (20): 1675–1682.

Feenstra, Robert C., and Akira Sasahara. 2018. The 'China Shock', exports and U.S. employment: A global input-output analysis. *Review of International Economics* 26 (5): 1053–1083 November.

Foon, Ho Wah. 2016. China investments to life Malaysia Outlook. *The Star Online*, April 17. http://www.thestar.com.my/news/nation/2016/04/17/china-investments-to-lift-malaysias-outlook.

Friedberg, Aaron L. 2018. Globalization and Chinese grand strategy. *Survival* 60 (1): 7–40.

Goh, Brenda, and Yawen Chen. 2017. China Pledges $124 billion for new silk road as champion of globalization. *Reuters*, May 13. https://www.reuters.com/article/us-china-silkroad-africa/china-pledges-124-billion-for-new-silk-road-as-champion-of-globalization-idUSKBN18A02I.

Guo, Wenxin, and Joseph A. Clougherty. 2015. The effectiveness of the state in chinese outward foreign direct investment: The 'Go Global' policy and state-owned enterprises. In *Emerging Economies and Multinational Enterprises*, eds. Laszlo Tihanyi et al., 28, 141–159.

Guo, Wenxin, Joseph A. Clougherty, and Tomaso Duso. 2016. Why are Chinese MNES not financially competitive in cross-border acquisitions? The role of state ownership. *Long Range Planning* 49 (5): 614–631 October.

Haley, Usha C.V., and George T. Haley. 2013. *Subsidies to Chinese Industry: State Capitalism, Business Strategy, and Trade Policy*. Oxford: Oxford University Press.

Harpaz, Marcia Don. 2013. China's WTO compliance in banking services. In *China and Global Trade Governance: China's First Decade in the World Trade Organization*, eds. Ka Zeng and Wei Liang, 69–102. London: Routledge.

He, Canfei. 2002. Information costs, agglomeration economies, and the location of foreign direct investment in China. *Regional Studies* 36: 1029–1036.

Holmes, R. Michael, Jr., et al. 2016. The effects of location and MNC attributes on MNCs' establishment of foreign R&D centers: Evidence from China. *Long Range Planning* 49 (5), October: 594–613.

Howell, Anthony. 2020. Picking 'Winners' in space: Impact of spatial targeting on firm performance in China. *Journal of Regional Science* 60 (5): 1025–1046 November.

Howell, Sabrina T. 2018. Joint ventures and technology adoption: A Chinese industrial policy that backfired. *Research Policy* 47 (8): 1448–1462 October.

International Monetary Fund (IMF). Direction of Trade Statistics (DOTS): Tables-Exports to and Imports from Counterpart Countries. https://data.imf.org/regular.aspx?key=61013712.

Jenkins, Rhys. 2019. *How China is reshaping the global economy*. Oxford: Oxford University Press.

Keupp, Marcus Matthias, Angela Beckenbauer, and Oliver Gassmann. 2009. How managers protect intellectual property rights in China using de facto strategies. *R&D Management* 39 (2) (2009): 211–224.

Lai, Hongyi, Sarah O'Hara, and Karolina Wysoczanska. 2015. Rationale of internationalization of china's national oil companies: Seeking natural resources, strategic assets, or sectoral specialization. *Asia Pacific Business Review* 21 (1): 77–95.

5 China and the Impact of Economic Globalization … 103

Lardy, Nicholas R. 2002. *Integrating China into the Global Economy*. Washington, D.C.: The Brookings Institution.

Lechmacher, Wolfgang. 2016. Why China could lead the next phase of globalization. *World Economic Forum*, November 22. https://www.weforum.org/agenda/2016/11/china-lead-globalization-after-united-states.

Liang, Wei. 2007. "China: Globalization and the emergence of a new status Quo power? *Asian Perspective* 31 (4): 125–149.

Liang, Yu. 2015. The determinants and structural change of FDI in China-a study based on city-level panel data. The Journal of Applied Business Research 31 (4), July/August: 1519–1530.

Long, Guoqiang. 2005. China's policies on FDI: Review and evaluation. In *Does Foreign Direct Investment Promote Development?*, eds. Theodore H. Moran, Edward M. Graham, and Magnus Blomstrom, 315–336. Washington, D.C. Institute for International Economics.

Marro, Nick. 2015. Foreign company R&D: In China, For China. *China Business Review*, June 1. https://www.chinabusinessreview.com/foreign-company-rd-in-china-for-china

Meunier, Sophie. 2014. 'Beggars can't be choosers': The European crisis and Chinese investment in the European Union. *Journal of European Integration* 36 (3): 283–302.

Naughton, Barry J. 2007. *The Chinese Economy*. Cambridge: The MIT Press.

Nicolas, Françoise. 2008. China and foreign investors: The end of a beautiful friendship?" *Asie Visions* 4, April 2008. https://www.ifri.org/sites/default/files/atoms/files/av4_nicolas_china_and_foreign_investors_2008.pdf.

O'Neill, Daniel. 2014. Playing risk: Chinese foreign direct investment in Cambodia. *Contemporary Southeast Asia* 36 (2): 173–205 August.

"Over 500 Multinational Set Up Regional Headquarters in Shanghai," *China Daily*, December 8, 2016. http://www.chinadaily.com.cn/business/2016-12/08/content_27609335.htm.

Paradise, James. 2013. The new intellectual property rights environment in China: Impact of WTO membership and China's "Innovation Society" makeover. *Asian Journal of Social Science* 3–4: 312–332 December.

Pearson, Margaret M. 1999. China's integration into the international trade and investment regime. In *China joins the world*, ed. Elizabeth Economy and Michel Oksenberg, 161–205. New York: Council on Foreign Relations Press.

Rodrik, Dani. 2012. Getting globalization right: China marches to its beat. *OECD Insights*, May 4. http://oecdinsights.org/2012/05/04/getting-globalization-right-china-marches-to-its-own-beat.

Prasad, Eswar, and Shang-Jin Wei. 2005. The Chinese approach to capital inflows: Patterns and possible explanations. *IMF Working Paper*, WP/05/79, April. https://www.imf.org/external/pubs/ft/wp/2005/wp0579.pdf.

Prater, Edmund, and Bin Jiang. 2008. The drivers of foreign R&D investment in China. *Journal of Marketing Channels* 15 (2 & 3): 211–233.

Shen, Wei, and Matthias Vanhullebusch. 2015. Where is the Alchemy?" The experiment of the Shanghai Free trade zone in freeing the foreign investment regime in China. *European Business Organization Law Review* 16 (2): 321–352 June.

Sidders, Jack, and Vinicy Chan. 2017. China's $246 Billion foreign buying spree is unraveling. *Bloomberg*, May 11. https://www.bloomberg.com/news/articles/2017-05-10/china-s-246-billion-takeover-spree-is-crumbling-as-sellers-balk.

Tan-Mullins, May. 2020. Smoothing the silk road through successful Chinese corporate social responsibility practices: Evidence from East Africa. *Journal of Contemporary China* 29 (122): 207–220.

Top 10 Largest Overseas M&A Cases for Chinese Firms. *China Daily*, May 9, 2019. http://www.chinadaily.com.cn/a/201905/09/WS5cd35ac0a3104842260ba996_1.html.

United Nations Conference on Trade and Development (UNCTAD), World Investment Report. http://unctad.org/en/Pages/DIAE/World%20Investment%20Report/Annex-Tables.aspx.

Wang, Huiyao. 2019. China and globalization: 40 years of reform and opening-up and globalization 4.0. *Journal of Chinese Economic and Business Studies* 17 (3): 215–220.

Wang, Jiang, and Xiao Wang. 2015. Benefits of foreign ownership: Evidence from foreign direct investment in China. *Journal of International Economics* 97 (2): 325–338 November.

Wang, Yong. 2016. Offensive for defensive: The belt and road initiative and China's new grand strategy. *The Pacific Review* 29 (3): 455–463.

Wei, William X., and Ilan Alon. 2010. Chinese outward direct investments: A study on macroeconomic determinants. *International Journal of Business and Emerging Markets* 2 (4): 352–369.

Wu, Ruirui et al. 2020. Effect of government R&D subsidies on firms' innovation in China. *Asian Journal of Technology Innovation* 28 (1): 42–59.

Yang, Monica, and Ping Deng. 2017. Cross-border M&A by Chinese companies in advanced countries: Antecedents and implications. *Thunderbird International Business Review* 59(3) (May/June 2017): 263–280.

Yu, Linhui, Junsen Zhang, and Yanbing Wen. 2019. Does foreign investment liberalization enhance women's economic status? *The World Economy* 42 (12): 3404–3429.

Yue, Jianyong. 2012. What does globalization mean for China's economic development. *Global Policy Journal*, May 24. http://www.globalpolicyjournal.com/blog/24/05/2012/what-does-globalization-mean-china%E2%80%99s-economic-development.

Zhang, Jianhong, Jiangang Jiang, and Chaohong Zhou. 2014. Diplomacy and investment: The case of China. *International Journal of Emerging Markets* 9 (2): 216–235.

Zheng, Yu. 2019. Foreign direct investment in China. In *Handbook on the International Political Economy of China*, ed. Ka Zeng, 61–75. Cheltenham: Elgar.

Zweig, David. 2001. China's Stalled 'Fifth Wave': Zhu Rongji's reform package of 1998–2000," *Asian Survey* 41 (2), March/April: 231–247.

Chapter 6
Geo-economics, Globalization and the Covid-19 Pandemic: Trade and Development Perspectives from Bangladesh

Mohammad A. Razzaque

1 Introduction

By unleashing a catastrophic health crisis for global economies including Bangladesh, the COVID19 pandemic has brought unprecedented disruptions in world economic activities including international trade, tourism, and investment flows. Before the pandemic impact, the U.S.–China trade war caused global trade to slow down significantly affecting almost all countries. All-out retaliatory measures employed by the world's two biggest economies against each other, bypassing multilateral rules for settling disputes, was a major manifestation of an undercurrent indicating that globalization and free trade policy regimes were at crossroads.

After rapid expansion since 1990, internationally trademarked a prolonged period of deceleration. Triggered initially by the global financial crisis of 2008, the trade-led development perspective was subject to a massive setback as the benefits of globalization were called into questions in Western developed countries leading to, among others, trade policy reversals in the United States, especially under President Trump during 2017–2020. The rise of China as a major trading and economic power has also had a profound impact on the geopolitical landscape marked by a proliferation of geoeconomic tools used by various countries in pursuit of their national interests and in protecting their regional and global influence. As most developed countries faced disruptions in emergency supplies in the immediate aftermath of the COVID19 crisis, there were concerns about the highly concentrated production network centering on China. This prompted proactive policy measures focusing on "reshoring", "onshoring", and "nearshoring" of production processes, to diversify supply sources away from China. While U.S. trade policy actions against China

---

The original version of this chapter was revised: Chapter title have been incorporated. The correction to this chapter is available at
https://doi.org/10.1007/978-981-16-7185-2_11

M. A. Razzaque (✉)
Research and Policy Integration for Development (RAPID), Dhaka, Bangladesh

© The Author(s), under exclusive license to Springer Nature Singapore Pte Ltd. 2022, corrected publication 2022
A. Palit (ed.), *Globalisation Impacts*, International Law and the Global South,
https://doi.org/10.1007/978-981-16-7185-2_6

started to have some impact, Japan rolled out a major economic support package to help manufacturers shift production out of China.[1] The possibility of a new cold war threatens to overshadow multilateral and regional cooperation as the disentangling of the so-called "Chimerica"—with China as the global manufacturing hub and the United States as the tech and finance headquarters—comes to the fore.[2] The rivalry between China and India has also generated new economic and security uncertainty in South Asia and the two neighboring economic giants vie for geopolitical gains, increasingly making use of geoeconomic tools.

With Asia set to propelling global economic growth for many decades to come, it will also be one of the most important fronts for geoeconomic and geopolitical rivalry. The existing global trade and investment regimes could change profoundly as global economic forces strive for economic and political competitive advantages. Despite the change in political leadership following the 2020 U.S. presidential election, it is not clear yet to what extent the policy reversals of the United States will backtrack given that China appears to have come out stronger amid the COVID19 pandemic. This could imply unsettling environments for global trade and other multilateral cooperation.

The emerging geoeconomic order brings a new spotlight on the development prospects for a country like Bangladesh, which has registered impressive socio-economic advancement—as reflected in its impending graduation from the group of least developed countries (LDCs)—and expects a credible, inclusive, and rules-based international trading system to strengthen its development transitions. Bangladesh also wants to benefit from being in the vicinity of the world's two largest growth centers in India and China. Over the past decades, international trade as a vehicle for economic growth became established in the development strategies of many developing countries. The United Nations' 2030 Agenda for Sustainable development recognizes it as a means for achieving various Sustainable Development Goals (SDGs). However, the WTO-led multilateral trading system (MTS) now faces an existential threat as the long-running Doha Development Round of negotiations, initiated in 2001, is now stalled and trade conflicts undermine existing rules and regulations. Along with it, geopolitical competition accentuated by the COVID19 pandemic has triggered global and regional powers to unleash intensified geoeconomic instruments. In this backdrop, the objective of this chapter is to discuss how the intensified geoeconomic rivalry can affect trade and development prospects for Bangladesh and discuss some policy options for navigating the unfolding geo-economics landscape.

---

[1] It has been reported that *Japan* has paid 87 *companies* to shift production back home or into Southeast Asia after the coronavirus pandemic disrupted supply chains and exposed an overreliance on *Chinese manufacturing* (The Washington Post dated 21 July 2020).

[2] Economic historian Niall Ferguson first coined the term "Chimerica" to explain the intricate interdependence between the world's two largest economies, China and America (United States). It was argued that the Chinese savings fuelled a massive U.S. overspend leading to an incredible period of wealth creation but eventually contributing to the global financial crisis of 2008.

2 Rise of Geo-Economics and the Multilateral Trading System

Geo-economics is a relatively new concept: the term was first coined in 1990 by Edward Luttwak who suggested that the main area of rivalry in the post-cold war system would be economic rather than military (Luttwak 1990). Military interventions have become very expensive and due to numerous countries having nuclear weapons to deter opponents' military approaches, the use of economic tools to realize geopolitical goals has become more pragmatic. Blackwill and Harris (2016) refer to geo-economics as "war by other means" and define it as "the use of economic instruments to promote and defend national interests, and to produce beneficial geopolitical results…" (Blackwill and Harris 2016; p.9). Although the term is relatively new, it has been argued that geo-economics has long existed in practice with the U.S. Marshall Plan after World War II to rebuild Europe and the most recent Chinese Belt and Road Initiative (BRI) to boost trade and connectivity at the continental scale having the same objectives of benefitting their originators economically and geopolitically (Beeson 2018). Recent real-world examples of geoeconomic tools are widespread including western countries' economic sanctions against Iran and Russian, China's aid to many low-income countries to gather political influence, U.S. restrictions on Huawei's 5G network, U.S.–China trade war, etc. Regional powers regularly make use of a wide variety of geoeconomic instruments targeting their neighbors to exert and maintain influence at a sub-continental level. Along with financial assistance and various state-supported investment projects, hyped-up diplomatic campaigns of India and China promising to make COVID19 vaccines available for neighboring countries can also be regarded as examples of geo-economics in play.

Despite its long existence, geo-economics is now attracting intense attention because of several reasons. First and foremost, China, which has become the world's largest economy in purchasing power (PPP) terms, is increasingly flexing its economic muscles to project power and gather influence. Its BRI initiative—regarded as one of the most ambitious transcontinental connectivity and trade infrastructure projects—has caused concerns among established global economic forces such as the United States, EU, Japan, and its regional rival, India.[3]

Second, the world is witnessing the shifting center of economic gravity in Asia. Even going beyond the largest economies of China, India, Japan, and the Republic of Korea, several other big Asian economies including Bangladesh, Indonesia, Vietnam, Pakistan, and the Philippines are growing fast. Asia's share in the world economy is projected to rise from 32% in 2018 to more than 50% by 2050. Therefore, it is inevitable that all global economies including the United States and the EU will have to engage more proactively with Asian growth centers to reorient their integration into the future world economy. Another reason for the interest in geo-economics

---

[3] There is no official definition of what qualifies as a BRI project. There are Chinese-funded projects in countries not participating directly in the BRI, sharing the same characteristics of the BRI projects. It is estimated that BRI-related infrastructure development will require investments worth of $26 trillion in the Asia-Pacific region, with the Chinese government pledging $1 trillion to date.

is that the deep integration of global economies makes geoeconomic tools more powerful than ever.

Geo-economics is gaining the most traction due to the complex manner through which the United States is considering its options in dealing with China. Blackwill and Harris (2016) argue that the United States, until recently, has dealt with international trade and investment treaties separately from economic and security issues. This was possible as it did never experience economic and strategic competition from a single country. It strongly campaigned for free trade, which was considered as the best possible option for itself and its allies. However, according to Blackwill and Harris (2016), with the rise of China, the United States has seen an economic and as well as strategic challenges. An inextricable economic interdependence between the two countries in which China's purchase of U.S. debts over many years to fuel American spending, and U.S. technology and investment flowing into China to generate global export production at an unprecedented scale means any U.S. measures against China would also cause adverse consequences for the United States and other global economies.[4] That is, decoupling of the U.S. and Chinese economies would require a lot of adjustments and would have far-reaching implications.

It is worth noting that the rules-based multilateral trading system led by the WTO should ideally constrict the scope of geo-economics and unilateral actions. It is generally held that, by taking advantage of WTO rules and legally binding dispute settlement decisions, China has been able to become a major trading power. The United States-led developed countries often argue that the WTO system has failed to deal with the problem of state capitalism, currency manipulations, etc. It, however, needs to be acknowledged that it is the WTO members that make rules through negotiations. In the past, not only China but the rapid growth of other large developing countries such as Brazil, India, Indonesia, Mexico, Russia, etc., also caused concerns because of shifting comparative advantages away from developed to developing nations. Developing countries enjoy certain privileges (e.g., commitments of lesser tariff cuts and longer transition periods in implementing various binding provisions) and operate under labor, intellectual property protection, and environmental standards that are viewed by developed countries as non-acceptable contributing to competitive advantages of the relatively advanced developing countries, especially China. The United States and its allies thus demand reforming the WTO system.

In a multilateral member-driven organization, negotiations are difficult, and bringing fundamental changes can be a lengthy process. On the other hand, China and other developing countries' rapid rise would require new rules and regulations to protect the competitiveness of the United States and other advanced economies. The United States attempted to develop such trading blocs as the Trans-Atlantic Trade and Investment Partnership (TTIP) and the Trans-Pacific Partnership (TPP) with more stringent provisions than those under the WTO. These new trading blocs, particularly TPP, would bring in new rules (beyond those in the WTO) in such areas as standards

---

[4] China currently holds a staggering $3.4 trillion as foreign exchange reserves. Of the total $7.04 trillion US debts held by foreign countries, China holds $1.07 trillion in U.S. securities followed by Japan $1.26 trillion.

and intellectual property protection where China is thought to have been involved in unfair practices and the current WTO system cannot provide remedial measures. In 2008, the United States began negotiating TPP with an expressed objective of counterbalancing China's growing influence in the region.[5] Under President Obama's "Pivot to Asia" strategy, the TPP would play a critical role as then U.S. Secretary of Defence Ashton Carter remarked "...TPP is as important to me as another aircraft carrier". It was a clear indication of the TPP being considered a major geoeconomic tool.[6]

However, the United States eventually withdrew from the TPP following the 2016 presidential election campaigns when the benefits of free trade policies and globalization were questioned. Although President Trump's drastic policy reversals led to the end of the TPP, it also became clear that global trade had changed profoundly, and new trading blocs alone would not give the United States enough leverage. China had become a formidable market for the rest of the world and accessing the Chinese market was lucrative for many countries.

Indeed, while the TPP failed to emerge, the Regional Comprehensive Economic Partnership (RCEP) agreement—widely perceived as a China-led initiative—came to fruition in November 2020 as 15 Asia-Pacific Nations including 10 Association of Southeast Asian Nations (ASEAN), as well as South Korea, China, Japan, Australia, and New Zealand, formed the biggest trade deal in history, comprising nearly one-third of the world's population and 30% of global GDP.

The collapse of the TPP in setting new rules to be regarded as global standards made it inevitable for the WTO system to become the target of geo-economics playing. The initiation of the trade war against China in 2018 and the U.S.-led western countries' imposing a ban on Huawei 5G technology on the ground of security risks marked a new era in geopolitical rivalry. China, on the other hand, has imposed strict censorship on many popular online and social media services such as Google, YouTube, and Facebook.

Rivalry in the field of technology will be a major bone of contention and the existing MTS system could struggle to find solutions to the problems. China has benefited from technology transfer from the United States through FDI and has also invested massively to transform its productive capacities. After several decades of deep integration between these countries, any policy-driven decoupling of the two economies will not be an easy one. The extremely intricate and complex web of supply chains means disentangling of business and investment linkages will have massive consequences. The interdependence of the two economies has led to worldwide fragmentation of production processes, in which countries specialize in specific tasks rather than manufacturing an entire product. For example, parts and components of the Boeing 787 Dreamliner are produced in at least 10 countries before the airplane

---

[5] The TPP members were Australia, Brunei, Canada, Chile, Japan, Malaysia, Mexico, New Zealand, Peru, Singapore, Vietnam, and the United States and the proposed TPP agreement was signed in February 2016. The U.S. withdrew from it in 2017. The other 11 countries later signed a revised version of the agreement, called the *Comprehensive and Progressive Agreement for Trans-Pacific Partnership*.

[6] Mr. Carter's speech at the McCain Institute at Arizona State University on 6 April 2015.

being assembled in the United States; the suppliers involved in the production of the Apple iPhone are from numerous countries; and even for relatively low-tech products such as t-shirts and footwear, supply chains involve several countries. Therefore, a grand scale geoeconomic architecture to decouple economies would disrupt production processes causing severe welfare consequences. It has been estimated that U.S. and Chinese companies together have around $550 billion in revenues at stake in each other's markets with U.S. companies having a much greater share of around $400 billion (Varadarajan et al. 2020). On the other hand, while the world remains dependent on China's manufacturing infrastructure, it has been pointed out that China cannot feed global markets without foreign technology (Weber 2020). Again, China's dependence on the U.S. dollar as foreign reserves exposes it to U.S. sanctions with crippling consequences. The emerging trends are thus gravely unsettling as Ferguson and Xu (2018) observe:

> Arrangements that made sense when China was merely a big emerging market now urgently need to be revised to take account of the new economic parity—and increasingly open strategic rivalry—between the two halves of Chimerica. There is a need, in short, for a new balance—and it will only be achieved if China gives ground. The alternative is a Chimerican divorce. That is unlikely to be amicable—and is bound to hurt not only the United States and China but also the world economy as a whole.

The policy shifts of the United States in response to trade and technology challenges, however, until now do not show any vision of future architecture. It is possible that any paradigm change can take place even within the WTO process. Keeping the recent rivalry and geo-economics aside, WTO members have for long failed to successfully conclude the Doha Round and thus many issues that were prominent when the round was launched have become less relevant while it has not been possible to deal with emerging issues effectively. Decision-making processes including the principle of "single undertaking" paralyzing the system have also been criticized. It is also true that many geoeconomic battles are in areas outside the purview of the WTO System. For example, the areas where rules are less than well-established, e.g., services trade, e-commerce, etc. Hence, there are important scopes for reforming the WTO to strengthen the rules-based system. However, another possibility for the United States to try to bring in a completely new system. Both the options are challenging, and some quick fixing may not work out. Overall, the possibility of a chaotic geo-economics powerplay to (mis)govern the future trade and technology cooperation affecting development prospects of many developing countries is a real one.

2.1 Bangladesh in the Unfolding Geo-Economics Landscape

Graduation from the Least Developed Countries and the Importance of Expanded Trading Opportunities

Bangladesh has achieved commendable socio-economic development over the past decades. From a fragile socio-economic setup at independence, it has emerged as a "development surprise" (Mahmud 2008). Despite confronted with numerous challenges, its record of solid macroeconomic stability, rising per capita income, improvements in child nutrition, decrease in child mortality, expansion of primary and secondary education, reduction of gender inequality in education, maintaining food production close to self-sufficiency level, sustained trends of decline in income-poverty, maintaining an external debt level much lower than many other developing countries, etc., is considered remarkable by development observers (Razzaque 2018). compared to many other countries at a similar stage of development, Bangladesh has attained faster progress in various social and human development indicators such as demographic, health, and gender equality outcomes, (Asadullah et al. 2014). Because of sustained economic growth over the past three decades, and economy of $35 billion of the mid-1990s has now grown to a sizeable $350 billion. At the same time, the proportion of the population living below the nationally defined poverty line income fell from more than 50% to about 21% while the per capita gross national income registered about a seven-fold rise from just $300 to above $2,000. Even amid the COVID19 global pandemic, Bangladesh has remained relatively resilient registering an impressive economic growth of 5.6% in 2019–20. In 2015, Bangladesh made an important transition from a low-income to a lower-middle-income country as per the World Bank's defined classification of global economies. It has attained qualification for graduating from the group of the least developed countries (LDCs) and is firmly set to leave the ranks of these poorest countries by 2026.

Bangladesh's impressive success story to a large extent is attributed to the performance of its export sector as merchandise exports expanded rapidly from less than $2 billion in 1990 to above $40 billion in 2018–19 before being hit by the global pandemic during 2019–20 when exports dropped to $34.1 billion. During the most recent past decade before COVID19 (2009–19), Bangladesh achieved an average yearly export growth twice as fast as the world average export growth, registering the second-highest export growth among global economies (WTO 2019). It is the apparel industry that has singlehandedly driven the export success leading to a remarkable transformation in which manufacturing exports rose to prominence to dominate the export basket, driving down the dependence on primary products to a very low level. This was a striking development as many low-income and lower-middle-income countries failed to make such a transformation happen. The expansion of readymade garment (RMG) exports has generated massive employment opportunities, particularly for women. Through increased exports, job creation, women's economic empowerment, and many other indirect linkages, the RMG sector emerged as a symbol of the trade-led development process for Bangladesh.

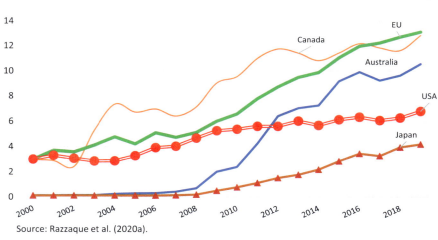

Fig. 1 Bangladesh's apparel market share in some major countries (%)

However, given the impending LDC graduation, the apparel export-led growth and development strategy poses a cause for concern because of several reasons. First, despite the garment industry's success, Bangladesh's exports remain modest in comparison with most countries of comparable size (in terms of population). For instance, the 91 million-strong Vietnam posts an export volume of more than $270 billion; Indonesia exports $170 billion with a population of 218 million; the Philippines, with a population of 101 million, have export earnings of around $70 billion. Again, much smaller countries in East Asia such as Malaysia and Singapore are extremely successful exporting nations, exporting $240 billion and $390 billion, respectively.[7] Therefore, Bangladesh will have to continue to maintain robust growth in exports. Second, Bangladesh's export earnings are heavily concentrated in garments (84%), as export diversification has proven to be a formidable task. Such a high dependence on a single category of exports can be quite risky in the face of any sector-specific shock.

Finally, and perhaps most importantly, Bangladesh is heavily dependent on export markets that offer preferences (such as duty-free market access and relaxed rules of origin) designed for the least developed countries (LDCs). It enjoys such preferential market access under various countries' generalized system of preferences (GSP) schemes in more than 40 countries with almost three-quarters of export earnings being sourced from these countries. In fact, among the most important economies, only the United States currently does not provide any preferential market access to Bangladesh. There is clear evidence that in such major economies as Australia, Canada, the EU, and Japan where Bangladesh has preferential market access in clothing, its export share has increased remarkably (Fig. 1).

---

[7] The export figures mentioned for comparison purposes are for 2019 and have been taken from the World Bank's World Development Indicators.

The loss of these preferences after graduation is likely to put export competitiveness under tremendous pressure. After graduation, new preferential trading opportunities must be sought through bilateral and regional free trade negotiations. Until now, Bangladesh does not have any bilateral free trade agreement (FTA) and it is a member of just one regional FTA, the South Asian Free Trade Area (SAFTA).

The European Union and the United Kingdom together is the largest export market, accounting for more than 60% of Bangladesh's exports.[8] Bangladesh's 90% exports to these markets are apparel items that have a zero-import duty under the EU's Everything But Arms (EBA) preferential scheme for LDCs while the comparable EU average most favored nation (MFN) tariff rate is around 12%. Canada, which is another important market, offers duty-free imports of textile and clothing items originating in LDCs, but non-LDC suppliers are subject to import tariffs of as high as 18%. Japan's average MFN import duty on apparel products is close to 9% while most LDC products are exempt from tariffs. In Australia, the LDC duty-free access is granted against an average 5% import duty regime. In recent times, China and India have become emerging apparel markets for Bangladesh. After LDC graduation, the average tariffs facing in the Chinese market would rise from zero to above 16%. In India, the duty-free LDC market access for most items will be replaced by the SAFTA non-LDC tariff regime which would see average tariffs rising to more than 8% while many items falling under the sensitive list with no preferential market access given. In some cases, it is possible to retain some preferences after LDC graduation. However, GSP donor countries provide relaxed and least stringent rules of origin (RoO) requirements for the products from LDCs. Even under FTAs, RoO provisions are more stringent for non-LDC countries.

Graduation from LDC status also seriously constrains a country's policy space to support its export and domestic sectors. Among others, providing direct export subsidies, as Bangladesh currently does, may not be possible given the provisions of the WTO. Similarly, like other countries, graduated LDCs are also expected to enforce stronger intellectual property protection that can also affect some of the currently available policy flexibilities. For instance, LDCs have been granted a transition period until 1 January 2033 to comply with WTO provisions of the Agreement on Trade-Related Intellectual Property Rights (TRIPS) concerning pharmaceutical products. However, as Bangladesh's graduation is expected to take place in 2026, the transition period would come to an end almost a decade earlier. There are many such areas where LDCs have been given the so-called special and different treatment (S&DT) to help them foster economic development. WTO members are also generally reluctant about raising concerns or lodging official complaints about individual LDCs' actions and/or policy regimes that would otherwise be deemed inconsistent or non-compliant with international trade rules and regulations. Graduation from the group of LDCs would however almost certainly trigger closer scrutiny to ensure conformity.

---

[8] The UK's share in Bangladesh's exports is about 10%. After Brexit, the UK is still matching a similar level of market access treatment for LDCs.

It is in the above backdrop that graduation from LDC status marks a major transition with important implications for external competitiveness. While an overwhelming majority of the LDCs do not have the required supply-side capacities to exploit various trade preferences, Bangladesh has been an exception making use of many of the available LDC privileges. However, this also means, among all graduating LDCs, any potential adverse implications arising from graduation could be more conspicuous for Bangladesh. Indeed, in a recent assessment by the WTO, it has been found that "LDC graduation will have the greatest impact on the exports of Bangladesh, which is estimated to see exports decline by 14%" (WTO 2020, p. 20).[9]

Therefore, building competitive supply-side capacities and exploring new trading and investment opportunities through bilateral and regional trade negotiations are the critical pathways for a smooth LDC graduation. It is widely recognized that LDC graduation is not any winning post, rather it is "the first milestone in the marathon of development" (UNCTAD 2016). The emerging geo-economics could make that process even more challenging.

2.1.1 Exploring Opportunities in Geo-Economics Minefields

Trade preferences, i.e., tariff advantages over competitors, add directly to recipient countries' competitive advantage. That is why countries negotiate bilateral and regional trade deals. When initial MFN tariffs are high, trade preferences can be exceedingly attractive for partner countries. In general, MFN tariffs in developed countries are low: around 3%. However, there are certain sensitive sectors, e.g., textile and footwear, where average tariff rates have been historically much higher than the average rate. As Bangladesh exports predominantly clothing items along with a small but growing shipment of footwear where MFN tariffs are also high, any forgone preferences would constitute a disproportionately large pressure on competitiveness. Gaining back the likely lost competitiveness through trade negotiations is not going to be easy partly because such negotiations could be lengthy and would require well-developed technical and negotiating capacities that most graduating LDCs like Bangladesh lacks. In certain instances, promoting development through trade and investment will be compromised due to unfolding geoeconomic and geopolitical issues while in other cases there can also be opportunities.

Among others, Bangladesh intends to pursue, through WTO processes, the possibility of continuing with LDC benefits and privileges even after graduation. The WTO-led trade multilateralism is, however, under intense pressure. One geoeconomic instrument being considered by the United States aims at reforming the system in a manner that would deal with China but could also include other relatively

---

[9] The same study finds that other graduating LDCs with expected sizeable reductions in exports (more than 1%) are Bhutan, Lao PDR, Myanmar, Nepal, and the Solomon Islands. The effects for Angola, Kiribati, Sao Tomé, and Principe, Timor Leste, Tuvalu, and Vanuatu (0.3% or less) are negligible. Apart from the WTO study, there are many other studies including those form UNCTAD and UN DESA that have found adverse consequences for Bangladesh. For a detailed review of LDC graduation issues, see Razzaque (2020c).

advanced developing countries that have become competitive and exerted tremendous supply response but are confronted with labor, environmental, and intellectual property rights related challenges. Under this circumstance, it would be difficult for WTO members to agree on further trade concessions for graduating LDCs. When one principal objective of the United States, supported by other developed countries, is to reform the WTO, it is difficult to perceive that WTO members could agree on the creation of a new group of countries—graduating LDCs—and provide them with preferences going beyond the current provisions.

Furthermore, in the absence of a strong multilateral trading system, countries could use trade policy options arbitrarily. The unilateral duty-free market access offers (to LDCs, for instance) are not bound by multilateral commitments and any preference donor countries can withdraw their schemes at any time. However, a vibrant MTS means developed countries and relatively advanced developing countries are under peer pressure to be predictable and consistent with their unilateral GSP schemes. While one could point out many limitations of the MTS, discussions did indeed take place in various WTO forums that resulted in far-reaching favorable outcomes, especially for LDCs. The Hong Kong Ministerial Conference in 2005, among others, urged "developing Countries in a position to do so" to offer duty-free and quota-free market access to LDCs. That was no binding commitment, but it resulted in, among others, China's and India's introducing their respective preferential market access packages for LDCs. The United States, however, opted not to "generalize" their preferential schemes as it discriminated between Asian LDCs and others, and sought a waiver from the WTO to legitimize its African Growth and Opportunities Act (AGOA) preferences for sub-Saharan African nations. In the absence of a strong rules-based WTO system, such arbitrary policy mechanisms will proliferate potentially exerting unfair competitiveness pressure on many developing countries including Bangladesh.

A weakened MTS would inevitably trigger a new bout of heightened protectionism. The stark realization that production networks being excessively concentrated in China has encouraged many countries to proactively look for protective policy stances. Furthermore, even before the pandemic hitting the Western economies, policy strategies like "Made in China 2025", "Make in India", and "America first" was being aggressively pursued by China, India, and the United States, respectively.[10] Even after President Trump, it is still not clear if there will be any major change in the U.S. stance as President-elect Joe Biden during the 2020 presidential campaign emphasized on ensuring "the future is made in all of America by all of America's workers" in which he is reported to have believed that "American workers can out-compete anyone, but their government needs to fight for

---

[10] Under Made in China 2025, China aims to upgrade its manufacturing capabilities and has set the target of increasing the domestic content in final output to 70% by 2025. Under Make in India, the government of India provides incentives for certain types of manufacturing production and aims to raise the manufacturing-GDP ratio to 25% by 2025. "America first"—a policy and slogan used by President Donald Trump—has a history of being used as a foreign policy stance emphasizing isolationism during the interwar period of 1918–1939. Under President Trump, it indicated a strong inward-looking trade policy stance.

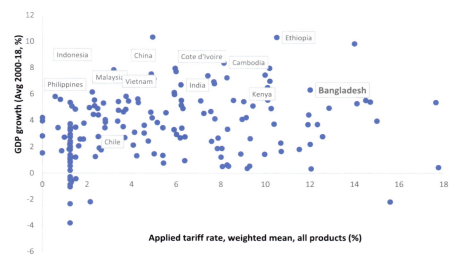

Fig. 2 Bangladesh achieved high growth despite maintaining much higher level of tariff protection

them."[11] Therefore, if the major economies are being more protectionist, exploring new trading opportunities for countries like Bangladesh would be quite challenging. It is also worth pointing out that Bangladesh's impressive growth has been accompanied by a much higher level of tariff protection than all other successful globalists including China, India, Indonesia, Malaysia, the Philippines, and Vietnam (Fig. 2). Therefore, Bangladesh is also in a paradoxical situation asking for openness in other countries while maintaining a high level of tariff protection in its domestic economy.

Compared to the United States and China, the EU is perceived to be less proactive in making use of geo-economics. Nevertheless, its trade preferences have featured various elements of geo-economics. EU GSP schemes are conditional upon fulfilling certain conditions. For example, graduating LDCs can apply for the "second-best"— after the most liberal, Everything But Arms (EBA scheme) for LDCs—preferential regime, known as the GSP Special Incentive Arrangement for Sustainable Development and Good Governance (GSP+), which grants duty-free access to 66% of EU tariff lines including textile and clothing items. However, EU GSP rules will change from the beginning of 2024 and the continued tariff-free market access for Bangladesh's apparel products after LDC graduation is not certain.[12] The complex provisions for accessing EU preferences do indicate its scope of using geoeconomic tools and given the current trends in the global economic landscape, it is likely to more frequently employ these while pursuing its interests through negotiated bilateral trade deals.

---

[11] This is taken from https://joebiden.com/made-in-america/. Accessed on 5 November 2020.

[12] Details of EU GSP provisions and Bangladesh's eligibility can be found in Razzaque et al. (2020a).

When unilateral trade preferences are not available, negotiating an FTA with the EU could be an option for securing duty-free market access. However, the choice of FTA partners can be motivated by geo-economics gains. For example, the EU was keen on having an FTA with Vietnam, which has become a part of the global production network based in East Asia. According to the signed FTA deal, EU tariffs on almost all Vietnamese products will gradually be eliminated by 2027. On the other hand, if Bangladesh is officially graduating from the group of LDCs in 2026, all EU LDC preferences for Bangladesh will cease to exist in 2029. Needless to mention that this will provide Vietnam with a huge competitive advantage over Bangladesh. On the other hand, even if Bangladesh would want to strike an FTA with the EU, the latter might not find it worthwhile.

The rise of geo-economics can be a double-edged sword. There can be opportunities as well. For example, if the share of China in global trade is affected due to geoeconomic tools being deployed by others, many developing countries are likely to benefit. When COVID19 induced policy measures were imposed targeting China, most diverted investments were reported to have shifted to Vietnam and Indonesia. Bangladesh was marginally benefited in terms of some increased export orders when in 2018 U.S. tariffs were imposed on China. However, as tariff wars got escalated disrupting global supply chains and investor confidence, global trade fell in 2019–20 even before the pandemic hit the Western developed economies. Indeed, in the eight months (July 2019–February 2020) preceding the onset of COVID19, Bangladesh experienced negative growth of exports for six months due to the U.S.–China trade war. It is also important to bear in mind that the same policies that undermine Chinese competitiveness could also be used against any other country. Another outcome of geo-economics-led policy mechanisms is that rival powers could compete between themselves to offer trade concessions, investment, and financial assistance to third countries to gain influence. Making use of such opportunities, however, could be a delicate task to avoid being a victim of geopolitical rivalry.

2.1.2 Bangladesh and Geo-Economics Powerplay in the Region

While Asia has been experiencing heightened geopolitical tensions on many fronts, the battle for Asia hegemony has strained the China-India relationship with profound implications for a country like Bangladesh, which aims to benefit from the growth dynamics of the two regional economic powers and enhanced regional cooperation from South to East Asia. Bangladesh's geographical location near two of the world's largest economies—China and India—provides enormous opportunities for boosting exports, attracting foreign investment, and achieving economic diversification. As an LDC, Bangladesh enjoys duty-free market access in most products in both countries but export growth to these markets has been much less than potential. Bangladesh's merchandise exports to India grew gradually over the past two decades from $80 million in FY01 to $1.25 billion in FY19. On the other hand, exports to China expanded from about $100 million in FY09 to reach a peak of $950 million in 2016–17 before falling to less than $700 million in FY19. In contrast to modest exports,

China and India are the two most important sources of Bangladesh's imports. In FY19, China accounted for more than 22% of Bangladesh's merchandise imports while India was the source of about 14% of such imports.[13] Therefore, Bangladesh holds large trade deficits with both China and India. Geographical proximity and other factors that determine bilateral trade flows seem to suggest large untapped export potential. It has been estimated that given the global experience of how countries trade with their partners, Bangladesh's current exports to India are at least $6 billion less than the potential, while the corresponding figure is $2 billion for exports to China.[14]

Geo-economics powerplay can come as both bane and boon for other countries. Over the past few decades, China, flaunted by its ambitious BRI project, has become the world's largest foreign investor in developing countries. Bangladesh needs investment in infrastructure and industries to stimulate export response and create jobs and thus the Chinese investment projects are of great interest especially now as LDC graduation is approaching. Cumulative Chinese investments pledged (through SOEs, foreign direct investment, and concessional loans) for Bangladesh during 2009–2019 was about $27.5 billion although only a small proportion (7.3%) of it has been materialized (Razzaque et al. 2020b). Nevertheless, Chinese investors provided more than $506 million as FDI in FY18 following President Xi Jinping's visit to Bangladesh and then $1.16 billion in FY19, making them the largest source of net FDI inflows into Bangladesh for the very first time. Very recently, China has also granted Bangladesh extended duty-free market access covering more than 97% of tariff lines.

The Chinese trade and investment initiatives have been causing unease in India— a country that considers itself as Bangladesh's natural, historic, and strategic ally. Over the past decade, the state-level relationship between Bangladesh and India has achieved a new height. India as part of its trade preference to LDCs also provides duty-free market access to Bangladesh. Along with resolving many disputes over land boundaries, both countries are also working on improving connectivity through various transit and transshipment facilities. While Bangladesh has allocated three special economic zones (SEZs) exclusively to Indian companies, India also offered three different credit lines worth around $7.5 billion together for development projects in Bangladesh (Byron and Adhikary 2019). Like the Chinese pledged investments, utilizing the Indian credit line has also been problematic due to various administrative, bureaucratic, and capacity-related issues. Overall, Bangladesh welcomes investment opportunities and support from all leading world economies, but many analysts perceive China's initiatives as geoeconomic tools to enhance geopolitical influence in the region. On the other hand, others are of the view that Bangladesh has not yet been proactively seeking Chinese investments due to the apprehension of political and economic backlash from India.

China and India have deployed "vaccine diplomacy", promising COVID19 vaccines for developing countries and Bangladesh. However, in the case of the

---

[13] Imports from China were valued at $22 billion, while those from India were worth of $7.6 billion.

[14] A detailed analysis of Bangladesh's export prospects to India and China can be found in Kabir et al. (2020) and Razzaque et al. (2020b).

Rohingya repatriation issue, passive stances by both India and China, despite having expressed concerns for the matter, have not been perceived as satisfactory by Bangladesh. China and India have self-interests that define their stances. China is Myanmar's second-largest investor and biggest trading partner, and Myanmar is one of China's oldest allies in the neighborhood. The geostrategic location of Myanmar is of great importance to China and India due to the access to the Indian Ocean and because of Myanmar's bridging between South and Southeast Asia. For India, Myanmar is also important due to the prevalence of insurgency issues in northeast India. Chinese investments in Myanmar are concentrated in the key natural resource sectors of hydropower, oil, gas, and mining. India has been trying to counter China's clout in Myanmar through the Government India's flagship policy "Act East"—that aims to strengthen India's relations with the Asia-Pacific region—by constructing a strategic port, taking initiatives to complete India-Myanmar-Thailand trilateral highways, and offering support for enhancing the petroleum sector of Myanmar. India also has enhanced defence cooperation with Myanmar.[15]

India has serious concerns about Chinese involvement in other Asian countries. Historically, China maintained close defense and security relations with Pakistan, and over the past decades, the two countries have deepened their economic ties. The China Pakistan Economic Corridor (CPEC) comprises various large scale infrastructure projects worth more than $62 billion which will connect China's largest province with a port in Pakistan that leads to the Arabian Sea, passing through a region that has been subject to disputes between India and Pakistan for many decades (Hussain 2017). Sri Lanka has also seen massive investment projects funded by China. Cumulative Chinese infrastructure investments in Sri Lanka since 2006 amount to more than $12 billion (Wignaraja et al. 2020).[16] Security analysts have perceived the Chinese activities in the island country to be both economic and security challenges for India. Furthermore, China and India have been dueling with geoeconomic tools in the Maldives, and there have been reports suggesting that it could scrap its FTA with China, signed in 2017, to enhance its ties with India (Chaudhury 2020). Finally, for centuries, Nepal has shared deep and historic cultural, economic, social, and political relations with India. However, ties between the two countries started to deteriorate due to various unresolved bilateral issues including border disputes. At the same time, growing engagements between China and the Himalayan country have disquieted India. Chinese investments increased substantially, comprising more than 90% of all FDI inflows into Nepal in recent times. Kathmandu is reported to have undertaken an initiative to curtail its dependence on Indian ports, where two-thirds of goods are being transported to and from the country, by signing a transit protocol with Beijing in

---

[15] Some diplomatic analysts are of the view that India's recent initiatives in Myanmar to counter China is due to it not having enough political influence in the country, which is not the case of Bangladesh where India has a very strong political foothold.

[16] It is often suggested that Sri Lanka has fallen into the Chinese "debt trap" following an incident of a constructed port being handed over to a Chinese company. Sri Lanka built the port of Hambantota, which turned out to be unprofitable and later was handed over to a Chinese company under a debt-equity swap deal (Moramudali 2020).

2019 which gives them access to several Chinese sea and land ports (Mukhopadhyay 2020).

The heightened tensions between China and India seem to be affecting regional cooperation. For instance, the Bangladesh-China-India-Myanmar (BCIM) economic corridor is now far from reality largely due to the regional geopolitics of China and India. China considered BCIM activities as part of the BRI while India argued that the regional cooperation idea of BCIM predated the BRI. Eventually, the Chinese government decided to remove BCIM activities from the BRI.

3 Policy Implications and Concluding Remarks

World trade and globalization are now passing through turbulent times. Since the global financial crisis of 2008, there has been a sustained deceleration in international trade and investment flows marked by globalization backlash, trade war, and heightened policy attempts to undo cross-border interlinked supply chains built over several decades. Along with causing devastating health and economic consequences, the COVID19 pandemic has prompted the widespread use of geoeconomic instruments by global and regional powers, putting the existing global trade and investment architectures under pressure. As Bangladesh is graduating out of the group of LDCs and aiming for consolidating its economic success while exploring new trading opportunities, the unsettling global trade environment is of particular concern. Based on the discussions above, some broad policy implications for Bangladesh are provided below.

First and foremost, given the unfolding landscape of geo-economics, Bangladesh will have to be proactive at multilateral, regional, and bilateral levels to maximize its development gains. At the multilateral level, the focus should be on monitoring the developments in international trade and global economic orders. A rules-based multilateral trading system with a transparent dispute settlement procedure should be the most preferred option for ensuring a stable global trading environment. Therefore, it should be a priority for Bangladesh to work with other countries to find out the means for strengthening the existing system, if needed, by bringing in some major reforms.

Bangladesh must also collaborate with other developing and advanced countries to help build a coalition in major areas where international consensus can be reached on the emerging issues affecting their trade and development interests. In this context that a broad and effective coalition of LDCs, graduating LDCs, sub-Saharan Africa, and small and vulnerable economies can be important in championing the role of development trade. Developing countries without geopolitical ambitions should press hard to secure a productive role of trade in international development. This group of countries should demand that meaningful dialogues and interactions among the world's largest economies (e.g., the G20) continue with the objective of finding solutions to trade conflicts, curb protectionism, and protect and promote the interests of capacity-constrained developing countries.

At the regional level, Bangladesh must re-emphasize its objective of ensuring regional prosperity through enhanced trade and improved connectivity so that all countries can benefit. The emergence of both China and India as the world's major economic powerhouses is a great opportunity from which Bangladesh and all other countries in the region can benefit profoundly. Trade and investment linkages with China and India offer new opportunities for specialization, efficiency gains, increased export earnings, and export market diversification. China and India have also become important sources of technical and financial assistance. Therefore, productive relations with both countries are critical. It is likely that because of the strategic rivalry both China and India will try to bring Bangladesh into their orbit, and it will only be prudent not to show any preference between the two giants (Anwar 2019).

Bangladesh must work closely with South Asian and South-East Asian countries to strengthen regional and intra-regional cooperation and to make sure that rivalry between China and India does not undermine the growth and development potential of the region. Bangladesh should press ahead with improved connectivity and enhanced trade and investment linkages that can help minimize geopolitical tensions.

Bangladesh should have an open mind about attracting foreign investment considering the merits of individual projects. While the current investment policy regime in the country is already quite attractive, certain policy reforms and creating a more enabling environment can make Bangladesh a lucrative investment destination. However, it is also important to carefully evaluate the returns from potential investment projects, considering likely export gains, prospects for employment generation, and environmental impact.

While pursuing foreign investment and concessional loans from emerging economic powers such as China and India, Bangladesh should be cautious about the rising external debt prospect to an unsustainable level. Emerging donors often overlook the risk of debt unsustainability. Several countries, including Pakistan and Sri Lanka, from the South Asian region, have faced difficulties in servicing debts incurred by Chinese-funded infrastructure projects. China and India offer attractive loan schemes/credit lines with conditions of procuring equipment and materials and technical assistance from their respective countries. This "tied aid" could be more expensive than it appears.

The heightened competition for regional hegemony between India and China can offer opportunities that can be materialized through judicious diplomatic engagements. Bangladesh until now has not been able to use the vast Indian and Chinese markets to expand exports. Currently, both countries provide attractive duty-free market access to Bangladesh as an LDC and it will be beneficial to maintain the existing market access after LDC graduation. Therefore, Bangladesh should pursue an extended LDC transition period from China and India. The EU, for example, allows an additional three-year period for graduating countries to continue with LDC-specific preferences. There is also a precedence of China's providing a similar transitional arrangement for Samoa, which graduated in 2014. On the other hand,

India allowed the Maldives to continue to enjoy LDC benefits after the latter's graduation in 2011. Bangladesh can ask for similar concessions from India.[17] It is possible that securing concessions from one of the regional powers could generate a matching offer from the other.

As Asia is going to dominate the world's economic activities, increased integration within the continent can bring economic opportunities and help benefit from spillover effects. Bangladesh should engage with China and ASEAN countries to become a member of the RCEP. This could be a game-changer given the presence of all major Asian economies (except India) that attach importance to trade openness and mutually reinforce the credibility of a trading bloc, facilitating cross-border investment flows within the region. Being part of a strong trading bloc can also act as a shield against being subject to indiscriminate geoeconomic tools deployed by any regional powers. However, negotiating membership in such a large trading bloc would not be an easy task for Bangladesh. Despite using the existing ASEAN (Association of the South-East Asian Nations) trade agreement as to the premise for RCEP, it took members eight years to reach a deal. Aligning with RCEP trade, investment, and other regulatory environments could also be quite challenging for Bangladesh.[18] RCEP members have kept the option open for India to join the bloc and this could also lead to an opportunity for Bangladesh to seek membership. Bangladesh should also be regarded by many other countries as a potentially attractive FTA partner. This is because Bangladesh has managed to expand fast by maintaining robust economic growth under rather a highly protected trade policy regime. A growing market shielded by high tariffs provides preferential partners with a large competitive advantage (over others who do not have such preferential access).

Along with pursuing RCEP membership, Bangladesh should also work with other partners to promote SAFTA and transform BIMSTEC into a full-fledged FTA. Geopolitical issues between India and Pakistan have been a major setback for promoting SAFTA further. However, high-level political engagements should continue if South Asian nations would want to take advantage of gains from expanded regional trade and economic cooperation in fostering growth and development. Bangladesh can work with such SAFTA members as Afghanistan, Bhutan, the Maldives, Nepal, and Sri Lanka to promote regional cooperation and connectivity, which should promote intra-regional trade and investment. As regards BIMSTEC, the prospect of trade opening and enhanced technical cooperation to a large extent

---

[17] Article 12 of SAFTA states, "Notwithstanding the potential or actual graduation of the Maldives from the status of a least developed country, it shall be accorded in this Agreement and in any subsequent contractual undertakings thereof treatment no less favourable than that provided for the least developed contracting states".

[18] There has been a suggestion that Bangladesh should have tried becoming part of the RCEP bloc. However, when negotiations began in 2012, it was not clear that Bangladesh would be graduating from the group of LDCs so soon. As an LDC, it was most prudent to secure duty-free market access under various GSP schemes of major economies without reciprocating any tariff cuts. In fact, all major RCEP economies, including Australia, China, Japan, Republic of Korea, and New Zealand provide duty-free market access to Bangladesh. Only after Bangladesh's LDC graduation has become so imminent, especially after meeting the qualification criteria for the first time in 2018, does the possibility of joining RCEP appear to be a missed opportunity.

depends on India. Whether this bloc can exert enough geo-economics leverage is a major consideration for India in this regard. Two BIMSTEC members Myanmar and Thailand have also become part of the RCEP deal. However, this should not derail the overall objective of transforming the existing scheme into an FTA as envisaged in the BIMSTEC Free Trade Area Framework Agreement. For Bangladesh, a major objective will be to expand the horizon of regional cooperation, which can cushion against unnecessary geopolitical and geo-economics rivalries in the region.

Given the rise of geo-economics and escalated geopolitical tensions, trade and development prospects facing Bangladesh in the immediate aftermath of its LDC graduation can be greatly insulated by securing a favorable post-LDC trading arrangement from the EU. Therefore, the single most priority should be to explore opportunities for an EU GSP regime that will be as close as the EBA. Although under the existing rules Bangladesh does not qualify for GSP+, the current GSP regime will be replaced by a new one in 2023. Therefore, proactive engagements with the European Commission and other stakeholders should be undertaken to influence any future changes in the EU GSP regime. Striking a free trade agreement—in the absence of a favorable GSP scheme—could be an option if the EU would be interested.

Along with China–India rivalry, Bangladesh will also have to manage a productive bilateral relationship with the United States, which—being the single most important export market, one of the largest sources of foreign direct investment, and a major provider of overseas development assistance—has been an indispensable trade and development partner for Bangladesh. As the United States does not provide any duty-free market access, LDC graduation as such will not bring any changes in the trade policy regime affecting Bangladesh's exports. While the United States—among others, through the legally non-binding Trade and Investment Cooperation Forum Agreement (TICFA)—has put pressure on improving intellectual property rights and other trade-plus issues such as labor standards, environment, and governance, this forum can be used for a promoting more proactive trade and economic cooperation schemes. As the U.S. stance on the global trade and investment regime and regional trade deals is still evolving and it is not clear how it would push for any likely bilateral cooperation. However, Bangladesh should be ready to consider participation in any possible FTA and/or regional trading bloc initiative like the TPP if the United States aims to pursue it.[19]

Finally, there is no denying that the emerging trade and development landscape is going to be associated with a great deal of uncertainty, which Bangladesh needs to take into consideration in preparing for LDC graduation and achieving other development objectives. Notwithstanding the challenges of the external environment, so much can be achieved on the domestic front to enhance the economy's overall competitiveness and to sustain export growth in the future. Tackling the much talked about the high cost of doing business in the country, dealing with weak and inadequate infrastructure facilities in conjunction with inefficient inland road transport

---

[19] It has been estimated that preferential market access, e.g., through an FTA, could increase Bangladesh's exports by more than $1.3 billion, i.e., almost 22% of Bangladesh's current exports to the United States.

and trade logistics, addressing intricate customs processes, making further improvements in investment climate-related indicators, strengthening institutions, among others, are critical factors promoting competitiveness. In the era of geo-economics and heightened geopolitical tensions, it is also important to build diplomatic and trade negotiation capacities so that country interests can be pursued without being a victim of geopolitical competition of rival economic powers.

Acknowledgements This chapter is a shorter and revised version of a paper that was originally prepared for the Friedrich-Ebert-Stiftung (FES) Bangladesh. Helpful comments and suggestions on an earlier draft were received from Tina Blohm and Shadhan Kumar Das. Research assistance was provided by Mahir Musleh. Any views expressed here are those of the author and do not necessarily reflect the official policy or position of the Friedrich-Ebert-Stiftung (FES) Bangladesh.

References

Anwar, A. 2019. How Bangladesh is Benefiting from the China-India Rivalry. *The Diplomat*, July 12, 2019.

Asadullah, M.N., A. Savoia, and W. Mahmud. 2014. Paths to Development: Is there a Bangladesh Surprise? *World Development* 62: 138–154.

Beeson, M. 2018. Geo-economics isn't back—It never went away. The Interpreter, 22 August 2018, The Lowy Institute.

Blackwill, R.D., and J.M. Harris. 2016. *War by Other Means: Geo-economics and Statecraft*. Cambridge, Massachusetts: Harvard University Press.

Byron, R.K., and Adhikary, T.S. 2019. First Indian Line of Credit: 8yrs gone, only 51pc utilized. The Daily Star, 21 February 2019.

Chaudhury, D.R. 2020. Maldives considers scrapping Free Trade Agreement (FTA) with China. The Economic Times, 12 October 2020.

Ferguson, N., and Xu, X. 2018. Making Chimerica great again. International Finance, vol. 21, Issue 3, accessed via Wiley Online Library. https://doi.org/10.1111/infi.12335.

Hussain, S. 2017. China's CPEC investment in Pakistan reaches $62 billion. Mint, 12 April 2017.

Kabir, M., and Razzaque, M.A. 2020. Promoting Bangladesh's Exports to India. Chapter 6 in Razzaque, M.A. 2020. *Navigating New Waters: Unleashing Bangladesh's Export Potential for Smooth LDC Graduation*, Bangladesh Enterprise Institute, Dhaka.

Luttwak, E. 1990. From Geopolitics to Geo-economics: Logic of Conflict, Grammar of Commerce. *National Interest* 20 (1990): 17–23.

Mahmud, W. 2008. Social Development in Bangladesh: Pathways, Surprises and Challenges. *Indian Journal of Human Development* 2 (1).

Moramudali, U. 2020. The Hambantota Port Deal: Myths and Realities. *The Diplomat*, 1 January 2020.

Mukhopadhyay, A. 2020. Nepal's delicate balancing act between China and India. DW, March 09 2020. https://www.dw.com/en/nepals-delicate-balancing-act-between-china-and-india/a-526 93835.

Razzaque, M.A. 2018. The Tipping Point: Bangladesh's Graduation from the Group of Least Developed Countries. *Harvard International Review, Summer* 2018: 34–38.

Razzaque, M.A., Akib, H., and Rahman, J. 2020a. Bangladesh's Graduation from LDCs: Potential Implications and Issues for the Private Sector. Chapter 2 in Razzaque, M.A. 2020. *Navigating New Waters: Unleashing Bangladesh's Export Potential for Smooth LDC Graduation*, Bangladesh Enterprise Institute, Dhaka.

Razzaque, M.A., Rahman, J., Akib, H. 2020b. Bangladesh-China Trade and Economic Cooperation: Issues and Perspectives. Chapter 7 in Razzaque, M.A. 2020. *Navigating New Waters: Unleashing Bangladesh's Export Potential for Smooth LDC Graduation*, Bangladesh Enterprise Institute, Dhaka.

Razzaque, M.A., Abbasi, P., and Rahman, J. 2020c. Partnering Up: Towards a Strengthened Bangladesh-U.S. Trade Relationship. Chapter 5 in Razzaque, M.A. 2020. *Navigating New Waters: Unleashing Bangladesh's Export Potential for Smooth LDC Graduation*, Bangladesh Enterprise Institute, Dhaka.

UNCTAD. (2016). The Least Developed Countries Report,. 2016. *The path to graduation and beyond: Making the most of the process*. Geneva: UNCTAD.

Varadarajan, R. Varas, A., Gilbert, M., McAdoo, M., Ruan, F., and Wang, G. 2020. What's at Stake If the US and China Really Decouple. Boston Consulting Group, October 20, 2020. https://www.bcg.com/publications/2020/high-stakes-of-decoupling-us-and-china.

Weber, I. 2020. Could the US and Chinese economies really 'decouple'? The Guardian, 20 September 2020. https://www.theguardian.com/commentisfree/2020/sep/11/us-china-global-economy-donald-trump.

Wignaraja, G., Panditaratne, D., Kannangara, P., and Hundlani, D. 2020. *Chinese Investment and the BRI in Sri Lanka*, Research Paper, London: Royal Institute of International Affairs. https://www.chathamhouse.org/sites/default/files/CHHJ8010-Sri-Lanka-RP-WEB-200324.pdf.

World Trade Organization. 2019. World Trade Statistical Review 2019, World Trade Organization, Geneva, Switzerland.

World Trade Organization. 2020. *Trade Impacts of LDC Graduation*, WTO, Geneva, Switzerland.

Chapter 7
Managing Globalization to National Advantage: The Case of Ireland

Louis Brennan

1 Background

Ireland gained its independence from Britain in the early 1920s to become an independent state. From the 1930s onwards, it embraced protectionism which delivered little in terms of development in the succeeding decades with high levels of emigration persisting right up to the 1990s. The Industrial Development Authority (today's IDA Ireland) was established in 1949 to attract foreign direct investment (FDI). IDA Ireland is today considered to be best in class among national Investment Promotion Agencies and has played, since its foundation, a key role in Ireland's development with its success in attracting foreign direct investment particularly in recent decades (O'Donovan and Rios-Morales 2006).

Initial steps toward opening up started to take place in the 1950s and this was followed by the signing of the Anglo–Irish free trade agreement in 1965 and Ireland's entry into the then European Economic Community (EEC) in 1973. An important education initiative was introduced in the second half of the 1960s with free second-level education being granted to all. This had the effect of increasing dramatically participation rates in second-level education. A further initiative related to education was initiated in the early 1970s with the establishment of third-level Regional Technical Colleges (later called Institutes of Technology and now in transition to Technological Universities) around the country.

Notwithstanding some economic progress during the 1960s, the 1970s, and 1980s proved to be harsh decades for Ireland with a series of deep recessions accompanied by high levels of unemployment, emigration, and national debt. Conventional wisdom concerning Ireland was stark as reflected in the following extract from the Economist in 1988:

L. Brennan (✉)
Trinity Business School, Trinity College, Dublin, Ireland
e-mail: brennaml@tcd.ie

© The Author(s), under exclusive license to Springer Nature Singapore Pte Ltd. 2022 127
A. Palit (ed.), *Globalisation Impacts*, International Law and the Global South,
https://doi.org/10.1007/978-981-16-7185-2_7

128 L. Brennan

Take a tiny open ex-peasant economy. Place it next door to a much larger one, from which it broke away with great bitterness barely a lifetime ago. Infuse it with a passionate desire to enjoy the same lifestyle and as its former masters, but without the same industrial heritage or natural resources. The inevitable result: extravagance, frustration, debt. Ireland is easily the poorest country in rich northwest Europe. Its gross domestic product is a mere 64% of the European Community average (Economist 1988).

The late 1980s saw a series of measures that included the resolute addressing of government debt and the institution of an inclusive partnership approach to the management of the economy. These measures were key to laying the foundation for the emergence in the 1990s and into the 2000s a period of very rapid economic growth that became known as the Celtic Tiger era. By 1997, the Economist noted that:

Just yesterday, it seems, Ireland was one of Europe's poorest countries. Today, it is about as prosperous as the European average, and getting richer all the time (Economist 1997).

Along with the measures mentioned above, a confluence of factors combined to create the circumstances that gave rise to the Celtic Tiger era. Those factors included a buoyant global economy, a demographic dividend, and an educated workforce as a consequence of the education initiatives that took place in earlier decades, significant fiscal transfers in the form of structural and cohesion funds from the European Union, the establishment of the Single European Market and the astute deployment of arbitrage on the part of the Irish government to take advantage of the then increasingly globalizing world. At the same time, Ireland signed up to the Maastricht treaty signaling its intention to participate in the European Monetary Union (EMU). By the end of the 1990s, Irish interest rates had harmonized with low German rates and Ireland was a member of the Eurozone.

2 Ireland's Economic Transformation

The transformation of the Irish economy during the 1990s was dramatic. It grew over the 1990s at over three times the European average and twice the U.S. average. The economy grew at an annual average rate of 9.4% from 1996 to 2000 (CSO 2016). By 1998, GDP per capita was 106.2 relative to an EU average of 100 compared to 64.2 in 1973 when Ireland first joined the then EEC. By 2003, it was 120% (CSO 2004).

While in 1987, central government debt was 107% of GDP,[1] over 50% of which was held externally, debt as a percentage of GDP was reduced to 36% by the early 2000s and below 24% by 2007.[2]

Employment grew from 1.183 million in 1993 to 1.671 million by the beginning of 2000 (CSO 2008) while the seasonally adjusted unemployment rate had fallen from double-digit figures to below 4% by late 2000.[3]

---

[1] OECD Database.

[2] CSO Database.

[3] Ibid.

7 Managing Globalization to National Advantage: The Case of Ireland

The country was recording a favorable balance of payments with the diversification of export markets and the peace process in Northern Ireland was taking hold which contributed to confidence across the whole island of Ireland.

Perhaps most noteworthy for a country whose most consistent export since the mid-1800s had been its people in the form of emigration, Ireland started to record by the mid-1990s net migration inflows as the rapidly growing economy served as a magnet for returning emigrants and economic migrants and outward migration declined.

Ireland had been a low-cost manufacturing base within Europe for maturing US enterprises, which were already exporting new products to the growing European market. It became an attractive base of operations with its tax incentives designed to make it an export platform (Buckley and Ruane 2006). From the late 1970s and early 1980s, Ireland's industrial strategy shifted from process and assembly operations to a concentration on newer and more high-tech industries. By the 1990s Ireland had become established as the most attractive base for foreign investment within Europe benefitting inordinately from the large flows of investment into Europe that coincided with the advent of the single European market. Flows of FDI from the US tripled from 1991 to 1993 while Ireland's US FDI stock per capita greatly exceeded those of France, Germany, and the UK. In 1997, Ireland ranked fifth in the world as a destination for US direct investment outflows (OECD 1999).

Such flows were encouraged by favorable tax policies toward foreign investment, a "high tech" focused industrial strategy, and the investment in education that had been in train since the late 1960s. By the end of the 1990s, almost all the largest international firms in information and communication technology (ICT) and pharmaceuticals had a presence in Ireland. The setting up of the International Financial Services Centre in the late 80 s led to Ireland becoming one of the two leading global locations along with Luxembourg for funds management.

Ireland was among a small group of countries where spending per student in primary and second-level education rose by 30% or more between 1995 and 2002 (OECD 2005). Between 2005 and 2010 expenditure per student rose by 33%, an increase above the OECD average of 17% (OECD 2013). Whereas the participation rate in tertiary education among the school-leaving cohort was 11% in 1965, by the middle of the last decade it was estimated that 66.9% of final year second-level students (public and private) in any given academic year transfer to publicly aided third-level institutions before reaching the mature student age of 23 (Department of Education and Skills 2015). Since this estimate does not include those transferring to private third-level institutions, the actual percentage is even higher.

In 2017, Ireland was one of the top three countries in the EU in terms of the percentage of the population aged 30–34 that had completed tertiary education with 55% having done so (Eurostat 2019). This compared to 32% in 2002 and 20% in 1992. In 2019, Ireland ranked joint first with Korea among the OECD countries for 25–34-year-olds with a tertiary degree at 70% of this age group. (OECD 2019). Ireland had the highest proportion of mathematics, science, and technology (STEM) graduates in the EU in 2014 with the proportion of graduates in these disciplines at 24.7 per 1,000 of the population aged 20–29 (CSO 2015).

2.1 Ireland and Globalization

While Ireland is a small island on the periphery of Europe, it is in the words of Ireland's Prime Minister Leo Varadkar "an Island at the center of the world" (Duggan 2017). The Economist noted in 1997 that what is most striking about Ireland's new economy is how tightly it is linked to Europe and the world (Economist 1997). Murphy (2000) has argued that globalization enabled Ireland to move from the periphery to the center of the global economy.

Globalization is enacted via the flows of trade, investment, information, knowledge, finance, and movement of peoples across borders. International integration represents the ongoing outcome of the process of globalization. In the context of globalization flows, Ireland's embrace of globalization is evident along the dimensions of Openness, Participation, Connectedness, and Integration.

2.1.1 Openness

Ireland is one of the most open economies in the world. Its ratio of trade (imports and exports) as a percentage of GDP has been consistently among the highest of all countries in the world. In 2019, the World Bank reported that in terms of trade openness, it ranked seventh among countries in the world with a ratio of trade to GDP of 239% (World Bank Data 2020). McWilliams (2017) has argued that commercially Ireland is more akin to a trading state than a nation-state and that rather than being on anyone's periphery it is at the center of the globalized trading world.

2.1.2 Participation

This refers to the extent that a country is involved in vertically fragmented production, both as a user of foreign inputs for its exports (measured as the value of imported inputs in the overall exports of a country) and as a supplier of intermediate goods or services used in other countries' exports (measured as the%age of exported goods and services used as inputs to produce other countries' exports). Participation can be assessed using the Global Value Chain Participation Index. The higher the foreign value-added embodied in gross exports and the higher the value of inputs exported to third countries and used in their exports, the higher the participation of a given country in global value chains. In 2009, Ireland ranked fifth among OECD countries on this index (Backer and Miroudot 2013). The extent of Ireland's participation in global value chains as a result of FDI is well illustrated by the following quote from a Washington Post article on Ireland in the early 2000s (Irish Times 2001):

> An American worker running Oracle's database software with Windows on a Dell computer with a Pentium IV microprocessor who takes Prozac in the morning and Viagra at night could have received all those products from Ireland

2.1.3 Connectedness

This relates to the degree of a country's participation by flow in goods, services, financial, people and data and communications as measured by flow intensity and share of the world total and is represented by the MGI Connectedness Index (McKinsey Global Institute 2016). In 2014, Ireland was ranked 5th among 139 countries on the MGI Connectedness Index while ranking number one in terms of services and financial flows.

2.1.4 Integration

This can be assessed using the A.T. Kearney/Foreign Policy Globalization Index. This Index tracks and assesses changes in four key components of global integration viz. economic integration, technological connectivity, personal contact, and political engagement. These components incorporate such measures as trade and financial flows, movement of people across borders, international telephone traffic, Internet usage, and participation in international treaties and peacekeeping operations (Foreign Policy 2009). During the 2000s, Ireland ranked among the highest countries in the world on this index including being ranked number one in 2002, 2003, and 2004.

Thus, Ireland is highly globalized as is evident from its strong positioning in terms of openness, participation, connectedness, and integration. Such positioning has not emerged by happenstance but is the result of decisions and policies that lead to it being highly globalized.

In the context of the various flows that represent the enactment of Globalization viz. trade, financial, foreign direct investment, and migration flows, Ireland has purposely encouraged such flows and has tended to implement policies that are supportive of those flows. Thus it has had in place policies to support the internationalization of its indigenous firms and their participation in international markets. As already mentioned, it has for decades implemented policies to make Ireland attractive to FDI. Through the International Financial Services Centre and related policies, it is a major player in global financial flows. In terms of migration, Ireland was one of a small number of EU countries that opened up its labor market to nationals from the new accession countries of Central and Eastern Europe in 2004.

In the context of managing globalization to national advantage, it has and continues to exploit cultural, administrative, geographic, and economic similarities and differences to its advantage. Ireland has been particularly adept at engaging in arbitrage to ensure that it benefits from globalization and its flows. As such, it has been enacting at a national level, the CAGE Distance Framework (Ghemawat 2001). For example, in relation to flows of foreign direct investment, it has leveraged cultural similarities via its ethnic ties to the USA, administrative differences via its tax and regulatory policies, its geographic location in terms of serving as a bridge between Europe and the USA, and economically its high-quality talent pool.

Through such judicious exploitation of similarities and differences and ongoing innovating of its model of internationalization (Rios-Morales and Brennan 2009), Ireland has reaped the benefits of globalization. Again, in the case of FDI flows, it has derived a myriad of benefits. These include:

(i) export-led contribution to economic growth and employment-intensive growth,
(ii) serving as a driver of business-friendly infrastructure, human resource development, regulatory change, and flexibility in the economy,
(iii) acting as a key source of new technology, skills, management, and business know-how, and instilling a global orientation,
(iv) serving as a breeding ground for Irish entrepreneurs,
(v) providing scale and critical mass in new technologies, and
(vi) contributing substantial tax revenues.

Critically Ireland's receptivity to FDI as evidenced by the consistency and continuity of a supportive approach to FDI by successive governments has led to agglomeration economies—powerful forces that produce the clustering of particular types of activity in particular locations viz. the development of deep and liquid labor markets in industry-specific skills, the emergence of specialist producers of the materials and services required by an industry and knowledge spillovers that arise from personal contact between people working in the same industry. Thus clusters have emerged in sectors such as the Internet, ICT, Medical Devices, and Pharmaceuticals which apart from providing demonstration effects also drive centripetal forces that serve to sustain and grow activity in these sectors.

From an economic development perspective, FDI is recognized as having delivered a portfolio of economic benefits to Ireland. The attraction of FDI has been a central part of Ireland's enterprise policy since Ireland first took proactive measures to attract internationally mobile investments in the 1950s. Today, foreign firms contribute substantially to Ireland's exports, jobs, expenditure in the Irish economy and to the exchequer. FDI has also:

I. played a key role in stimulating the development of new enterprise sectors and activities in Ireland;
II. helped to raise the bar in terms of RD&I performance and management capabilities;
III. contributed to balanced regional development.

Ireland continues to attract high-value investment from overseas with principal investment determinants still in place—much improved infrastructure, high skills, and an investment-friendly regulatory environment combined with a forward-looking investment promotion effort. The establishment of Science Foundation Ireland in the early 2000s represented an important initiative. This was directed at ensuring a vibrant research infrastructure in the country driving basic and applied research in the areas of science, technology, engineering, and mathematics with a strategic focus, advancing highly skilled human capital development, and spurring academic-industry collaborations. In 2015, Ireland attracted 4.3 percent of all FDI entering

7 Managing Globalization to National Advantage: The Case of Ireland 133

the EU even though it only accounts for 1.7% of the EU economy (Financial Times 2017).

2.2 From Boom to Bust

The early 2000s saw some potentially destabilizing events for the Irish economy in the form of the downturn in the technology sector and the slowdown in the US economy and Foot and Mouth disease in Britain. These events together with an infrastructure deficit, labor shortages, and a high rate of growth in government spending raised some concerns around continued economic growth. Nonetheless, growth continued until 2007 albeit at reduced rates compared to the 1990s. The average GDP growth rate over the period 2000–2004 was 6.2%—the highest among the OECD countries (CSO 2016). Employment continued to show strong growth with an increase of 5% in 2005 alone and by 2007 stood at over 2.1 million (CSO 2008). Ireland retained one of the lowest unemployment rates in Europe. Population growth continued with a growth of 8.1% in the four years 2002–2006[4] driven in part by sizable inflows of migrants especially from the new EU states of Eastern Europe.

However, these positive outcomes disguised the fact that the nature of growth in the economy had changed from the earlier years of rapid growth in the 1990s. It is possible to classify the era of Ireland's rapid economic growth into two stages:

1. Export-led with Ireland benefiting from its position as a small, open, and competitive economy in a booming global market place until the early part of the 2000s
2. Less reliance on exports and more on domestic growth, housing and consumption from 2001 to 2007

Though economic growth remained strong, national competitiveness weakened with a 32% decline in international price competitiveness between 2000 and 2008. Ireland was the second most expensive place in the EU in 2008—25% above the EU average (National Competitiveness Council 2009). Housing costs more than tripled in the 10 years 1998–2007. While public sector debt declined private sector debt increased substantially.

The real Celtic Tiger Period of the 1990s saw solid growth with the attainment of full employment and high incomes. Beyond the 1990s, easy availability of credit, low-interest rates, property tax incentives, and light-touch regulation generated a bubble. The OECD housing price-to-income ratio (a measure of the affordability of house purchase for the average buyer) which stood at 78.38 in 1998 peaked at 144.13 by 2007.[5] From 1953 to 1996, the average ratio of the price of new houses in Dublin to average industrial earnings was 5.3. In 2006, it was 12.98 and by 2010 it had

---

[4] CSO Database.
[5] OECD Data.

fallen back to 7.88.[6] At the peak of the property boom, 13.4% of the workforce were employed in construction (CSO 2008). The bursting of the property bubble led to a collapse in the property sector and, along with the advent of the global financial crisis, was instrumental in the collapse of the banking sector with government intervention required to rescue the banking sector. Unemployment which had been as low as 3.6% in 2001, jumped to 6.4% in 2008 and finally peaked at close to 15.0%.[7] Government debt which had been at 24% of GDP in 2007 increased to 43% in 2008 and peaked at over 124% of GDP in the first half of 2013.[8] The current government budget balance moved from surplus to a deficit of 7% of GDP in 2008 and continued to grow rapidly (Department of Finance 2017). New house dwellings which were above 93,000 in 2006 were under 52,000 in 2008 and bottomed out in the low thousands in succeeding years contributing to today's acute housing shortage.[9]

The economy went into a deep recession with GDP falling precipitously in 2008 and 2009. GDP continued to fall in 2010 but at a much-reduced rate. By early 2011, GDP was down some 13% from its peak in Q4 2007 while GNP was down some 17% from its peak in Q1 2007.[10]

The collapse in government revenues from property taxes and the costs of its bailing out of the banking sector created a crisis of confidence in the government's finances. The government budget deficit for 2010 was 32% of GDP (Department of Finance 2017). By the fourth quarter of 2010, Government debt as a % of GDP reached 86.1% and continued to rise.[11] This ultimately led to the government being forced to agree on a bail-out package from the international institutions which included bailing out the Irish banks' creditors. In November 2010, Ireland was forced to agree to a financial package from the European Commission, the ECB, and the IMF. The banking system had to be overhauled and government expenditure had to be greatly reduced. However, in 2010, Ireland was still the third richest country in the EU with a GDP per capita 25% above the EU average (Central Statistics Office 2011).

2.3 The Economy Recovers

The Economy adjusted rapidly with major downward cost adjustments that restored cost competitiveness. Ireland's export performance was largely unaffected by the Global Recession and exports continued to grow. Flows of inward FDI continued to be recorded into the Irish economy. At the same time, GDP growth returned in 2011 with more robust GDP growth rates being recorded in more recent years including

---

[6] Author calculations based on CSO data.

[7] CSO Database.

[8] Ibid.

[9] Ibid.

[10] Ibid.

[11] Ibid.

7 Managing Globalization to National Advantage: The Case of Ireland   135

8.3 and 5.1% in 2014 and 2016, respectively, rising again to 8.2% in 2018.[12] Time magazine hailed Ireland's recovery as "the Celtic Comeback" in a front cover article in October 2012 (Time 2012). By the end of 2013, Ireland successfully exited from the bail-out program having met or exceeded all of the program requirements.

Ireland's national debt stood at just over 204 billion euro at the end of 2019, equating to 59% of GDP. At the height of the crisis, Ireland's debt was more than 120% of GDP.[13] The Government ran a budget surplus for 2019 of 0.4% of GDP (Department of Finance 2020). However, the national debt has expanded since the onset of the global pandemic, and the government is forecast to run a budget deficit of 6.1% in 2020.

Employment has been increasing in Ireland since 2012 with 2.372 million people recorded as being in employment in Ireland in January 2020, surpassing the peak of the Celtic Tiger era. The rate of unemployment had seen a year-on-year decline since 2012 until the advent of the COVID19 pandemic. Unemployment which had peaked at close to 15% had fallen to 4.6% by April 2020, although this has subsequently risen again to 17.3% in October 2020 due to pandemic-related layoffs. The rate of youth unemployment had also fallen from 19% in the second quarter of 2016, to 10.7% in November 2019,[14] however, this has also risen substantially after the pandemic's onset.

The collapse of Ireland's economy was in part a function of its openness to the global system and its integration into the European monetary system. The former meant that its banking sector was heavily funded by foreign creditors during its boom period while the latter meant that interest rates determined externally as a result of its membership of the Eurozone were unsuited to Ireland's economy. These two factors were key in driving the expansion of credit in the Irish economy that led to the emergence of the bubble and its subsequent bust.

However, Ireland's globalized economy was also key to Ireland's rapid recovery and its renewed high levels of economic growth. Along with its well-established Economic and Institutional Framework, Quality Education System, Dynamic Information Infrastructure, and Innovation Systems, the capacity of Ireland's economy to recover was aided by its deep integration into the global economy that saw robust inward investment, strong exports performance and surging tourism underpin the recovery.

2.4 Ireland and Migration

As noted earlier, Ireland had long been an emigrant country. Up to the early 1990s, only a small percentage of the country's population was foreign-born and Ireland was

---

[12] Whereas a GDP growth rate of 26.3% (subsequently adjusted to 25.6%) was recorded for 2015, this was an anomaly due to the impact of one-off transactions conducted by the MNE sector.

[13] CSO Database.

[14] Ibid.

a very homogenous society. With the phenomenon of inward migration flows that started in the 1990s and peaked in 2007, Ireland ceased to be a net exporter of people and the foreign-born share of the population increased to 16.4% by 2011 (OECD 2015). This represents a quite extraordinary transformation of the population in terms of both the scale and pace of change. Outside of regions where conflict prevails, this represents an unprecedented development.

With the rise in unemployment in the late 2000s, the flows of inward migration decreased while the flows of outward migration increased so that Ireland became again a net exporter of people. As the Irish economy has recovered in recent years, there has again been a reversal in migration flows with inflows again increasing while outflows have decreased (Fig. 1). The number of immigrants to Ireland in the year to April 2020 is estimated to have decreased slightly year-on-year by 3.6% from 88,600 to 86,400, while the number of emigrants increased from 54,900 to 56,500 (CSO 2020a; b), although the travel embargoes implemented worldwide and suspension of visa processing in early 2020 may have affected these numbers negatively. These flows have resulted in net inward migration for Ireland in 2020 (+28.900), the third-highest level of net inward migration since 2008. Together with a natural population increase of 27,100, there was an overall increase in the population in the year ending April 2020 of 55,900 bringing the population estimate to 4.98 million.

Today Ireland is a changed country from just over two decades ago with a multiplicity of nationalities and diverse cultures.

Notwithstanding the dramatic increase in inward migrant flows to Ireland over the past two decades, Ireland's experience of migration has been relatively friction-less. This continued to be the case even in the years of recession that following the collapse of the boom. Unlike many other developed economies, there has been a little manifestation of anti-migrant sentiment even in the years of recession and migration is not a political issue of contestation.

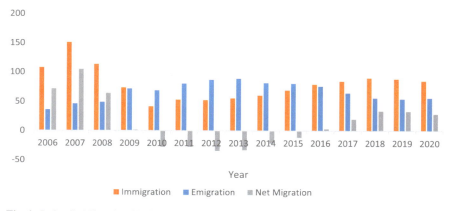

Fig. 1 Ireland's Migration 2006–2020. *Source* CSO

7 Managing Globalization to National Advantage: The Case of Ireland

The absence of any substantive tensions concerning migration can be attributed to Ireland's long history of emigration that continues up to the present with its citizens seeking refuge and fortune in other countries around the globe. As a result, there resides in the Irish psyche a keen appreciation and understanding of the challenges that face migrants and intrinsic solidarity with them. This has helped to ensure the relatively seamless integration of migrants into Irish society.

At the same time, the rapid growth in inward migration flows took place during the boom years of the Celtic Tiger when Ireland had effectively full employment and labor shortages abounded. Thus migration was not seen to lead to job displacement for local workers. With just over a quarter of the workforce unionized compared to an OECD average of 17 percent (OECD 2017), this greater trade union density has tended to counter the incidence of reduced wages and poorer working conditions, factors which have tended to lead to negative reactions elsewhere. The fact that Ireland operates a substantial social safety net and implements significant distributional measures via the tax and welfare systems thus reducing income inequality is also likely to explain the relative absence of anti-migrant sentiment even in recessionary times.

2.5   Current Challenges Including Those Posed by Brexit

Competitiveness: Pre-pandemic, Ireland had enjoyed one of the highest growth rates in Europe. However, costs are rising rapidly in key areas thus threatening the competitiveness of the economy. The construction sector has still not completely recovered from its crisis-era collapse and the construction of new homes continues to fall far short of need, further hindered by the closure of construction sites for several months early in the pandemic. This combined with policy decisions taken years before the collapse including relying on the market for housing and with decisions concerning the disposal of indebted assets has produced in recent years a housing shortage and steep increases in rents thus leading to a housing crisis. This has not only severe social consequences but also implications for the future development of the economy. A recent report from the American Chamber of Commerce in Ireland has highlighted the significance of housing for the country's competitiveness (American Chamber of Commerce 2017).

FDI has long been attracted to Ireland because of the availability of a highly educated and qualified talent pool. That talent pool is not just the product of a young population and the Irish education system. It is also the product of substantial flows of migrant talent into the country from overseas particularly other EU countries where high rates of unemployment persist. Ireland has always been attractive to such talent and in turn, it serves to reinforce the attractiveness of Ireland to FDI.

However, there are indications that the current challenges associated with housing may have the effect of Ireland been seen in a less favorable light by potential migrants, whether those from overseas or returning Irish migrants. If that were to lead to such talent deciding not to migrate to Ireland, then it poses a risk to one of the key elements of Ireland's attractiveness to FDI viz. the availability of talent.

As Globalization has evolved through the stages of globalization of markets, sources and now intellect, today's location decisions by MNEs can be strongly influenced by access to talent. Thus firms locate in sites where they are assured of access to the best talent. Ireland has been ranked first in the world in attracting high-value FDI projects from 2012 to 2017, dropping to third place behind Singapore and the Netherlands in 2018, (IBM 2019). Such high-value investment inevitably needs high levels of talent further emphasizing the importance of Ireland maintaining its attractiveness to potential migrant talent. The speedy resolution of the current housing crisis is therefore imperative if Ireland's continued attractiveness to FDI is not be imperiled.

Ireland's favorable tax regime has long been a core element of its competitiveness as a location for inward investment. Recent years have seen several multilateral initiatives seeking to reduce the incidence of tax avoidance on the part of MNEs. The Base Erosion and Profit Shifting (BEPS) project being undertaken by the OECD at the behest of the G20 is one such initiative. Of likely greater potential significance in the context of Ireland's competitiveness is the renewed push on the part of the EU Commission and some EU member states notably France for the introduction of the Common Consolidated Corporation Tax Base (CCCTB). Were that system to be introduced, it would not only impact Ireland's corporation tax receipts leading to pressure on the public finances, but it would also have the effect of rendering its tax regime including the low corporation tax rate of 12.5% considerably less effective as an element of Ireland's attractiveness to investing MNEs. Recent revelations concerning Apple (Financial Times 2017) affirm that tax minimizing strategies continue to be a major consideration for MNEs in their investment location decisions. Accordingly, any substantial lessening of Ireland's current tax advantage could harm future investment inflows. However, Ireland is today less reliant on tax as an element of its attractiveness for foreign investment than in the past.

Ireland's future within the context of Brexit: The implications of Brexit for Ireland are potentially profound. Despite the EU Withdrawal Bill being passed by the UK Parliament in January 2020 after a series of revisions and deadline extensions being granted by the EU, the challenge of squaring the circle that Brexit requires across so many aspects is particularly acute in the case of Ireland. While it is impossible to have certainty around the medium to long-term effects of Brexit, it is already possible to identify some negative short-term impacts. As of November 2020, the EU and UK have yet to reach an agreement on a post-Brexit trade deal and the Irish Government has instructed the Irish industry to assume the worst case, no-deal scenario (Irish Times 2020a).

The uncertainty that Brexit has created has been most manifest concerning the lower valuation of sterling. This has generated negative impacts for the Irish tourism sector which has played a key role in Ireland's recovery and for an indigenous industry dependent on the UK market. The UK is the largest source of tourists to Ireland and with the fall in the value of sterling, the numbers of British tourists coming to Ireland have already fallen.

The UK accounts for 18% of Ireland's total exports and is the most important market for Ireland's food and drink sector. Already, there have been reports of several firms closing due to the reduction in their competitiveness in the British market as a result of the loss of value in Sterling. Other firms are reported to be struggling to adjust to this change in their competitiveness.

Beyond the short-term, several issues arise for Ireland concerning the trade, travel, and rights of Irish migrants in the UK. In relation to trade, the importance of the UK as an export market has already been highlighted. However, it is important to note that the UK is a significantly more important market for indigenous firms that are a major source of employment than for multinational firms. Hence that sector is particularly vulnerable if post-Brexit, the current trading arrangements cease to apply. Of equal, if not greater importance, is the fact that the overwhelming bulk of Irish exports transit through the UK. Again if barriers were to put in place post-Brexit, this would represent an enormous encumbrance for exporters potentially adding to costs and the time taken to ship exports to their market destinations. In that regard, it is noteworthy that the joint report from the negotiators of the EU and the UK Government on progress during phase 1 of negotiations issued on December 8th, 2017 committed to addressing "issues arising from Ireland's unique geographic situation, including the transit of goods (to and from Ireland via the United Kingdom)".

As part of its Brexit Readiness Action Plan,[15] the Irish Government has dramatically stepped up investment in port facilities and upgraded customs capacity in preparation for a no-deal outcome (Irish Times 2020b). Official government advice to exporting firms is to examine options for shipping directly to continental Europe as an alternative to UK trans-shipment routes to mitigate the additional costs in time and bureaucracy. These Brexit-related changes in logistics are expected to increase costs for Irish exporters in the event of a no-deal scenario.

While Irish goods exports continue to grow to the EU and other non-EU destinations, in 2019 Great Britain accounted for only 9% of Ireland's goods exports, down 11% compared with 2018 (CSO 2020b). At the same time, the share of Ireland's imports from Great Britain represented 21% of total imports. Some of those imported goods would have been for immediate consumption, but with Ireland's high participation in global value chains, others would inevitably have been inputs into production processes whose outputs would then be exported to markets outside Ireland. Given the interwoven nature of today's supply chains, some of that import trade can represent just one stage of a supply chain that can extend into and then out of Ireland and in some cases (such as in those chains that cross the border between the Republic of Ireland and Northern Ireland) may do so several times.[16] Consequently, the potential for severe disruption in those supply chains in a post-Brexit context is great.

In relation to travel and the rights of Irish migrants in the UK, there has been since the 1920s a free travel area between the UK and Ireland. Irish migrants in the UK

---

[15] From 1st January 2021, any business that moves goods from, to or through the UK will be subject to a range of new customs formalities, SPS checks and other regulatory requirements, that do not apply in any form today to such trade. (Department of the Taoiseach 2020).

[16] Connelly (2017) offers graphic illustrations of the intricacies of such supply chains.

have essentially enjoyed the same rights as British citizens. In recent years, the UK has represented the destination for some 20% of Irish emigrants.

Brexit raised the possibility of restrictions on the free movement of people between Ireland and the UK for work, despite the stated position of both the Irish and British governments of maintaining the longstanding common travel area. As noted above, since the UK continues to be a significant destination for Irish emigrants particularly at times of high unemployment, such restrictions could have implications for the Irish labor market. However, the aforementioned joint report "recognizes that the United Kingdom and Ireland may continue to make arrangements between themselves relating to the movement of persons between their territories (Common Travel Area)".

A significant number of Irish-born people are residents in the UK and likewise, a substantial number of UK-born people are residents in the Republic of Ireland. Recent estimates indicate that almost 400,000 people residing in the UK in 2011 were born in the Republic of Ireland while close to 230,000 British-born people were residents in Ireland. (Davy Research 2016). However, many of these migrants will have passports that relate to their current residencies as opposed to their places of birth (for example, there were only 112,259 United Kingdom nationals usually resident and present in the State in 2011 (CSO 2016)). Initial fears that others could find themselves post-Brexit being resident in a country where their right to residency might come into question post-Brexit have largely been allayed by both the EU and Britain.

The post-Brexit status of the North–South border on the island of Ireland has posed a particular challenge. From a practical perspective, that border no longer operates today. While the term "frictionless border" has been used to describe the nature of the border that could operate post-Brexit, squaring this particular circle is especially challenging. Furthermore, there have been concerns that changes to the status of the border post-Brexit could have an impact on the Peace Process. Nonetheless in the December 8th joint report of the negotiating parties, there is a reaffirmation by the UK to protecting cooperation between the North and South of the island and to the avoidance of a hard border. The joint report states that "any future arrangements must be compatible with these overarching requirements".

However, the current UK Government has raised concerns regarding its plans to abandon sections of the EU negotiated Withdrawal Agreement thereby breaking international law as set out in the Good Friday (Belfast) Agreement, a document signed in 1998 which effectively ended the period of violence known as "the troubles" in Northern Ireland. As of November 2020, the UK Parliament's upper chamber (the House of Lords) has overwhelmingly rejected such proposals in the interest of maintaining peace on the island of Ireland.

There are however some positive benefits that potentially could apply from Brexit. Over the past 15 years, the UK has received more than 20% of FDI to the EU. Were full access to the EU's internal market to cease post-Brexit, future FDI flows that would have gone into the UK had it remained a member of the EU might locate elsewhere in the EU 27. Ireland could potentially capture some FDI currently located in Britain as well as future FDI that in the absence of Brexit would have located in Britain.

By September 2019, some 29 financial services firms have already relocated staff or offices to Dublin, principally in the insurance, banking, and asset management sectors, making Ireland the number one choice for relocation of UK financial services firms ahead of Luxembourg and Frankfurt (Irish Times 2019).

Related to Brexit, Kobrin (2017) has noted that with the rise of populist nationalism in advanced economies, there are possible impacts on the multinational enterprise. He highlights that in such conditions, policy toward MNEs and FDI will be much less predictable, uncertainty will be increased, and "economically rational" arguments will have less traction. A key feature of the Irish landscape however is the lack of any discernible shift toward such populist nationalism and thus the absence of the factors instanced by Kobrin. In that light, the suggestion by Johns (2017) that the dominance of political centrism in Ireland could be a major factor of attraction for investing MNEs in the future has substance.

2.6 The Impact of the Global Pandemic on Ireland

While the medium to long-term impact of the pandemic on Ireland's economy and global connectivity is uncertain, in the short term Ireland has been negatively affected by the emergence of COVID19 in 2020. In terms of GDP, initial forecasts for robust annual growth of 5.6% have been revised downwards to -1.8%, reflecting reduced demand in the retail and hospitality sectors, for example, and the loss of productivity from the closure of businesses during periods of government-imposed travel restrictions and work-from-home advisories. Similarly, both private consumption expenditure and investment levels are forecast to witness negative growth of -9.2% and -17%, respectively, down from the positive growth rates of 3.2% and 74.8% in 2019 (ESRI 2020).

The impact of the pandemic on supply chains, and particularly on the global value chains in which Ireland plays an important role is also negative. The pandemic has disproportionately affected indigenous sectors typically comprising of SMEs, whereas other sectors such as technology and pharmaceuticals characterized typically by large MNEs have in many instances flourished during the pandemic with little impact on their Irish operations. The construction sector, which is key to addressing the shortfall in housing stock discussed above, has yet to return to full capacity due to additional health and safety measures implemented to curb the spread of the pandemic.

In relation to the flows of people in and out of Ireland, global travel restrictions have curtailed travel in the short term thereby reducing both business travel and migration, hence reducing Ireland's physical connectivity internationally. Anecdotal evidence suggests that Q1 2020 saw high levels of repatriation of Irish expatriates driven by uncertainty around the pandemic, however, this has stabilized as flights have remained grounded in many instances.

Unlike the austerity budgetary policies introduced in the wake of the Global Financial Crisis, the Irish Government's response to the pandemic has been expansionary with spending dramatically increased in Budget 2021. Several measures have been implemented by the Government aimed at supporting indigenous businesses and retaining jobs in the short term, and an emergency welfare payment has been introduced to support lower-skilled workers who have been disproportionately affected by the pandemic.

3 Conclusion

Through the decades of globalization, Ireland has firmly embraced it and has reaped considerable benefits as a result. These have not accrued by chance but have been a product of a deliberate approach on the part of Ireland to capitalize on the potential inherent in the myriad of flows that are intrinsic to the enactment of globalization. This approach has involved the leveraging of both similarities and differences to capture significant shares of those flows. Of particular note has been Ireland's exceptional application of arbitrage.

With the fraying of globalization as exemplified by Brexit, Ireland has already incurred some costs. Into the future of a post-Brexit world, major uncertainties prevail. The incurrence of costs particularly related to trade represents a real prospect impacting Ireland's economic growth and employment. The global pandemic has added further uncertainty to the future of Ireland's connectivity and participation in complex global value chains.

While Ireland's managing of globalization has delivered in many respects a distinct set of largely positive outcomes in the context of globalization, it nonetheless offers some lessons for other nations. Ireland's embrace of openness and greater integration with the rest of the world was accompanied by proactive policies geared toward national advantage. The adoption of such a strategy by other nations likewise offers the possibility of garnering national advantage.

References

American Chamber of Commerce in Ireland. 2017. Growing Great Teams in Ireland: The Role of the Residential Rental Sector, November.

Backer, K.D., and Miroudot, S. 2013. Mapping Global Value Chains, *OECD Trade Policy Papers*, No. 159, OECD.

Buckley, P.J., and F. Ruane. 2006. Foreign Direct Investment in Ireland: Policy Implications for Emerging Economics. *The World Economy* 29 (11): 1611–1628.

Central Statistics Office. 2004. Ireland and the EU 1973–2003.

Central Statistics Office. 2008. Statistical Yearbook of Ireland 2008. October.

Central Statistics Office. 2011. Measuring Ireland's Progress 2010, September. http://www.cso.ie/en/media/csoie/releasespublications/documents/otherreleases/2010/progress2010/Measuring_Ireland's_Progress_2010.pdf.

Central Statistics Office. 2015. Measuring Ireland's Progress 2015. http://www.cso.ie/en/releasesandpublications/ep/p-mip/mip2015/edu/ed/#d.en.124353.

7 Managing Globalization to National Advantage: The Case of Ireland 143

Central Statistics Office. 2016. Brexit: Ireland and the UK in numbers, December.

Central Statistics Office. 2020b. Population and Migration Estimates, September 28, 2020. https://www.cso.ie/en/releasesandpublications/er/pme/populationandmigrationestimatesapril2020/.

Connelly, Tony. 2017. Brexit & Ireland: The Dangers, the Opportunities, and the Inside Story of the Irish Response, Penguin Ireland.

Central Statistics Office. 2020a. Government Finance Statistics (A). October 21, 2020. https://www.cso.ie/en/statistics/governmentaccounts/governmentfinancestatisticsa/.

Davy Research. 2016. The economic impact of Brexit on Ireland, March 31.

Department of Education and Skills. 2015. Projections Of Demand For Full Time Third Level Education, November. https://www.education.ie/en/Publications/Statistics/Statistical-Reports/Projections-of-demand-for-full-time-Third-Level-Education-2015-2029.pdf.

Department of Finance. 2017. Expenditure report Budget 2018.

Department of Finance. 2020. Expenditure report Budget 2021. http://www.budget.gov.ie/Budgets/2021/Documents/Budget/Part%20I%20-%20Public%20Expenditure%20Strategy%20.pdf.

Department of the Taoiseach. 2020. Trade in Goods: Brexit Readiness Action Plan, September 9. https://www.gov.ie/en/publication/e10c9-trade-in-goods-brexit-readiness-action-plan/.

Duggan, Jennifer. 2017. Q&A: Ireland's Leo Varadkar on Brexit, Trump and Keeping Ireland 'At the Center of the World', Time, July 13.

Economist. 1988. Poorest of the rich. (Ireland Survey), January 16.

Economist. 1997. Ireland shines. Lessons and questions from an economic transformation, May 15. Economic & Social Research Institute (Ireland), 2020. Quarterly Economic Commentary Autumn 2020, September 28.

Eurostat. 2019. 40% of 30–34 year-olds have tertiary education, 24 January, 2019. https://ec.europa.eu/eurostat/web/products-eurostat-news/-/EDN-20190124-1.

ESRI. 2020. Quarterly Economic Commentary, Autumn.

Financial Times. 2017. Ireland sees FDI rising as investors shrug off Brexit and tax fears, January 3.

Financial Times. 2017. Paradise Paper allege Jersey role in Apple tax strategy, November 7.

Foreign Policy. 2009. How the Index is Calculated, October 29.

Ghemawat, Pankaj. 2001. *Distance Still Matters: The Hard Reality of Global Expansion*, Harvard Business Review, 79, 8, September, pp.137–147.

IBM Institute for Business Value. 2019. Global Location Trends 2019 Annual Report.

Irish Times. 2001. People are still Republic's trump card when it comes to attracting US companies to invest here, March 2, 2001.

Irish Times. 2019. Brexit: Almost 30 financial groups move operations from London to Dublin, September 19, 2019

Irish Times. 2020a. Ireland poised for greater likelihood of no-deal Brexit, September 11, 2020.

Irish Times. 2020b. Rosslare Europort in line for €30m upgrade from Irish Rail, July 3, 2020.

Johns, Chris. 2017. Populism, free-trade zealots and the future of western democracy, November 6.

Kobrin, Stephen. 2017. The rise of nationalism, FDI and the multinational enterprise Columbia FDI Perspectives, No. 212, November 6.

McKinsey Global Institute. 2016. Digital Globalization: The New Era of Global Flows, March.

McWilliams, David. 2017. A new economic plan for Ireland, Irish Times, November 18.

Murphy A. 2000. The "Celtic Tiger"—An Analysis of Ireland's Economic Growth Performance, EU Working Papers RSC No. 2000/16, Robert Schuman Centre for Advanced Studies.

National Competitiveness Council. 2009. Annual Competitiveness Report 2008.

O'Donovan, David and Rios-Morales, Ruth. 2006. Can the Latin American and Caribbean countries emulate the Irish model of FDI attraction? Cepal Review 88, April 49–66.

OECD. 2017. OECD Employment Outlook 2017, OECD Publishing. *Paris. Available at:* https://doi.org/10.1787/emploutlook-2017-en.

OECD. 1999. OECD Economic Surveys 1999 Ireland.

OECD. 2005. 'Education at a Glance', OECD Indicators 2005.

OECD. 2013. Education at a Glance 2013: OECD indicators.

OECD. 2015. OECD Economic Surveys IRELAND, September. http://www.oecd-ilibrary.org/docserver/download/1015171e.pdf?expires=1510378813&id=id&accname=ocid195199&checksum=AADE63F5794C72DFAA8C888B5A2E0258.

OECD. 2019. Education at a Glance Report, 2013.

Rios-Morales, R., and L. Brennan. 2009. Ireland's Innovative Governmental Policies Promoting Internationalization. *Research in International Business and Finance* 23 (2): 157–168.

Time. 2012. The Celtic Comeback, October 15.

World Bank Data. 2020. https://data.worldbank.org/indicator/NE.TRD.GNFS.ZS.

Chapter 8
Multilateralising Regionalism: The ASEAN Experience

Jayant Menon

1 Introduction

As a regional organisation, the Association of Southeast Asian Nations, or ASEAN, is different, in many ways. Previous assessments of ASEAN may not have fully recognised how different ASEAN's objectives may have been from most, if not all, other regional arrangements. This is mainly because in assessing regionalism, it has become customary to look to the European experience to serve as a benchmark against which all other regional integration programs are judged. Despite recent challenges, there is little doubt that Europe has made great strides in the economic sphere, as well as in preserving the peace and security of the region. It is clearly the most integrated region in the world, and there was a time when regional groupings everywhere looked on in awe, aspiring to emulate its many achievements. So how does ASEAN compare to this so-called model of regionalism?

Unlike Europe, regionalism for ASEAN has evolved to become more of a means, rather than an end. With markedly different objectives in mind, any comparative assessment needs to employ criteria and metrics that measure intended outcomes, rather than assumed outputs. In this paper, we look closely at what ASEAN has tried to achieve through the way in which it has implemented its economic protocols. By doing this, we try and delineate the true objectives of ASEAN, rather than simply assuming that they must be the same as other regional arrangements. Put simply, this paper argues that any comparison with the European or other regional arrangements

---

I am grateful to participants at the ISAS-BASC Workshop "Revisiting Globalisation: Comparing Country Experiences from South Asia and the World" on 12 October 2017 for their comments, particularly Vinod Aggarwal. Any remaining errors are mine.

This chapter draws heavily from the author's working paper—"ASEAN's limited regional Integration spells globalisation, not Failure", *Working Papers in Trade and Development*, No. 2020/02, Australian National University, Australia.

J. Menon (✉)
Visiting Senior Fellow, ISEAS-Yusof Ishak Institute, Singapore, Singapore

© The Author(s), under exclusive license to Springer Nature Singapore Pte Ltd. 2022
A. Palit (ed.), *Globalisation Impacts*, International Law and the Global South,
https://doi.org/10.1007/978-981-16-7185-2_8

145

is likely to yield flawed results if the underlying objectives differ, and therefore the metrics used in the assessment should align with true objectives.

The paper is in five parts. Section 2 provides a brief background of ASEAN, and argues the importance of differentiating between stated and true objectives in evaluating progress towards goals. In Sect. 3, we examine ASEAN's trade performance using traditional and non-traditional indicators, and assess performance accordingly. This section brings out the practical importance of identifying true objectives and then applying the correct metrics in assessing performance. The same is done for foreign direct investment (FDI) in Sect. 4. A final section concludes.

2 Understanding ASEAN's Objectives: Stated Versus Real

Born as a politico-security pact during the Viet Nam War in 1967, it took a while before ASEAN decided to get serious about pursuing an economic agenda. It was only at the Bali Summit of the five leaders in February 1976 that a formal set of regional cooperation measures were introduced. None of the economic cooperation programs had any significant impact on regional economic relations, however (Imada and Naya 1992). They had little effect because they were explicitly designed that way. Member countries were not ready, willing, or interested in forging greater economic ties amongst each other and the implementation of these agreements reflected that. An outsider observing these outcomes would have declared the program a failure, while an insider would have understood that they achieved exactly what they were designed to achieve: very little.

The first serious attempt at pursuing economic objectives commenced in 1992 when ASEAN leaders announced at their Summit that they would pursue the establishment of an ASEAN Free Trade Area, or AFTA. This marked a clear break with the past, and the stated emphasis was on stronger economic cooperation: for the first time, 'free trade' was the regional objective, there was a clear timetable for implementation, and a 'negative list' approach was adopted, in that all goods traded would be included within AFTA unless explicitly excluded.

On the trade liberalisation front, AFTA succeeded in doing much more than mandated, again drawing the contrast between stated and actual objectives, but this time in a more positive way. But AFTA had a much wider agenda, covering areas such as services, investment, intellectual property rights, and the like, but progress in all of these areas remained limited.

Instead of backing down, ASEAN decided to double down, and announced an even more ambitious agenda labelled the ASEAN Economic Community (AEC). In 2007, ASEAN leaders signed the AEC Blueprint defining the actions, measures, and timelines leading up to the AEC's creation. An AEC Scorecard was drawn up to track progress in implementing specific measures within the Blueprint's timelines.

Like with the AFTA agenda (except for tariffs), ASEAN fell short of its target of realising the AEC by end-2015. By 2015, the full list of AEC Scorecard measures had grown from 316 to 611; of this total, 506 were identified as the focused base of measures for implementation between 2008 and 2015. At end-October 2015, ASEAN had reportedly implemented 92.7% of these 506 measures. The remaining 105 measures were deferred until after 2015 (ASEAN 2015). A successor Blueprint called AEC 2025 had to be introduced, laying out the work for ASEAN economic integration that remained to be done.

Some see this as a failure on ASEAN's part, but should they? An alternative view could be that ASEAN was never going to meet the deadline of 2015, which had been moved forward from 2020, as it had been overly ambitious by design. With this explanation, the real objective was never to realise the AEC by 2015 or even 2020, but to create sufficient momentum to get as close as possible to it than would otherwise have been possible. Given ASEAN's mixed record, this is not an implausible explanation.

Other assessments of ASEAN as a regional integration program may also have failed to delineate true underlying objectives from those that appear on the surface. It is often assumed, quite understandably, that the primary purpose of regional integration agreements is to increase regional integration outcomes. If this were the case, then traditional measures of integration such as changes in the shares of intra-regional trade and investment over time would be the appropriate metrics for assessing performance or measuring progress. But if it is not the primary objective, then these metrics alone may not be sufficient in delivering an accurate assessment of performance.

3 Assessing Trade Performance

There are both price and quantity indicators that are used to measure the extent of integration. Price indicators are not as common as quantity indicators because data is limited. But when sufficient data on prices are available, they can be employed to examine the degree of price convergence across markets as a measure of market integration, with the law of one price setting the theoretical limit for perfect convergence. The most commonly used quantitative indicators of integration are measure of intra-regional trade. These measures are often used as indicators of inter-dependence, and equally to indicate a capacity for self-reliance and independence.[1] They can also be used to indicate the degree of resilience to global shocks, or shocks emanating from other regions.

In ASEAN, the share of intra-regional trade has remained low and relatively unchanged at around 20–25% for almost two decades (Fig. 1). Other similar indicators such as trade intensity measures are less gloomy but still point in the same direction.[2] If we rely only on these traditional indicators of trade integration, ASEAN

---

[1] Measures of business cycle synchronisation such as output correlations are often used as indicators of macroeconomic interdependence (see Capanelli et al. 2009).

[2] The trade intensity index is used to determine whether the value of trade between two entities is greater or smaller than would be expected on the basis of their importance in world trade. It is usually measured as the ratio of two export shares. The numerator is the share of the destination of

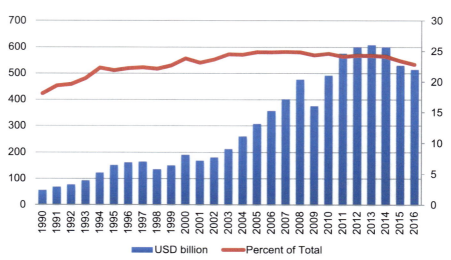

Fig. 1 Share of intra-ASEAN trade has remained below 25% and has declined in recent years. *Source* ADB ARIC integration indicators database. https://aric.adb.org

would be judged a failure. But what if there are broader objectives being pursued? What if regionalism is only a means towards greater ends?

This is indeed the case for ASEAN. To illustrate, consider the implementation of the ASEAN Free Trade Agreement, or AFTA. ASEAN's original members have used the agreement as a stepping stone to pursue broader liberalisation and thereby promote globalisation. The data suggests that the original members have been multi-lateralising their tariff preferences over time, narrowing or eliminating the difference between preferential and most favoured nation (MFN) tariff rates. This began initially with multilateralising the Common Effective Preferential Tariff (CEPT) rates, and then continued with the ASEAN Trade in Goods Agreement (ATIGA) rates.[3] This has significantly reduced, and often eliminated, the margins of preference (Fig. 2). In a comparison of external tariffs of major regional trade agreements, the World Bank (2005) found that only the North American Free Trade Agreement or NAFTA had lower external tariffs than AFTA. Since then, it is quite likely that the ASEAN's external tariff rates have been reduced to be currently lower than NAFTA's.

As a result, more than 90% of tariff lines have a margin of preference of zero (Feridhanusetyawan 2005), and more than 70% of intra-ASEAN trade is conducted at MFN zero (Table 1). On average, ASEAN members had 96% of their tariff lines at 0% by August 2017 (ASEAN 2017), and this share is expected to reach 98.7% by 2018 (ASEAN 2016).

---

interest in the exports of the region under study, while the denominator is the share of the destination of interest in the exports of the world as a whole.

[3] ATIGA replaces the CEPT scheme of AFTA, and was signed in February 2009 and entered-into-force in May 2010.

8 Multilateralising Regionalism: The ASEAN Experience

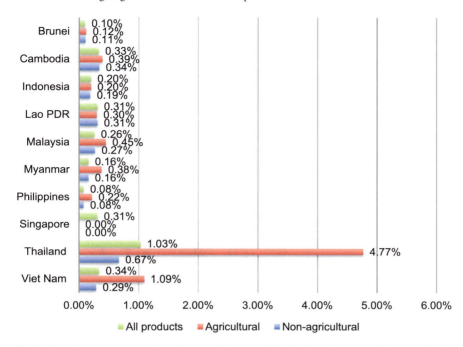

Fig. 2 Margins of preference have been declining in ASEAN. *Note* Latest available year. In the calculation of MFN tariff averages, general tariffs (for non-WTO members) and non-MFN tariffs are included. *Source* ITC market access map country tariff averages, downloaded 9 October 2017

There is an unusual amount of discussion about how ASEAN needs to raise the rates of utilisation of preferences within the agreement. To a certain extent, preference utilisation would overcome the so-called attribution problem; i.e., to be able to say that such trade would not have otherwise taken place if not for the preferences provided by the trade agreement. It does not fully overcome this problem because there is no definitive way of determining that such trade would not have occurred anyway. The case may be strengthened if intra-regional trade shares had increased significantly over time, but this has not been the ASEAN experience.

Furthermore, rates of utilisation of preferences in ASEAN remain low by international standards. Table 2 provides utilisation rates for Japanese affiliates operating in ASEAN reported by Hayakawa et al. (2009). They employ the results of a survey conducted by JETRO to examine the utilisation of ASEAN FTAs by Japanese affiliates. The authors restrict the sample to Japanese affiliates that are actually exporting to or importing from ASEAN countries. They find that average utilisation rates for exports is rarely above 25%, averaging 22%, and it is even lower for imports. Another survey by JETRO (2003) found that in 2002, the rate was only 4% for Malaysia, and 11% for Thailand. Manchin and Pelkmans–Balaoing (2007) cite estimates based on firm interviews conducted for the ASEAN Secretariat that showed an AFTA tariff preference utilisation rate of about 5% of total trade. ISEAS (2010) reports AFTA

Table 1 Preferential trade by agreement/type of regime, 2008 (selected regimes)

Regime	Share of trade by preferential margin (PM) and MFN rate (in percent of total trade)								Trade weighted pref. margin (percentage points)
	Preferential trade						Total non-pref, > 0	Total MFN zero	
	Total preferential	PM > 20%	PM 10.1–20%	PM 5.1–10%	PM 2.6–5%	PM 0.1–2.5%			
Intra-ASEAN	20.1	2.0	2.0	2.6	4.7	8.7	3.6	72.9	1.7
Singapore-USA	7.2	0.2	0.2	0.6	4.8	1.4	0.0	92.7	0.3
Japan-Singapore	3.1	0.0	0.0	0.1	2.4	0.6	1.9	94.0	0.1
Australia-Singapore	6.4	0.0	0.0	0.2	6.1	0.0	0.0	93.6	0.4
India-Singapore	20.0	0.0	0.0	8.7	6.6	4.6	16.2	59.6	1.0

Source WTO (2011)

8 Multilateralising Regionalism: The ASEAN Experience

Table 2 Utilisation rates of Japanese affiliates

	Exporter			Importer		
	Use (%)	Intend to use (%)	No intention to use (%)	Use (%)	Intend to use (%)	No intention to use (%)
ASEAN	22	28	50	18	27	55
Indonesia	26	35	39	24	37	39
Malaysia	25	21	53	16	18	66
Philippines	15	23	61	10	20	70
Singapore	35	22	44	NA	NA	NA
Thailand	22	34	44	21	33	46
Viet Nam	9	28	62	14	28	59

Note NA = Not available
Source Hayakawa et al. (2009)

tariff preference utilisation rates of around 15–17% for the Philippines and 20% for Viet Nam. The average utilisation rate for ASEAN was 23% in 2008. To put this in comparative perspective, utilisation rates of below 50% are considered low in European preferential trading agreements (see, for instance, Augier et al. 2005).

Why are rates of utilisation of preferences so low in ASEAN? There are factors on both the cost and benefit side of the equation that account for these low rates in ASEAN. On the cost side, often complex rules of origin (ROO) and limited information and lack of firm-level skills to comply with requirements discourage the use of ATIGA. On the benefit side, the low and often non-existent margin of preference limits the value of using the FTA for trade. The most compelling reason for low utilisation rates is because of irrelevancy—there are hardly any preferences to utilise. When this is the case, improving information flows or simplifying rules-of-origin or other similar measures will be misplaced as they will not improve utilisation rates.

Most previous studies on the welfare effects of FTAs have assumed that utilisation is complete, or 100%.[4] This is a serious limitation given the evidence summarised above. Exceptions in the East Asian context are Petri et al. (2011) and Menon (2014a). These studies find that actual utilisation rates significantly diminish the benefits from preferential liberalisation, but in a non-linear way. For instance, when a utilisation rate of 25% is applied, the results suggest that the welfare impacts are less than 25% of the impacts when full utilisation is assumed (Menon 2014a).

Reciprocity is an important motivation for pursuing FTAs over unilateral actions such as multilateralisation of preferences. Proponents of FTAs argue that unilateral multilateralism reduces the bargaining power of countries looking to gain greater access to traditional and new markets through the exchange of concessions. To isolate the impact of reciprocity, Menon (2014a) compares the welfare impacts of pure preferential liberalisation with a scenario where preferences are multilateralised.

---

[4] See Ando (2009) for a summary of these studies.

The findings suggest that preferential liberalisation delivers greater welfare benefits through reciprocity over multilateralisation of preferences only when utilisation rates are high or complete. That is, with 25% utilisation, multilateralisation of preferences (without reciprocity) still delivers greater benefits to members compared to preferential liberalisation with reciprocity.

Furthermore, the potential for trade deflection combined with possible retaliatory actions may further reduce benefits to members, and to the world as a whole. Multilateralisation of preferences is not subject to either trade deflection or retaliation. In general, when members extend their preferential reductions to non-members on a non-discriminatory basis, welfare is enhanced because of three primary effects: (i) the extent of the liberalisation is greater, (ii) the broader liberalisation undoes the welfare-reducing trade diversion resulting from the preferential liberalisation, and (iii) the productivity of scarce resources within each member country is allocated more efficiently across its industries.

As a further plus, because the preferential tariff reduction schedules have been ambitious and rapid, AFTA has accelerated the pace of multilateral trade liberalisation in the original ASEAN member countries. Instead of jeopardising multilateralism, it has hastened the speed at which these countries have moved towards their goal of free and open trade. In this way, AFTA's greatest achievement may have less to do with what it is required or mandated to do, but rather what more it has been able to achieve, through the long-standing commitment of its members to open regionalism.

To illustrate, Fig. 3 compares, in stylised form, trade liberalisation outcomes under various scenarios involving WTO or unilateral liberalisation, with a preferential approach through a regional trade agreement, in this case AFTA. WTO negotiations and outcomes or unilateral actions reduce the amount of time required for countries to move towards their goal of free and open trade (defined here as 0–5% average tariff rates). How does a preferential trade agreement like AFTA affect this objective?

If AFTA is implemented on a purely minimalist basis, or without any multilateralisation of tariff preferences, then the time taken to arrive at the aforementioned goal is unchanged. Average tariff rates do fall more rapidly however, particularly up to AFTA's 2003 deadline for 0–5% internal tariff rates, but this gain could be offset by the trade diversion that it would also induce. If, however, members choose to fully multilateralise their preferences for all tariff lines soon after AFTA's commencement, then the deadline for free and open trade is moved forward to coincide with AFTA's deadline of 2003 (Menon 2007).

As noted earlier, preferences for the vast majority of tariff lines have been fully multilateralised and if the remaining few tariff lines are dealt with in the same way relatively soon, then the deadline will fall somewhere between 2003 and the WTO-based deadline. If this happens, AFTA would have served as a building block that enables countries to pursue multilateral goals at a faster pace.

Emulation of the approach taken by the original members would be in the interest of the Mekong economies. Indeed, they will need to emulate this approach if they are not to be left behind, and if they are to succeed in deepening regional integration. Regionalism through ASEAN membership could then provide the GMS economies

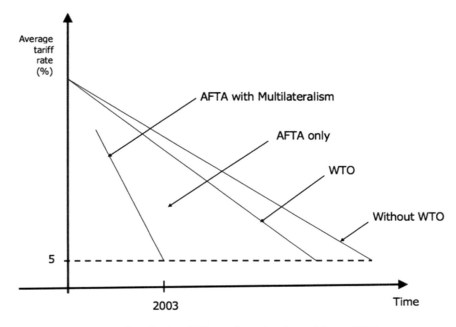

Fig. 3 WTO and AFTA liberalisation: Different Scenarios. *Source* Menon (2007)

with an opportunity to pursue multilateralism aggressively and thus allow regionalism through AFTA to be a building block rather than stumbling block toward free and open trade. However, whether the worldwide proliferation of regional trade agreements will eventually integrate rather than fragment the world economy remains a separate and open question.

Multilateralisation has minimised trade diversion, and may account for the stubbornly low intra-ASEAN trade shares. This being the case, low intra-regional shares may be a sign of success rather than failure, as far as producing welfare-enhancing outcomes are concerned. Most of intra-ASEAN trade is supply-chain related trade in parts and components, which mostly travel duty-free because of zero tariffs provided by the Information Technology Agreement for electronic parts and components, Special Economic Zone privileges, or duty drawback schemes (Menon 2017). ASEAN's ambitious tariff reduction and trade facilitation programs have supported value-chain driven trade, as has multilateralisation, because final markets for the finished goods are predominantly outside the region.

If multilateralisation has subdued intra-regional trade, it has promoted rapid growth in overall trade, raising ASEAN to be the fourth largest exporting region in the world, next only to the European Union, North America, and China (Hill and Menon 2014). Although ASEAN accounts for just 3.3% of world GDP, it produces more than 7% of world exports. Indeed, according to the McKinsey Global Institute's 2016 Connectedness Index, four ASEAN member countries rank among the world's 50 most connected nations: Singapore (ranked first), Malaysia (20th), Thailand (22nd), and Viet Nam (37th). Indonesia and the Philippines are not too far behind, ranking 51st and 54th, respectively (MGI 2016).[5] ASEAN member countries fared even better in DHL's 2016 Global Connectedness Index, with five member countries ranking among the top 50: Singapore (2nd), Malaysia (19th), Thailand (22nd), Viet Nam (36th), and Cambodia (44th).[6]

After all, it is how much trade that takes place, and on what terms, that matters for welfare, and not who you trade with (Menon 2014b). Trade preferences are designed to affect who you trade with through trade diversion, which is welfare reducing. ASEAN has largely avoided this outcome by multilateralising its trade preferences, and removing most or all of the margin of preference.

If the share of intra-ASEAN trade is to increase in the future, it should be driven by factors other than trade preferences. When intra- or extra-ASEAN trade increases as a result of factors such as comparative cost advantage, product differentiation, or scale economies, then this growth is welfare enhancing. There is also great potential to increase trade in services by reducing barriers, which remain the second highest in the world, in a non-discriminatory manner. Any increase in intra-ASEAN trade resulting from these factors would be welfare-enhancing.

For all of services, and increasingly for goods as well, non-tariff barriers (NTBs) are the problem today. For goods, achievements in tariff liberalisation have been offset by the rise in non-tariff impediments to trade, which increased from 1,634 to 5,975 between 2000 and 2015 (Ing 2016). The data points to a clear negative correlation between the fall in tariff rates and the increase in non-tariff barriers (NTBs) (Table 3). Whether or not NTBs have been rising because tariffs have been falling, in an attempt to restore protection, is unclear. Irrespective of whether the link between the two is causal or coincidental, this poses a challenge for ASEAN program of trade liberalisation. Not only are NTBs likely to be more restrictive, providing more protection to domestic producers, they are also opaque and more difficult to dismantle. In addition, NTBs are a moving target, as they can evolve to take on new forms as soon as they are targeted or dismantled. It is likely that, for many sectors, the loss in protection resulting from reductions in tariffs have been more than compensated for by the increase in NTBs.

4 Assessing FDI Performance

As with trade, less than a quarter of foreign direct investment (FDI) flowing to ASEAN countries originate from within the region (Fig. 4). ASEAN had flirted with the idea of providing preferential treatment to investors from member countries in the

---

[5] The MGI Connected Index measures countries' integration into the global economy based on their inflows and outflows of goods, services, finance, people, and data and communication.

[6] The DHL Global Connectedness Index captures cross-border flows of trade, capital, information, and people.

8 Multilateralising Regionalism: The ASEAN Experience

Table 3 ASEAN NTM measures and tariffs

Country	Total (number)	SPS (%)	TBT (%)	Export related measures (%)	Others (%)
Brunei	516	31	56	9	4
Cambodia	243	15	50	29	7
Indonesia	638	20	51	12	18
Lao PDR	301	13	30	27	30
Malaysia	713	36	47	10	7
Myanmar	172	44	24	20	12
Philippines	854	27	42	17	13
Singapore	529	24	59	9	7
Thailand	1630	48	34	8	9
Viet Nam	379	37	37	17	8
ASEAN total	5975	29	43	16	12

Notes SPS = Sanitary and Phytosanitary Standards; TBT = Technical Barriers to Trade
Source Ing (2016)

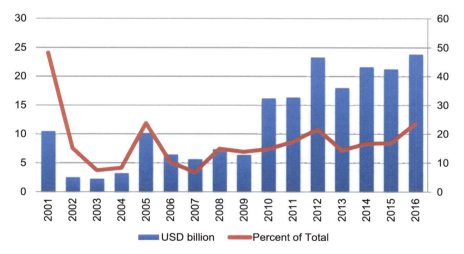

Fig. 4 Intra-ASEAN flows of FDI, USD billion and percentage shares, 2001–16. *Source* ADB ARIC integration indicators database. https://aric.adb.org

original design of the ASEAN Investment Area. But it quickly abandoned the idea, reaffirming its commitment to a non-discriminatory and open foreign investment climate, mirroring the national regimes in member countries.

Total inflows of FDI flourished as a result, even if flows from each other remained relatively unchanged. Again, as with trade, it is not where the FDI comes from that matters, but how much and what form it takes. The massive structural transformations

Table 4 ASEAN's Intra-regional trade, FDI, equity and bond holdings (%), 2016

	Trade (%)	FDI (%)	Equity holdings (%)	Bond holdings (%)
Within subregions				
ASEAN	**22.8**	**23.7**	**7.4**	**7.9**
ASEAN + 3 (including HKG)	47.0	57.8	16.3	9.9
Central Asia	7.0	2.9	0.0	0.0
East Asia	36.9	53.5	11.5	6.7
South Asia	5.8	0.6	0.3	2.2
With the rest of Asia and the Pacific				
ASEAN	**45.2**	**42.5**	**32.2**	**17.1**
ASEAN + 3 (including HKG)	10.8	5.2	3.2	5.8
Central Asia	24.1	11.4	11.7	15.0
East Asia	18.9	8.2	3.2	7.3
South Asia	33.2	36.6	21.1	9.6
With the rest of the world				
ASEAN	**32.1**	**33.9**	**60.4**	**75.0**
ASEAN + 3 (including HKG)	42.2	37.0	80.5	84.3
Central Asia	68.9	85.7	88.2	85.0
East Asia	44.1	38.3	85.3	86.0
South Asia	61.0	62.8	78.6	88.2

Source ADB ARIC Integration Indicators Database. https://aric.adb.org

that we have observed in the original ASEAN member countries, and continue to observe in the newer members, would probably have been compromised if ASEAN had not retained an open and non-discriminatory investment climate.

In the financial sphere, other purported measures of inter-dependence such as intra-regional equity and bond holdings also suggest shallow integration (Table 4). Intra-regional equity or bond holdings are less than 10%, while three-quarters of bond holdings emanate from outside the Asia–Pacific region.

5 Conclusions

As a regionalism project, ASEAN is different. Compared to Europe, it is outward-rather than inward-looking, more market than government driven, and institution light rather than heavy. These differences reflect the very different motivations, ambitions, and objectives of the two regional programs.

8 Multilateralising Regionalism: The ASEAN Experience

ASEAN's success lies in its almost unique achievement of being able to use regionalism to promote globalisation. Therefore, the metrics used to assess regionalism should reflect these broader objectives, even if they operate indirectly.

In the economic sphere, widely used indicators such as changes in the share of intra-regional trade and investment not only fail to capture the real story, but may point in the wrong direction. Instead of focusing on the failure to strengthen regional economic ties, attention should be paid to the strengthening of extra-regional links. The fact that the regional program may have been implemented in a manner that minimises trade and investment diversion is another sign of success. The lesson from the ASEAN experience is that it is overall trade and investment, rather than where it originates from, that should matter. Therefore, measures of total trade and investment, that include intra- and extra-regional flows, should be used in place of a subset that captures only intra-regional flows, in assessing performance of the regional initiative.

When the metrics used in the assessment properly reflect the broader objectives being pursued, then what appears as failure can turn into success. This is the case for ASEAN, where traditional indicators of regionalism would deem it a failure. This view is confirmed by empirical analyses that compare welfare impacts of different approaches to implementing ASEAN's program of liberalisation. The welfare gains from multilateralisation of preferences is greater than from pure preferential liberalisation when actual (low) utilisation rates are taken into account. In the end, it is welfare measures that matter in ranking outcomes, and non-discriminatory approaches such as multilateralisation come out unambiguously ahead.

While the multilateralisation approach has worked well with reducing tariffs, the benefits have been offset by the concomitant rise in NTBs. Whether or not the NTBs have risen to replace the protection lost from lower tariffs remains unclear. Whatever the reason, the rise in NTBs poses a serious challenge for ASEAN's liberalisation effort because they are more difficult to identify, track, and dismantle. Nevertheless, this does not imply the need for a change in approach, however. Unlike tariffs, it is either difficult or costly to exchange concessions in NTBs in a preferential manner, given the public goods nature of a lot of these reforms and the consequent ease of free riding. Therefore, whether it is tariffs or NTBs, the multilateralisation approach remains the best way forward.

References

Ando, M. 2009. Impacts of FTAs in East Asia: CGE simulation analysis. *RIETI Discussion Paper Series* 09-E-037. Tokyo: RIETI.

ASEAN. 2017. Joint media statement. In *The 49th ASEAN economic ministers' (AEM) meeting.* Available at http://asean.org/storage/2017/09/49th-AEM-JMS_FINAL11.pdf.

ASEAN. 2016. Joint media statement. In *The 48th ASEAN economic ministers' (AEM) meeting.* Available at http://asean.org/storage/2016/08/00-AEM-48-JMS-FINAL.pdf.

ASEAN. 2015. A blueprint for growth ASEAN economic community 2015: Progress and key achievements Jakarta: ASEAN secretariat. Available at: http://www.asean.org/wp-content/

uploads/images/2015/November/media-summary-ABIS/AEC%202015%20Progress%20and%20Key%20Achievements_04.11.2015.pdf.

Augier, P., M. Gasiorek, and Charles Lai Tong. 2005. The impact of rules of origin on trade flows. *Economic Policy* 43, July.

Capanelli, G., J-W Lee, and P. Petri. 2009. Developing indicators for regional economic integration and cooperation. In *UNU-CRIS working papers* W-2009/22

Feridhanusetyawan, T. 2005. Preferential trade agreements in the Asia-Pacific region. In *IMF working paper* 149, Washington, DC: IMF. Available at https://www.imf.org/en/Publications/WP/Issues/2016/12/31/Preferential-Trade-Agreements-in-the-Asia-Pacific-Region-18370.

Hayakawa, K., D. Hitarsuka, K. Shiino, and S. Sukegawa. 2009. Who uses free trade agreements? In *ERIA discussion paper* no. 2009–22. Jakarta: Economic Research Institute for ASEAN and East Asia (ERIA). Available at http://eria.org/pdf/ERIA-DP-2009-22.pdf.

Hill, H., and J. Menon. 2014. ASEAN commercial policy: A rare case of outward-looking regional integration. In *ADB working paper series on regional economic integration* 144. Manila: ADB. Available at https://www.adb.org/sites/default/files/publication/150385/reiwp-144.pdf.

Imada, P., and S. Naya (eds.). 1992. *AFTA: The way ahead*. Singapore: Institute of Southeast Asian Studies (ISEAS).

Ing, L.Y. 2016. Non-tariff measures in ASEAN. Jakarta: ERIA. Available at http://www.eria.org/non-tariff-measures-in-asean.pdf.

Institute of Southeast Asian Studies (ISEAS). 2010. ASEAN businesses and ASEAN economic integration. Summary of the brainstorming session on achieving the AEC 2015: Challenges for ASEAN businesses. Accessed 23 Sept 2010. Singapore: ISEAS.

Japan External Trade Organisation (JETRO). 2003. Current status of AFTA and corporate responses. November 2003. Tokyo: JETRO.

Manchin, M., and A. Pelkmans-Balaoing. 2007. Rules of origin and the web of East Asian free trade agreements. In *World bank policy research working paper* No. 4273. July 2007. Washington, DC: World Bank. Available at http://www-wds.worldbank.org/servlet/WDSContentServer/WDSP/IB/2007/07/06/000016406_20070706154708/Rendered/PDF/wps4273.pdf.

McKinsey Global Institute (MGI). 2016. Digital globalisation: The new era of global flows. March 2016. http://www.mckinsey.com/business-functions/digital-mckinsey/our-insights/digital-globalization-the-new-era-of-global-flows.

Menon, J. 2007. Building blocks or stumbling blocks? The GMS and AFTA in Asia. *ASEAN Economic Bulletin* 24(2): 254–266. August 2007.

Menon, J. 2014a. Multilateralisation of preferences versus reciprocity when FTAs are underutilised. *The World Economy* 37: 1348–1366.

Menon, J. 2014b. How should we measure ASEAN's success? *East Asia Forum*. 10 April.

Menon, J. 2017. Supporting the growth and spread of international production networks in Asia: How can trade policy help? In *South Asia-East Asia Integration,* ed. Menon, J., and T.N. Srinivasan. Oxford: Oxford University Press.

Petri, P., M. Plummer, and F. Zhai. 2011. The trans-Pacific partnership and Asia–Pacific integration: a quantitative assessment. In *East–West Center Working Paper* No. 119. Hawaii.

World Bank. 2005. *Global economic prospects 2005: Trade, regionalism and development*. Washington, DC: World Bank.

Chapter 9
COVID19, Supply Chain Resilience, and India: Prospects of the Pharmaceutical Industry

Amitendu Palit and Preety Bhogal

The outbreak of COVID19 has had far-reaching implications for the global economy. One of the most significant repercussions is observed in global supply chains. For several years, even before the outbreak of COVID19, global businesses have been trying to enhance resilience of supply chains to minimize the adverse impact of disruptions arising from unanticipated events. The COVID19 pandemic has reinforced and accelerated these tendencies. Supply chain resilience has also become a geopolitical priority as several countries are keen on reducing their economic dependence on China. This chapter examines the supply chain resilience initiative (SCRI) in the Indo-Pacific region and its prospects for India in the context of the pharmaceutical industry. Identifying the prospects of India's pharmaceutical industry, as it seeks to decouple substantively from China, reveals important insights on the impact of economic and political factors in repositioning supply chains post-COVID19.

Economic Ministers from Australia, India, and Japan announced a joint initiative for enhancing resilience of supply chains on 1 September 2020.[1,] Noting the context provided by the COVID19 pandemic, the announcement emphasized the importance of enhancing resilience of supply chains in the Indo-Pacific region through regional cooperation. Nearly 8 months after the announcement, the initiative was formally launched on 27 April 2021. The statement issued on the occasion mentioned

---

[1] "Australia-India-Japan Economic Ministers' Joint Statement on Supply Chain," 1 September 2020, Department of Foreign Affairs and Trade, Australian Government, https://www.dfat.gov.au/news/media-release/australia-india-japan-economic-ministers-joint-statement-supply-chain.

[2] "Australia-India-Japan Trade Minister' Joint Statement on Launch of Supply Chain Resilience Initiative," 27 April 2021, Press Information Bureau, Government of India, https://pib.gov.in/PressReleseDetail.aspx?PRID=1714362.

A. Palit
Trade and Economics, National University of Singapore, Singapore, Singapore

P. Bhogal (✉)
Economics, Kansas State University, Manhattan, USA
e-mail: preetybhogal@ksu.edu

© The Author(s), under exclusive license to Springer Nature Singapore Pte Ltd. 2022
A. Palit (ed.), *Globalisation Impacts*, International Law and the Global South,
https://doi.org/10.1007/978-981-16-7185-2_9

sharing of best practices and investment promotion activities for moving forward on diversifying supply chains and increasing their resilience.[2]

1 Supply Chain Resilience: The Academic Perspective

Resilience of supply chains has been a widely discussed subject in business, psychology, ecology, and industrial engineering literature.[3] The focus on "resilience" for cross-border supply chains increased in the last decade. The disruptions caused by various natural calamities and socio-political developments in the early years of the past decade were responsible for the enhanced focus.[4] The academic literature on supply chain management has since devoted considerable attention to the unforeseen events and disruptions that create a range of uncertainties of varying degrees for supply chains, leading to concomitant adverse impacts for firms and businesses engaged in these chains.[5] Such disruptions are often a result of unforeseeable external shocks, such as natural disasters, pandemics, and terrorism. Indeed, the large variety of causes capable of disrupting supply chains has led to the academic literature focusing extensively on the importance of production networks becoming *resilient*.

Resilience, in this regard, has been variously defined: the definitions largely converge on the broad premise of abilities of supply chains to develop sufficient adaptive capacities to withstand unforeseen disruptions and their ability to return to normal operations.[6] A working definition could be the one used by the World Economic Forum (WEF): "Resilience is the ability of a global supply chain to reorganize and deliver its core function continually, despite the impact of external and or internal shocks to the system."[7]

---

[3] Martin and Sunley (2015) provide different definitions of "resilience" employed in various disciplines ranging from ecology to psychology.

[4] Some of the major catastrophes were the earthquake and tsunami in Fukushima in Japan, Hurricane Sandy in the US, floods in Thailand, the famines in Africa, outbreak of the Arab Spring in the Middle East, and prolonged social unrests in Europe and Africa. Disruptions also occurred as a state strategy of coercing partners and adversaries. China's use of the rare earths supply chain to force Japan's release of its fisherman during the 2012 Senkaku Island dispute. An Expert Group set up by the World Economic Forum (WEF) for studying supply chain resilience identified natural disaster and extreme weather, and conflict and political unrest and terrorism, as the most important risks for smooth functioning of supply chains. WEF (2013).

[5] Karl et al. (2018) provides a detailed review of the supply chain management literature, including the risks involved for supply chains, and the importance of various affected non-financial parameters, such as those relating to capacity, stocks, and quality of goods and services. Singh et al. (2019) canvass deeper on the academic reflections on resilience, and the parameters influencing resilience, while proposing a conceptual framework for expanding resilience and enhancing performance of supply chains.

[6] See Brandon-Jones et al. (2014) and Day (2014) for illustration of the concept of resilience in supply chains.

[7] WEF (2013), 18.

9 COVID19, Supply Chain Resilience, and India: Prospects ... 161

The research on the firm-level analysis of supply chains has identified various characteristics of supply chains that contribute to their resilience. Some of these include agility, in terms of the ability to respond quickly to unforeseen changes in demand and supply; flexibility, or the ease with which chains can adjust to new conditions; redundancy, as in the ability of chains to use up existing stock in emergencies; visibility, or the ability of supply chain managers to clearly visualize functions across the entire length of the chain for addressing disruptions; and information sharing on potential risks across various actors of the chain. In addition, a critical factor contributing to resilience, as noted by various studies, is collaboration.[8]

Collaboration among firms across the supply chain is variously noted to be critical for identifying risks and locating strategies for tackling disruptions arising from these risks. From a business perspective, partnerships are considered crucial for improving supply chain resilience. It can be achieved through greater security, increased sharing of information and knowledge,[9] along with institutionalizing multi-stakeholder supply chain risk assessment processes.

1.1 Resilience and Collaboration Between Countries

Supply chain disruptions can result from state strategies seeking to influence or coerce adversaries. Geopolitics has often disrupted economic exchanges resulting in significant dislocation of supply chains and trade patterns.[10] In recent history, the Chinese blockade of rare-earth elements to Japan, and Russia's disruption of flow of natural gas into Ukraine, following their territorial disputes over the Senkaku Islands and Crimea, respectively, demonstrate such state-sponsored disruptions in supply chains.[11] States use monopolies over supply chains to distort trade and extract economic and diplomatic leverage over adversaries, as was seen in President Trump's trade wars with China.[12]

Global supply chains underpin the complex and intricate network of economic interdependence enabled by economic globalization.[13] The emergence and perpetuation of these supply chains have been enabled by the logic of economic efficiency, emanating from "disintegration of production" through vertical specialization, revolution in information and technology, falling transport costs, and differentials in labor costs.[14] But in addition to economic efficiency, cross-border supply chains are products of political choices made by states in a particular historical context. The context

---

[8] Hsieh (2019), Papadopoulos et al. (2016).

[9] WEF (2013), 22, 27.

[10] Oldrich and Hodulak (2019).

[11] Bradsher (2010), Kirby (2014), Huang (2019) and Tabeta (2021).

[12] Woo (2007). Yukon and Smith (2020).

[13] Gereffi et al (2018).

[14] Nathan (2019).

was provided by the post-Cold War Washington Consensus envisioning liberal political ideas manifesting in outward-oriented economic strategies enabling countries to access global markets, capital, and technology through global supply chains.[15] The vision would be unfulfilled without countries cooperating with each other and minimizing geopolitical and geoeconomic tensions that hinder cooperation.[16]

It is important for countries to mutually cooperate for reducing supply chain vulnerabilities produced by geopolitical uncertainties and increasing resilience of supply chains. State-specific efforts in this regard can focus on increasing resilience by reducing lengths of supply chains and moving production in-shore, or re-shoring production to different geographies.[17] These are considered essential for reducing excessive dependencies on a particular location. Such dependencies can empower the sourcing location to exert supplier-driven monopolistic influence over those sourcing and capitalize the influence for political gains.[18]

India's efforts to make pharmaceutical supply chains more resilient involve both in-shoring of more production, by incentivizing greater domestic production of pharmaceutical raw materials and intermediate inputs, and collaborating with Japan and Australia on the SCRI. The ostensible objective behind both strategies is to reduce sourcing dependence on China and ameliorate the geopolitical advantage that China derives from being the world's largest source of pharmaceutical inputs.

2 Collaboration and SCRI

The emphasis on collaboration for expanding resilience of supply chains resonates with a similar emphasis in the articulation of the SCRI. As mentioned earlier, the proposed SCRI between Australia, Japan, and India, highlights regional cooperation for enhancing resilience of supply chains in the Indo-Pacific. In this respect, the purported goal of SCRI—enhancing resilience through multi-country cooperation—is not at variance with the thoughts echoed by academics and policy practitioners on supply chain resilience.

Two contexts, however, are extremely important for the SCRI. First, the stated collaboration between *countries*, which is distinct from the collaboration between autonomous businesses and firms in supply chains. However, as the previous section points out, country-specific collaborations for resilience can be spurred by geopolitical motivations. Such collaborations, while being distinct from those between firms, are not unusual.

Key supply chain decisions like aligning incentives, synchronizing production and distribution between firms,[19] and partnering and planning for anticipated disruptions

---

[15] Solingen (2021).

[16] Ibid.

[17] Aanstoos (2021).

[18] Solingen (2021).

[19] Papadopoulos et al. (2016).

and risks[20] are taken by the management of lead firms in the supply chain. The SCRI construct, as an instrument for minimizing disruptions and making supply chains resilient, extends the firm-specific notion of collaboration to a broader canvas of countries.

The second context that becomes specifically important is the articulation of SCRI in the aftermath of COVID19. Various supply chains across the world, such as in automobiles, food, textiles, information technology (IT), and energy, have suffered from disruptions on various occasions. Academic studies of resilience for supply chains operating in different parts of the world point to the importance of collaboration in anticipating disruptions, resisting them, and preparing for turnarounds.[21] The contexts of these academic studies, however, never included disruptions arising from momentous developments like the outbreak of the COVID19 pandemic. The annunciation of the RSCI in the aftermath of COVID19 is, therefore, significant.

Indeed, the outbreak of COVID19, and the collaboration between Japan, Australia, and India in announcing SCRI for enhancing supply chain resilience, underscores the geopolitics that has shaped the economic rationale of SCRI. Understanding the origins of SCRI, therefore, necessitates an enquiry into its political economy.

3 Political Economy of SCRI

The outbreak of COVID19 in early 2020 caused severe disruptions in major regional supply chains. The primary reason behind such disruptions was the disturbance experienced in sourcing key materials and inputs from China. The stringent lockdown announced in the Wuhan province, and many other parts of China led to various supply chains snapping at different points of sourcing.[22] These disruptions drew attention to the serious vulnerabilities inherent in the regional supply chains due to their excessive dependence on procuring from a single location—China, in this instance. Such extreme dependence—given the exponential spread of the pandemic and systemic unpreparedness in dealing with the unanticipated external shock—stretched resilience of supply chains to their farthest limits. Anxieties over the abilities of supply chains to resume normal operations forced several countries to consider prospects of lowering supply chain risks by reducing dependence on China.[23]

China is the largest source of imports for Japan, Australia, and India—the three proponents of SCRI. The heavy reliance of the three countries on imports from

---

[20] Qian et al. (2018).

[21] Singh et al. (2019).

[22] More than 50,000 companies have direct suppliers in Wuhan, while around 5 million companies have tier-two suppliers located in the province. More than 900 Fortune 500 companies have supply links with Wuhan (Braw 2020).

[23] Similar concerns, arising from very specific dependencies on a location, had earlier been experienced for natural calamities like floods in Thailand in 2011. Thailand was the source for a critical component used in the Lexus model of the leading Japanese automobile assembler Toyota. Disruption in supplies from Thailand halted production of Lexus (DBS 2020).

China, including finished products and raw materials and intermediates, makes them vulnerable to risks of shortages if supplies cease from China. The risks are for both final products and essential inputs to be further processed for making final products. For the latter, a typical example to be discussed at length in the chapter are bulk drug imports from China, which are used extensively in producing finished formulations by India's pharmaceutical industry.

The onset of COVID19 also marked a sharp escalation in geopolitical tensions with China for the proponent countries of the SCRI. India's relations with China touched their lowest point in several decades after a catastrophic border clash in the high Himalayas in June 2020, resulting in loss of several lives.[24] Australia's relations with China soured over a bitter trade war that saw Beijing imposing heavy restrictions on prominent Australian exports, such as barley, grain, and beef.[25] Japan's ties with China further complicated over rising friction around claims for disputed islands in the Pacific. Japan and Australia's support of the United States and other Western nations demanding an independent enquiry by the World Health Organization (WHO) over China's role in the spread of COVID19 further estranged China's relations with both countries.[26]

A realization of the economic dependence on China for the smooth functioning of supply chains, at a time when geopolitical tensions with China soared, would have made the proponents of SCRI wary of China's intention to weaponize economic dependence for strategic advantage. Political economy literature points to the power effects of asymmetric interdependence.[27] Economic interdependence is never symmetrical; states that are more dependent upon others for supply of critical goods may be vulnerable to economic coercion by the latter, especially if those critical supplies cannot be produced internally at a bearable cost and in a reasonable timeframe, and if no alternative sources of supply exist in the international market.[28]

The global economic integration witnessed in the last couple of decades transformed China into the critical node of global supply chains. It also bestowed upon Beijing an extraordinary heft in controlling critical supply chains, through key ingredients for finished products and intermediate components.[29] China's active use of economic coercion has only highlighted the vulnerability of extreme dependence of other economies on Chinese-controlled supply chains. The COVID19 pandemic not

---

[24] "India China clash: 20 Indian troops killed in Ladakh fighting," BBC, 16 June 2020; https://www.bbc.com/news/world-asia-53061476.

[25] "How China's trade restrictions are affecting the Australian economy," 26 November 2020, https://www.bt.com.au/insights/perspectives/2020/australia-china-relations.html. A particularly bitter spat between China and Australia was over China's use of social media in highlighting alleged war crimes by Australian armed forces, drawing sharp rebuke from the Australian Prime Minister Morrison. "Australia demands China apologise for posting 'repugnant' fake image," BBC, 30 November 2020, https://www.bbc.com/news/world-australia-55126569.

[26] Arase (2020).

[27] Gilpin (2017); Copeland (2015); Barbieri (2002); Farrell and Newmann (2019).

[28] For differences in sensitivity and vulnerability interdependence, see, Keohane and Nye (2011), 231–233.

[29] Oya (2021), WEF (2016).

only laid bare the power dynamics of control over critical medical and health-related supply chains but also the vulnerability of Asia's other major economies accruing out of their extreme dependence on China and the lack of alternative sources of supply.

In the light of the pandemic and global supply chain disruptions, strategic opinions across the globe have started weighing the pros and cons of such extreme dependence.[30] The underlying motivation for pushing the SCRI is arguably geopolitical with the initiative encouraging businesses to shift production from mainland China to other countries in the region. For Japan, Australia, and India, this would result in diversifying the procurement of supplies and reducing the risk of disruptions from over-dependence on a single source. It would also increase their strategic leverage of responding to an assertive China.

The wider ramifications of the geopolitical urge to decouple from China extend to the Indo-Pacific region. Australia, Japan, and India are major stakeholders in the Indo-Pacific construct. The mention of Indo-Pacific in the joint statement of Economic Ministers of the three countries referenced earlier underlines their intentions of extending the importance of realizing the vulnerability of supply chains arising due to over-dependence on China to all countries around the Pacific and Indian oceans adding up the Indo-Pacific geography. The slow and gradual institutionalization of the Quadrilateral Security Dialogue (Quad) in the last couple of years did indeed help the SCRI process. Though Quad was primarily a security hedge against China's military and territorial assertiveness in the region, the pandemic has also provided it with an economic rationale.[31] From a regional geopolitical competitive perspective, this seems as an effort to counter the weaponization of economic interdependence pursued by China through the Belt and Road initiative (BRI). By being a huge provider of funds for correcting infrastructure deficits in Asia and Africa, China aims to create a pan-continental network of economic markets and institutions.

India has not only committed to the SCRI but also has, in recent months, clearly expressed its intention to decouple from China. After its border clashes with China in Galwan Valley in June 2020, it has severely restricted Chinese inward investments and banned more than a hundred popular Chinese apps, such as TikTok and WeChat. It is also an active participant in collective efforts with the United States and several Western and Asian democracies to keep the Huawei out of their strategic domestic 5G telecommunication space.[32] Its enthusiastic participation in the RSCI, therefore, is unsurprising.

---

[30] Braw (2020) reflects on specific concerns with respect to China in terms of the control it has on global supply chains. As such, weaponizing economic superiority, particularly market access, has been highlighted with respect to the trade policy approach of the US under President Trump with the US using its dominance in the international economic order to coerce those countries acting against its national interests Mullan (2020).

[31] Mathur (2020), Bagchi (2020).

[32] "The UK is forging a 5G club of democracies to reduce reliance on Huawei," *Atlantic Council*, 2 June 2020, https://www.atlanticcouncil.org/blogs/new-atlanticist/the-uk-is-forging-a-5g-club-of-democracies-to-avoid-reliance-on-huawei/

The apparent effort to decouple and reduce economic dependence on China would impact the nature of the development of some of its major industries. Reorganization of regional and global supply chains featuring Indian businesses would be adversely affected, especially those that currently have close links with China. The pharmaceutical industry, perhaps, is the most important in this regard. The importance arises from pharmaceuticals being one of India's major exports and foreign-exchange-earners, with several Indian firms having developed pronounced capacities for exporting to global markets.

India's abilities to supply cheap medicines to the rest of the world, as well as its own large population, makes pharmaceuticals one of its most strategically important industries. The critical sourcing dependence of the industry on China makes it vulnerable to deleterious impacts of poor geopolitical ties with China. The prospects have been sharply highlighted following the outbreak of COVID19, which has seen worsening of China-India relations and India heavily augmenting efforts to produce vaccines and health products for internal and external use. The imperatives make the pharmaceutical industry a significant one for being analyzed closely. The next section analyzes the global role of India's pharmaceutical industry and its close supply chain links with China.

3.1 Section 3: India's Pharmaceutical Industry

The pharmaceutical industry in India took great strides under the post-TRIPS arrangements that came into force after the formation of the WTO.[33] From merely US$ 2 billion in 1996, India's total trade in pharmaceutical products has increased to US$ 21 billion in 2020, out of which exports comprised US$18 billion.[34] India has the largest number of USFDA-recognized drug manufacturing facilities outside of the USA. The Indian pharma industry's readiness to embed into global supply chains has been responsible for its rapid growth and structural transformation. The latter has involved fragmentation of production, in which Indian pharma has been outsourcing bulk drugs and APIs from China, and specializing in production of generic formulations for high-income OECD markets, while retaining focus on research and development (R&D).[35]

The growth of several local firms with efficient generic formulation production capacities was a result of the patent laws that prevailed in India in the 1970s and 1980s allowing patenting on pharmaceutical processes as opposed to products. During the 1970s, Indian firms pursued strategic decoupling from the global pharma industry to functionally upgrade.[36] Once these laws changed after the WTO and the TRIPS

---

[33] Dhar and Joseph (2019).

[34] Author's calculations using ITC Trade Map.

[35] Abrol and Singh (2019).

[36] Horner (2014).

9 COVID19, Supply Chain Resilience, and India: Prospects …

Table 1 World's top pharmaceutical exporting countries ($billion, 2017–2019)

Exporters	2017	2018	2019
Germany	83.8	96.4	90.3
Switzerland	70.4	75.2	83.0
United States of America	44.9	48.3	53.6
Ireland	38.3	53.5	53.4
Belgium	42.6	47.5	52.7
France	31.5	33.9	35.6
Italy	25.5	27.8	33.6
Netherlands	25.7	28.5	30.1
United Kingdom	32.7	30.1	27.1
Denmark	12.9	14.4	17.5
India	12.9	14.3	16.3
Spain	11.4	11.6	12.8
World	**528.6**	**587.1**	**617.5**

Source ITC Database

agreement came into force, Indian pharma stayed focused on its large-scale generic formulation production expertise.

Recoupling with global supply chains in the 1990s allowed Indian industry to shift from "copying products for developing markets to producing medicines for high-end markets."[37] At the same time, China's emergence as the world's largest producer of bulk drugs and APIs created enabling conditions for the emergence of a global pharmaceutical supply chain where Chinese and Indian specializations blended well. The blending has been organic making India's decoupling from China a difficult proposition.

4 India's Trade in Pharmaceuticals and Vaccines

India stands out among major global pharmaceutical exporters. It is the only developing economy, and the only economy from Asia, to have come close to figuring among the top ten global pharmaceutical exporting countries. As such, global pharmaceutical exports are dominated by the advanced Organisation for Economic Co-operation and Development (OECD) economies (Table 1). European countries, led by Germany and Switzerland, are the top-most pharmaceutical exporters. The United States is also one of the leading exporters along with Ireland and Belgium. Indeed, other than the United States, all the remaining top pharmaceutical exporters are from Europe.

---

[37] Huakonsson (2009).

Table 2 India's main destinations for pharmaceutical exports ($billion, 2017–2019)

Export Destinations	2017	Share in India's pharma exports to world (in %)	2018	Share in India's pharma exports to world (in %)	2019	Share in India's pharma exports to world (in %)
United States of America	4.6	35.6	5.0	35.2	6.4	39.1
South Africa	0.5	3.8	0.5	3.8	0.5	3.2
Russian Federation	0.4	3.1	0.4	2.9	0.5	2.9
United Kingdom	0.4	3.3	0.6	3.8	0.5	2.8
Nigeria	0.4	2.9	0.4	2.9	0.4	2.4
Germany	0.2	1.4	0.2	1.5	0.3	1.7
Brazil	0.2	1.6	0.3	1.8	0.3	1.7
Canada	0.2	1.3	0.2	1.7	0.3	1.7
Australia	0.2	1.7	0.2	1.7	0.3	1.5
Philippines	0.2	1.5	0.2	1.5	0.2	1.5
World	12.9		14.3		16.3	

Source Calculated by authors using ITC Database

India's pharmaceutical exports in 2017 were $12.9 billion, which were as much as those of Denmark, making Denmark and India the tenth largest pharmaceutical exporters globally in 2017. Since then, notwithstanding an increase in exports, India has slipped behind Denmark and was the eleventh largest pharmaceutical exporter for 2018 and 2019. Over time, India's share in global pharmaceutical exports has steadily increased from 1.4 percent in 2010 to 2.6 percent in 2019.[38] This increase has been largely due to the proficiencies that India's pharmaceutical industry has developed in large-scale production of generic drugs. India has become reputed as a major source of affordable off-patent generic drugs for the entire world owing to patent law reforms starting with the Patents Act of 1970.[39]

The United States is the largest destination of Indian pharmaceutical exports (Table 2). Indian pharmaceutical exports have obtained significant access in the US market due to the Generalized System of Preferences (GSP) scheme.[40] Apart from the United States, Indian exports have obtained significant market access in Europe (e.g. United Kingdom, Germany), Africa (e.g. South Africa, Nigeria), Asia (e.g. Australia, Philippines), and other major global markets like Russia, Canada, and Brazil (Table 2).

---

[38] Computed by Authors from the ITC Database.

[39] He (2019), 258.

[40] The withdrawal of the GSP scheme by the US from June 2019 might impact access prospects of some Indian medical exports according to industry opinions. Viveka Roychowdhury, "A silver lining to withdrawal of GSP benefits?," *Express Pharma*, 21 June 2019, https://www.expresspharma.in/editors-note/a-silver-lining-to-withdrawal-of-gsp-benefits/.

Table 3 World's top ten vaccine exporting countries ($billion, 2017–2019)

Exporters	2017	2018	2019
Belgium	6.0	6.3	9.4
Ireland	4.6	5.8	5.3
France	3.1	3.8	4.3
United Kingdom	4.2	4.3	3.4
United States of America	1.4	2.4	2.0
Italy	1.2	0.9	1.1
India	0.6	0.7	0.8
Netherlands	0.5	0.4	0.6
Poland	0.5	0.6	0.6
Germany	0.4	0.7	0.5
World	**24.3**	**28.0**	**30.2**

Source ITC Database

India's global reputation as a source of quick supplies of large amounts of essential medicine was visible during the escalation of the COVID19 pandemic.[41] India's decision to stop exports of hydroxychloroquine—an anti-malarial drug initially used for treating patients infected with COVID19—created a major stir in the international community as countries looked forward to obtaining the medicine from India. The US President Donald Trump reached out to Indian Prime Minister Narendra Modi for lifting the ban and allowing Indian firms to export.

The large-scale domestic capacity to produce generic formulations and vaccines has influenced India's ability to expand its pharmaceutical exports and earn the tag of being the "pharmacy of the world." India is positioned to play a vital role in supplying vaccines to the rest of the world for tackling COVID19.

As seen for overall pharmaceutical exports, India again, is an exception among a group of advanced OECD economies from Europe and United States, in being one of the largest vaccine exporters of the world (Table 3). India was the seventh-largest vaccine exporter (Table 3) during 2017–2019 with its share in global vaccine exports increasing from 0.8 percent to 3.9 percent during 2010–2019.[42] It is noteworthy that India's share in global exports of vaccines has increased at a much faster rate than its share in overall global pharmaceutical exports mentioned earlier.

---

[41] India handed over about 13 essential medicines, including hydroxychloroquine, azithromycin, and paracetamol, approx. 22 million metric tons, to Mozambique to support its efforts against the coronavirus pandemic. "India hands over 13 essential medicines to Mozambique in COVID19 fight," *The Economic Times*, 19 September 2020, https://economictimes.indiatimes.com/news/politics-and-nation/india-hands-over-13-essential-medicines-to-mozambique-in-covid-19-fight/articleshow/78198779.cms?from=mdr.

[42] Computed by Authors from the ITC Database.

Table 4 India's main destinations for vaccine exports ($billion, 2017–2019)

Export Destinations	2017	Share in India's vaccine exports to world (in %)	2018	Share in India's vaccine exports to world (in %)	2019	Share in India's vaccine exports to world (in %)
Nigeria	0.1	8.3	0.1	8.1	0.1	9.1
Bangladesh	0.0	2.9	0.0	3.5	0.1	7.6
Brazil	0.0	5.9	0.0	5.2	0.0	6.0
Pakistan	0.0	4.3	0.0	5.4	0.0	5.2
Congo, Democratic Republic of the	0.0	2.1	0.0	0.9	0.0	3.8
Philippines	0.0	2.7	0.0	2.7	0.0	3.0
Uganda	0.0	0.6	0.0	0.9	0.0	3.0
Egypt	0.0	2.1	0.0	3.1	0.0	2.9
Mexico	0.0	1.1	0.0	3.6	0.0	2.7
Turkey	0.0	0.9	0.0	0.7	0.0	2.5
World	0.6		0.7		0.8	

Source ITC Database

India's vaccine-making capacities, including that of the Serum Institute of India, the world's largest vaccine-maker,[43] and producer of the Covishield vaccine developed in collaboration with leading pharmaceutical firm AstraZeneca and the Oxford University, put it in a commanding position for leading the world's fight against COVID19. The capacities are complemented by the Covaxin vaccine developed by the Indian firm Bharat Biotech and more vaccines that are being developed by local firm Biological E, in collaboration with Johnson & Johnson of the US and Providence Therapeutics of Canada.[44] A sense of the international markets in India's neighborhood and elsewhere that are awaiting India's vaccines can be obtained from India's current top vaccine exporting destinations (Table 4).

It's important to note that unlike India's main markets for pharmaceutical exports (Table 2), which include the United States and several European economies (e.g. United Kingdom, Germany, Canada, Australia), the largest markets for India's vaccines include Latin American (e.g. Brazil, Mexico), African (e.g. Nigeria, Congo, Uganda), and other developing countries from Asia (e.g. Bangladesh, Pakistan, Egypt, Philippines). India's main vaccine export markets do not include the United States and European countries like Belgium, United Kingdom, Germany, France,

---

[43] Bird (2021).

[44] "India's Bilogical E to produce J&J COVID19 vaccine alongside its own candidate," *Mint*, 18 May 2021 https://www.livemint.com/news/india/indias-biological-e-to-produce-j-j-covid-vaccine-alongside-its-own-candidate-11621349774812.html; "COVID19: India's Biological E to manufacture Providence Therapeutics' mRNA vaccine," *Business Today* 1 June 2021 https://www.businesstoday.in/sectors/pharma/covid-19-indias-biological-e-to-manufacture-providence-therapeutics-mrna-vaccine/story/440586.html.

9 COVID19, Supply Chain Resilience, and India: Prospects …

Table 5 World's top vaccine importing countries ($billion, 2017–2019)

Importers	2017	2018	2019
Belgium	4.6	6.6	7.7
United States of America	5.1	5.8	7.3
United Kingdom	2.2	2.2	2.1
China	0.5	0.8	1.5
Germany	1.0	1.2	1.2
France	1.1	1.1	0.7
Brazil	0.7	0.7	0.7
Poland	0.7	0.8	0.7
Canada	0.5	0.5	0.6
Italy	0.5	0.6	0.6
Spain	0.4	0.4	0.5
Nigeria	0.0	0.1	0.5
India	0.2	0.3	0.4
World	24.6	28.5	32.3

Source ITC Database

Italy, and Spain that are the world's largest importers of vaccines (Table 5). Except for Brazil and Nigeria, none of India's top vaccine export destinations figure among the world's largest vaccine importers.

The prospects for India's pharmaceutical industry, including its role as a global supplier of COVID19 vaccines, need to be looked at in the light of India's commitment to the reorganization of regional supply chains for reducing dependence on China. In this regard, it is important to note that China does not figure as a major destination for India's pharmaceutical exports, not even vaccines, though it is one of the world's largest importer of vaccines (Table 5). The complex connection of India's pharmaceutical industry to China needs to be understood by studying the links in the pharmaceutical supply chain. It is interesting to note that India's efforts to reduce sourcing dependency on China in the pharma supply chain is not accompanied by similar efforts with respect to the US and EU, which are major suppliers of vaccine ingredients to India, and also likely to be major export markets for India-made COVID19 vaccines. Thus the overall tendency to decouple in pharma supply chain is clearly selective—focused on China—and with primary emphasis on formulations, as opposed to biological products like vaccines.

5 Supply Chain and Dependence on China

A close look at the pharmaceutical supply chain reveals interesting insights about India and China's positionings in the chain. The upstream, or the initial part of the chain, involves sourcing bulk drugs used as active pharmaceutical ingredients (APIs) in formulations, which are manufactured downstream, for retail sales to consumers. Almost all major global pharmaceutical firms are located in Europe and the United States, accounting for the dominance of the latter in global pharmaceutical exports. These firms control the supply chains through their proprietary knowledge of know-hows in making the finished formulations as well as the marketing and global distribution of the latter. Over time, many of these firms have become critically dependent on the supply of APIs from elsewhere. China in this regard has become an indispensable actor in global pharma supply chains by becoming the world's largest producer of APIs.[45] While India also produces APIs, China is by far a larger and wide-ranging producer of these items.

India, in contrast, has developed remarkable indigenous capacities for making formulations, especially cheaper versions of original formulations,[46] once they are no longer bound by intellectual property protection. India has been supplying these generic drugs to the global market by large amounts. Around a fifth of India's pharmaceutical exports comprise generic drugs that are sold to various markets of the world and are widely accepted because of their affordability.[47]

The markets for India's generic exports include, ironically, the United States and European markets, where many of the generic drugs are originally discovered and patented. These are also markets that are likely to become major destinations for affordable COVID19 vaccines produced in India, in the foreseeable future. The objective of enhancing supplies to home markets would have encouraged European and North American vaccine developers like Astrazeneca, Johnson & Johnson, Prudence, and Novavax to tie-up with Indian firms for utilizing the latter's large vaccine-making capacities.

India's capability as a major global pharmaceutical producer has been driven significantly by its access to APIs from China. This is evident from its large volume of antibiotic imports, sourced significantly from China (Tables 6 and 7). India was the world's largest importer of antibiotics,[48] which include bulk drugs used as APIs for producing formulations, along with Italy, in 2018 (Table 6). These large antibiotic imports highlight the Indian pharmaceutical industry's critical dependence on imports. The reliance on imports has increased over time with India's share in global antibiotic imports increasing from 6.6 percent to 10.8 percent during 2010–2019.[49] Indeed, India's imports of antibiotics are more than those of Germany, the United States, France, Belgium, and Switzerland, which are much larger pharmaceutical

---

[45] Medicines and Regulatory Products Healthcare Agency, International Strategy, 2017, United Kingdom (UK), https://assets.publishing.service.gov.uk/government/uploads/system/uploads/att achment_data/file/609425/Item_10__2017-OB-05__International_Strategy.pdf.

[46] Hill et al. (2018). For more information on prices of different medicines in India, United Kingdom, and South Africa, see supplementary appendix 1 of the paper. https://gh.bmj.com/content/3/1/e00 0571#DC1.

[47] Handbook of Pharmaceutical Export Promotion Council of India, Pharmexcil (2019) https://pha rmexcil.com/uploadfile/HandBook2019.pdf.

[48] The International Trade Centre (ITC) trade data classifies antibiotics under code HS2941 and lists them under organic chemicals.

[49] Computed by Authors from the ITC Database.

9 COVID19, Supply Chain Resilience, and India: Prospects …

Table 6 World's top ten antibiotics importing countries ($billion, 2017–2019)

Importers	2017	2018	2019
Italy	1.2	1.4	1.5
India	1.1	1.4	1.3
Germany	0.7	0.9	1.2
United States of America	0.7	0.9	0.9
China	0.5	0.5	0.7
France	0.8	0.8	0.6
Belgium	0.6	0.5	0.5
Japan	0.4	0.3	0.4
Switzerland	0.3	0.4	0.3
Spain	0.3	0.4	0.3
World	11.6	12.6	12.5

Source ITC Database

Table 7 India's main sources of antibiotics imports ($million, 2017–2019)

Import Sources	2017	Share in India's antibiotics imports from world (in %)	2018	Share in India's antibiotics imports from world (in %)	2019	Share in India's antibiotics imports from world (in %)
China	877.1	79.7	1120.2	77.3	1078.8	80.1
United States of America	34.1	3.1	60.6	4.2	31.5	2.3
Italy	30.5	2.8	39.1	2.7	31.4	2.3
Hong Kong, China	3.5	0.3	43.0	3.0	27.4	2.0
Spain	20.0	1.8	19.7	1.4	22.9	1.7
Mexico	17.2	1.6	17.8	1.2	19.4	1.4
United Kingdom	16.6	1.5	19.3	1.3	17.9	1.3
Denmark	6.1	0.6	14.8	1.0	17.8	1.3
Korea, Republic of	16.1	1.5	16.4	1.1	16.4	1.2
Slovenia	0.4	0.0	6.0	0.4	15.8	1.2
World	1100.1		1448.3		1346.6	

Source Calculated by authors using ITC Database

exporters than India (Table 1). It is noteworthy that India's rising share in global antibiotic imports has been in tandem with its rising share of global pharmaceutical, and vaccine exports, as mentioned in this section earlier. Finally, what is especially striking is India's overwhelming reliance on China for import of antibiotics to be used as APIs (Table 7).

China's traditional comparative advantage in being able to produce large volumes at low costs has enabled it to dominate the global APIs market. India, on the other hand, as mentioned earlier, benefitted from the global intellectual property rules that patented processes, not products, enabling the growth of an indigenous pharmaceutical manufacturing industry capable of producing large amounts of formulations cheaply.[50] But such capacities rely heavily on imports from China due to insufficient availabilities of APIs at home.

Both China and India, in their respective areas of specific competences, have emerged as significant actors in global pharma supply chains. These chains would disrupt from production setbacks in either China or India. From a global perspective, functioning upstream capacities in China for producing APIs, accompanied by similar utilization of downstream capacities in India for churning out formulations in bulk, are required by the world in tackling the COVID19 pandemic and other global health demands.[51] The next section explores by what extent efforts to reposition global supply chains might affect the current linkages between India and China in pharmaceutical supply chains with implications for supplies of medicines necessary for the world.

6 China Dependence, SCRI, and Vaccines

6.1 Reducing China Dependence: Domestic Efforts

India has committed its efforts for increasing resilience of regional supply chains by promoting the SCRI with Japan and Australia. Its current political ties with China are at their lowest ebb, making India's geopolitical intention to join projects for reducing supply dependencies on China, an urgent necessity. China's tendency to weaponize economic dependence, as mentioned earlier, is a major concern for India, given its import dependencies on the country. Nearly 80 percent of India's merchandise trade with China comprises India's imports in 2019, raising serious concerns over India's inability to reduce economic dependence on a neighbor,[52] with whom bilateral relations are turning more and more hostile.

The pharmaceutical industry's dependence on China symbolizes much of India's current anxiety over how economic linkages might prevent India from standing up to an assertive China. Organic chemical imports, particularly those of pharmaceutical intermediates, such as antibiotics and heterocyclic compounds, are among India's

---

[50] Horner (2020).

[51] Ibid.

[52] Calculated by authors using trade data from the World Integrated Trade Solution (WITS) database, World Bank. In 2019, the value of exports and imports for India from China was $17.2 and $68.4 billion, respectively.

largest imports from China, after machinery, and mechanical parts and components.[53] These imports are essential as India doesn't produce enough of some of the antibiotics for supplying the large requirements of its domestic formulation producing industry.[54]

The Modi government is looking to reduce India's overt dependence on China for the pharmaceutical supply chain through specific efforts targeted at increasing domestic manufacturing of drug intermediates and APIs. The efforts include creating bulk drug parks that would host facilities supporting various upstream functions of the pharmaceutical supply chain.[55] The primary objective of the scheme is to create an effective infrastructure for reducing the costs of producing APIs and drug intermediates in India—one of the main reasons behind the domestic industry's import dependence on China. At present, production costs of APIs in China is substantially less than that in India,[56] making imported intermediates from China a far more rational business decision for Indian formulation makers.[57]

Bulk drug parks are visualized with integrated infrastructure facilities that include effluent treatment plant, common warehouse, steam generation and distribution system, common logistics, laboratory testing center, intellectual property management services, etc.[58] The focus on building bulk drug parks with the facilities envisaged is an attempt to facilitate a conducive eco-system for encouraging domestic production of APIs. While laudatory, it is important to note that such infrastructure facilities will take several years to be implemented and become functional. The cost–benefit analysis justifying cheaper imports from China as opposed to home-grown products, is therefore likely to persist.

The government has also announced financial incentives, described production-linked incentives (PLI) for enhancing domestic production of a large number of APIs, bulk drugs, and drug intermediates that are currently being extensively imported.[59]

---

[53] Export Import Data Bank, Department of Commerce, Ministry of Commerce and Industry, Government of India. https://tradestat.commerce.gov.in/eidb/Icntcom.asp.

[54] According to the trade statistics from the International Trade Centre (ITC) Database, India is importing about $34.0 billion of Amoxycillin and its salts (used to treat bacterial infections) and $226.5 billion of 6-APA (used as an intermediate for producing antibiotics) from China.

[55] Guidelines of the Scheme Promotion of Bulk Drug Parks, Department of Pharmaceuticals, Ministry of Chemicals and Fertilizers, Government of India, https://pharmaceuticals.gov.in/sites/default/files/Guidelines%20of%20the%20Scheme%20Promotion%20of%20Bulk%20Drug%20Parks_1.pdf.

[56] "Govt expands PLI scheme: India seeks to cull China reliance with latest move to boost bulk drug manufacturing," *Times Now Digital*, 30 October 2020,
    https://www.timesnownews.com/business-economy/industry/article/govt-expands-pli-scheme-india-seeks-to-cull-china-reliance-with-latest-move-to-boost-bulk-drug-manufacturing/674904.

[57] Palit (2021b).

[58] Ibid.

[59] "Revised Guidelines Dated 29.10.2020 for the Production Linked Incentive (PLI) Scheme for promotion of domestic manufacturing of critical Key Starting Materials (KSMs) I Drug Intermediates (Dis) I Active Pharmaceutical Ingredients (APIs) in India," Department of Pharmaceuticals, Ministry of Chemicals and Fertilizers, Government of India.
    https://pharmaceuticals.gov.in/schemes.

Rising geopolitical tensions with China even before the onset of the COVID19 pandemic was agitating Indian policymakers over the necessity of developing home-grown capacities for APIs and intermediates as indicated by industry experts.[60] Announcement of PLIs soon after the outbreak of COVID19, and the violent border clashes in June 2020, reflect the policy materialization of deep-rooted anxieties over China dominating pharmaceutical supply chains.

The incentives have attracted several investors and the first round of proposals for the production of major APIs like penicillin G and erythromycin thiocyanate—at present being fully imported by India—have been approved for implementation.[61] However, like bulk drugs parks, the current and subsequent investments into producing APIs would take several years to mature—both by volumes and scales—to a level where India becomes self-sufficient by reducing its import dependence on China.

Indian pharmaceutical producers cannot afford to wait for domestic supplies of APIs to expand and then respond to the rising demand for their products in the world market. This underpins a distinct character of the Indian pharmaceutical industry and its integration in global supply chains—the dependence on imported sourcing upstream—that is unlikely to change in the foreseeable future.

The limited prospects of decoupling from China in API sourcing for finished formulations, however, doesn't apply to biological products like vaccines. Indian producers manufacturing vaccines are more reliant on the West for supply of essential ingredients than on China.[62] The API dependence on China, therefore, is unlikely to affect Indian pharma industry's ability to supply vaccines.[63] This perhaps explains the policy urge to ramp up domestic production of APIs through PLI and bulk drug parks, whereas no such urgency is noted for expanding local production of inputs being used in vaccines. India did, however, urge the US—a major source of its essential vaccine raw materials—to lift export restrictions on the latter for enabling faster production of vaccines by the SII and other local firms.[64] These restrictions, notwithstanding great demand for vaccines, did not activate the kind of policy urgency in India that perceived disruptions from China did. The "selective" urgency is obviously more a product of geopolitical angst, and hardly of economics!

---

[60] "India working to reduce reliance on Chinese drugs as tensions rise," The Straits Times, June 21, 2020. https://www.straitstimes.com/asia/south-asia/india-working-to-reduce-reliance-on-chinese-drugs-as-tensions-rise.

[61] "First set of five bulk drug, pharma input projects under PLI scheme cleared," *The Hindu Business Line*, 22 January 2021, https://www.thehindubusinessline.com/companies/first-set-of-five-bulk-drug-pharma-input-projects-under-pli-scheme-cleared/article33637838.ece

[62] Evenett, et al. (2021).

[63] L-histidine—a non-key ingredient used in the AstraZeneca vaccine being made by the Serum Institute of India—is sourced significantly from China. Ministry of Commerce and Industry Export–Import Data Bank, https://tradestat.commerce.gov.in/eidb/default.asp. For components of AstraZeneca vaccine, see Toufexi (2020).

[64] "US defends restrictions on export of COVID19 vaccine raw materials amid India's request to lift ban," *The Hindu*, April 23, 2021. https://www.thehindu.com/news/international/us-defends-restrictions-on-export-of-covid-19-vaccine-raw-materials-amid-indias-request-to-lift-ban/article34391251.ece

7 Can SCRI Reduce Dependence?

Does the SCRI offer India any opportunities for sourcing substantial APIs from other countries? The SCRI, until now, is looking to come up around East Asia, Oceania, South, and Southeast Asia. These are the regions that include Japan, Australia, and India, as well as countries that the RSCI is incentivizing for investors to relocate from China.[65] India's current imports of APIs do reflect some sourcing from countries in this geography, such as from Japan, Australia, Hong Kong, Indonesia, Korea, Vietnam, Singapore, Taiwan, and Thailand.[66] But except for Hong Kong and Korea, none of these countries are among India's major sources of antibiotics (Table 7). Even Hong Kong and Korea are not as large sources of antibiotics for India as China.

India's procurement possibilities and the prospects of switching antibiotic imports from China would increase if the SCRI expands to include countries from Europe, as several European countries—Italy, Spain, United Kingdom, Denmark, and Slovenia (Table 7)—are among India's major sources for antibiotics. However, much will depend on the costs of procuring antibiotics from Europe as compared with China.

The possibility of SCRI facilitating a broad coalition of countries for engaging in pharmaceutical trade excluding China is evident from the Quad announcing a vaccine partnership. While India is envisaged the hub of vaccine production in the initiative, the US and Japan are providing financial support for making of, and storage of vaccines, and Australia the logistics for "last mile" delivery in the Indo-Pacific.[67] The partnership couldn't have been envisaged had the Quad members not been confident of sourcing vaccine ingredients among themselves without relying on China. Thus vaccines, clearly, are different from formulations, in the extent of their supply chain sourcing dependencies on China. This explains why US vaccine developers are tying up with Indian firms for vaccine production without worrying over supplies from China being disrupted.

Besides vaccines, being a part of the SCRI can help the Indian pharmaceutical industry in obtaining greater access to SCRI member country markets as these countries look to engage more with India for reducing their reliance on China. Australia, Vietnam, Philippines, Japan, and Thailand, which are currently India's top twenty-five export destinations, but not among the top ten, could start importing more from India, as they look towards participating in regional efforts for increasing the resilience of the supply chains. Over time, India and some of these countries might explore the possibility of a harmonious relationship along the pharmaceutical supply chain, where some of these countries start supplying more APIs to India, and India ramps up its formulation exports to them.

---

[65] "Japan adds India and Bangladesh to China exit subsidy destinations," *Nikkei Asia,* 4 September 2020, https://asia.nikkei.com/Economy/Japan-adds-India-and-Bangladesh-to-China-exit-subsidy-destinations

[66] These are for antibiotics mentioned in footnote 53 earlier.

[67] "Fact Sheet: The Quad Summit," The White House, 12 March 2021. https://www.whitehouse.gov/briefing-room/statements-releases/2021/03/12/fact-sheet-quad-summit/

8 Conclusion

Efforts to increase resilience of regional supply chains have accelerated in Asia after the outbreak of COVID19. The economic rationale of achieving higher resiliency by minimizing supply dependence on a single source has converged with the geopolitical intention to diminish possible weaponization of such dependence by China. The result has been the formation of the SCRI by India, Japan, and Australia. SCRI not only aims to reduce economic dependence on China but also neutralize China's strategic leverage through its monopolies on supply chains. However, even as India commits such collective efforts to economically decouple from China, the prospects appear limited in the foreseeable future. This is particularly evident for India's pharmaceutical industry that depends heavily on China for sourcing APIs.

Indian pharmaceutical industry's strategic dependence on China, and the inability to shake off such dependence in the foreseeable future, underpins the concerns of a prominent global rising power like India, in feeling constrained to resist the assertive intent of an economically mightier major power like China. The anxiety has precipitated collaborative efforts to delink supply chains from China. However, efforts like SCRI won't lead to significant relocation of the pharmaceutical supply chain unless India emerges a more efficient producer of bulk drugs and APIs from the perspective of its own finished formulation producers. India's challenge in this regard remains substantial.[68]

Indian pharmaceutical industry's dependence on China is historical. Such dependence, arising from specific comparative advantages, in upstream sourcing from China, and downstream final formulation production for India, has served the supply chain well. Reorganizing the supply chain by overlooking the distinct comparative advantages would be counterproductive. Indeed, the study of the Indian pharmaceutical industry and its supply chain linkages to China underpin the limited success that geopolitical drivers to decouple economies might have,[69] if supply chain connections are firmly embedded to specific production efficiencies.

References

Aanstoos, Kristen. 2021. "Hidden economic costs of geopolitical disputes for supply Chains in East Asia". In: Solingen, E. (Ed.). (2021). *Geopolitics, supply chains, and international relations in East Asia.* Cambridge: Cambridge University Press.

Abrol, D., & Singh, N. (2019). Indian pharmaceutical industry: Policy and institutional challenges of moving from manufacturing generics to drug discovery. In: D. Nathan, M. Tewari, & S. Sarkar (Eds.), *Development with global value chains: Upgrading and innovation in Asia* (Development Trajectories in Global Value Chains, pp. 279–315). Cambridge: Cambridge University Press. https://doi.org/10.1017/9781316221730.012.

---

[68] Palit (2021a).

[69] Palit (2021b).

9 COVID19, Supply Chain Resilience, and India: Prospects …

Arase, David. 2020. The COVID-19 pandemic complicates Japan-China relations: Will this benefit ASEAN?. Perspective 83. ISEAS Yusof Ishak Institute: Singapore.

Bagchi, Indrani. 2020. India, quad-plus countries discuss Covid-19 battle, economic resurgence. *The Times of India*, 28 March. https://timesofindia.indiatimes.com/india/india-quad-plus-countr ies-discuss-covid-19-battle-economic-resurgence/articleshow/74861792.cms.

Barbieri, Katherine. 2002. *The liberal illusion: Does trade promote peace?* Ann Arbor: The University of Michigan Press.

Bird, Mike. 2021. India's vaccine colossus is a model for the world to follow. *The Wall Street Journal*. https://www.wsj.com/articles/indias-vaccine-colossus-is-a-model-for-the-world-to-follow-11609930891

Bradsher, Keith. 2010. Amid tension, china blocks vital exports to Japan. New York Times. 22 September. https://www.nytimes.com/2010/09/23/business/global/23rare.html;

Brandon-Jones, Emma, Brian Squire, Chad W. Autry, and Kenneth J. Petersen. 2014. A contingent resource-based perspective of supply chain resilience and robustness. *Journal of Supply Chain Management* 50 (3): 55–73.

Braw, Elisabeth. 2020. Blindsided on the supply side. *Foreign Policy*. 4 March. https://foreignpo licy.com/2020/03/04/blindsided-on-the-supply-side/

Copeland, Dale C. 2015. *Economic interdependence and war*. New Jersey: Princeton University Press.

Day, Jamison M. 2014. Fostering emergent resilience: The complex adaptive supply network of disaster relief. *International Journal of Production Research* 52 (7): 1970–1988.

DBS. 2020. Navigating supply chain disruptions. 2020 Asian insights conference Notes #4, 3 August; Economics & Strategy, DBS Flash. https://www.dbs.com/aics/templatedata/article/gen eric/data/en/GR/082020/200803_insights_aic_notes4.xml

Dhar, Biswajit, and Joseph, Reji.K. 2019. The challenges, opportunities and performance of the Indian pharmaceutical industry post-TRIPS," K.-C. Liu, U. S. Racherla (Eds.), Innovation, economic development, and intellectual property in India and China, ARCIALA Series on Intellectual Assets and Law in Asia, pp. 299–323. https://doi.org/10.1007/978-981-13-8102-7_13.

Evenett, Simon J, Bernard Hoekman, Nadia Rocha and Michele Ruta. 2021. The COVID-19 vaccine production club', 9565, policy research Working Paper, World Bank Group, March. https://openknowledge.worldbank.org/bitstream/handle/10986/35244/The-Covid-19-Vaccine-Production-Club-Will-Value-Chains-Temper-Nationalism.pdf?sequence=1&isAllowed=y

Farrell, Henry, and Abraham L. Newmann. 2019. Weaponised interdependence: How global economic networks shape state coercion. *International Security* 44 (1): 42–79.

Gereffi, G., Humphrey, J., & Sturgeon, T. (2018). The governance of global value chains. In G. Gereffi (Author), Global value chains and development: Redefining the contours of 21st Century Capitalism (Development Trajectories in Global Value Chains, pp. 108–134). Cambridge: Cambridge University Press. https://doi.org/10.1017/9781108559423.005

Gilpin, Robert. 2017. The nature of the political economy. In: *International politics: Enduring concepts and contemporary issues,* Robert J Art and Robert Jervis (eds.) London: Pearson

He, Juan. 2019. Indian patent law and its impact on the pharmaceutical industry: What can china learn from India?. In: *Innovation, economic development, and intellectual property in India and China*, edited by Kung-Chung Liu, Uday S. Racherla. Singapore: Springer.

Hill, Andrew M., Melissa J. Barber, and Dzintars Gotham. 2018. Estimated costs of production and potential prices for the WHO Essential Medicines List. *BMJ Glob Health* 3:e000571.

Horner, Rory. 2014. Strategic decoupling, recoupling and global production networks. *Journal of Economic Geography* 14 (6) : 1117–1140.

Horner, Rory. 2020. The world needs pharmaceuticals from China and India to beat coronavirus. *The Conversation*, 25 May 2020. https://theconversation.com/the-world-needs-pharmaceuticals-from-china-and-india-to-beat-coronavirus-138388

Hsieh, Fu-Shiung. 2019. Dynamic configuration and collaborative scheduling in supply chains based on scalable multi-agent architecture. *Journal of Industrial Engineering International* 15: 249–269.

Huakonsson, Stine Jessen 2009. The changing governance structures of the global pharmaceutical value Chain. *COMPETITION & CHANGE* 13(1): 77.

Huang, Yukon and Jeremy Smith. 2020. In U.S.-China trade war, new supply Chains Rattle Markets. *Carnegie Endowment for International Peace,* 24 June. https://carnegieendowment.org/2020/06/24/in-u.s.-china-trade-war-new-supply-chains-rattle-markets-pub-82145

Huang, Eustance. 2019. Shares of rare earth miners skyrocket after Beijing threatens to cut off the minerals. *CNBC*, 28 May. https://www.cnbc.com/2019/05/29/rare-earth-miners-shares-rise-after-china-threatens-to-cut-off-supply.html;

Karl, Alexandre Augusto, Julio Micheluzzi, Luciana Rosa Leite, and Carla Roberta Pereira. 2018. Supply chain resilience and key performance indicators: a systematic literature review. *Production* 28: e20180020.

Keohane, Robert O., and Joseph S. Nye. 2011. *Power and interdependence*, 4th ed. New York: Longman, Pearson.

Kirby, Paul. 2014. Russia's gas fight with Ukraine. *BBC*, 31 October. https://www.bbc.com/news/world-europe-29521564.

Martin, Ron, and Peter Sunley. 2015. On the notion of regional economic resilience: Conceptualization and explanation. *Journal of Economic Geography* 15: 1–42.

Mathur, Kanchi. 2020. The quad and Covid-19. *Australian Outlook,* 28 May. https://www.internationalaffairs.org.au/australianoutlook/the-quad-and-covid-19/.

Mullan, Terrence. 2020. The corrosion of world order in the age of donald trump. *Council on Foreign Relations*, 13 February. https://www.cfr.org/blog/corrosion-world-order-age-donald-trump

Nathan, D. (2019). GVCs and development policy: Vertically specialized industrialization. In D. Nathan, M. Tewari, & S. Sarkar (Eds.), *Development with global value Chains: Upgrading and innovation in Asia* (Development Trajectories in Global Value Chains, pp. 373–408). Cambridge: Cambridge University Press. https://doi.org/10.1017/9781316221730.015.

Oldrich, Krpec and Vladan Hodulak. 2019. War and international trade: Impact of trade disruption on international trade patterns and economic development. *Brazilian Journal of Political Economy* 39(1): 152:172.

Oya, Shin. 2021. It's time to reduce the world's trade dependence on China," *The Japan Times,* 26 January 2021. https://www.japantimes.co.jp/opinion/2021/01/26/commentary/world-commentary/api-china-trade/.

Palit, Amitendu. 2021a. Will India's disengaging trade policy restrict it from playing a greater global role? *World Trade Review* 1–17.

Palit, Amitendu. 2021b. COVID19, Supply Chains and Dependence on China: The Indian perspective. In: *Questioning the pandemic's impact on the indo-Pacific: Geopolitical Gamechanger? Force for Deepening National Identity Clashes? Cause of Shifting Supply Chains?*; Joint US-Korea Academic Studies, 2021, Vol 32; Korea Economic Institute of America. 30 July 2021. https://keia.org/wp-content/uploads/2021/07/KEI_Joint-US-Korea_2021_210728.FINAL_.pdf

Papadopoulos, Thanos, Angappa Gunasekaran, Rameshwar Dubey, Nezih Altay, Stephen J. Childe, and Samuel Wamba. 2016. The role of big data in explaining disaster resilience in supply chains for sustainability. *Journal of Cleaner Production* 142: 1108–1118.

Qian, Xueming, Yanqiao Ma, and Huan Feng. 2018. Collaboration space division in collaborative product development based on a genetic algorithm. *Journal of Industrial Engineering International* 14: 719–732.

Singh, Chandra, Gunjan Soni, and Gaurav Kumar Badhotiya. 2019. Performance indicators for supply chain resilience: Review and conceptual framework. *Journal of Industrial Engineering International* 15 (Suppl): S105–S117.

Solingen, E. (2021). Introduction: Geopolitical Shocks and Global Supply Chains. In E. Solingen (Ed.), *Geopolitics, Supply Chains, and International Relations in East Asia* (pp. 1–20). Cambridge: Cambridge University Press. doi:https://doi.org/10.1017/9781108985468.002

Tabeta, Shunsuke. 2021. "China tightens rare-earth regulations, policing entire supply chain," *Nikkei Asia*, 16 January. https://asia.nikkei.com/Business/Markets/Commodities/China-tightens-rare-earth-regulations-policing-entire-supply-chain;

Toufexi, Ioanna. 2020. "Covid-19: What are the ingredients in the Oxford/AstraZeneca vaccine?," Cambridge-News, 30 December 2020, https://www.cambridge-news.co.uk/news/uk-world-news/covid-19-what-ingredients-oxfordastrazeneca-19538759

Woo, Wing Thye. 2007. "Dealing Sensibly with the Threat of Disruption in Trade with China: The Analytics of Increased Economic Interdependence and Accelerated Technological Innovation." Working Paper. Washington, DC: Brookings Institution. https://www.brookings.edu/wp-content/uploads/2016/06/1018_trade_woo.pdf;

World Economic Forum (WEF). 2013. "Building Resilience in Supply Chains." http://www3.weforum.org/docs/WEF_RRN_MO_BuildingResilienceSupplyChains_Report_2013.pdf

World Economic Forum. 2016. "The Age of Economic Coercion: How Geo-politics is Disrupting Supply Chains, Financial Systems, Energy Markets, Trade and the Internet." http://www3.weforum.org/docs/WEF_Age_of_Economic_coercion.pdf

Chapter 10
Globalization and New Developments: Towards a More Fragmented World?

Amitendu Palit

1 The Crisis of Interdependence

Over the last three decades, the world has become interconnected in a manner hardly witnessed before. The scale and speed of the interconnection have been remarkable, more so because it happened after four decades of disconnection between countries, as a result of the ideological split inflicted by the Cold War. Looking back, the four decades after the end of the Second World War in the 1940s, were years during which the world competed over parallel systems, ideologies, practices, and politics, created by the US-Russia divide. The end of the Cold War and the commencement of economic globalization in a liberal world order led to the astonishingly fast growth of global interconnections.

An interconnected world has also produced significant interdependences. Nothing symbolizes these interdependences better than global supply chains. Over time, 'made in' labels sporting names of specific countries have become largely meaningless, as supply chains ensure items are no longer manufactured in 'a' country but are produced by multiple countries, each distinct by the value it contributes to production. The steady obliteration of 'country' from the understanding of global production has been complemented by the growth of a global workforce, the emergence of a group of 'global' cities (e.g. London, New York, Sydney, Shanghai, Singapore, Dubai, Hong Kong, Mumbai), and the growth of 'global' citizens, benefitting significantly from the opportunities and possibilities created by globalization.

Economic globalization of the last three decades has led to national economies becoming significantly dependent on other countries, both as producers and consumers. Liberal trade policies have led to countries specializing in areas of their comparative advantages, often using imports for boosting such efficiencies. A populous country like India, while being deficient in domestic availability of crude oil and resorting to large imports, has developed notable capacities for refining crude and

---

A. Palit (✉)
National University of Singapore, Singapore, Singapore

© The Author(s), under exclusive license to Springer Nature Singapore Pte Ltd. 2022   183
A. Palit (ed.), *Globalisation Impacts*, International Law and the Global South,
https://doi.org/10.1007/978-981-16-7185-2_10

producing petroleum products (e.g. petrol, diesel, aviation turbine fuel) for domestic consumption as well as large-scale exports. In industries employing large numbers of workers, such as readymade garments, India's greatest prominence has been in exports of textile yarn, which have been ably worked upon by Bangladesh, Cambodia, Vietnam, and China to produce fabric and garment, on the back of designs supplied by supply chain managers based in the US and Europe. More such examples of countries enmeshing in a closely integrated network of production and consumption relationships are in abundance. The short point of such interconnection is countries today are no more in a position to live without each other.

The realization of interconnectedness leading to interdependence, and the concomitant imperative to 'work' with other countries, is not always a welcome option for individual countries. Given the necessity of sustaining 'bad marriages' due to economic compulsions, countries do explore ways and means for either hedging against the possibility of such marriages failing, or making the coexistence work for individual gains. The current post-liberal world order, characterized by rivalries between major powers—US and China—underlines these scenarios vividly, more so in the post-COVID19 scenario.

Reorganization of global supply chains for reducing economic dependency on China, as witnessed in the aftermath of COVID19, is a typical example of countries' resorting to hedging—striking alliances with friendly countries—to avoid the possibility of overdependence on China compromising their capacities to respond to China's assertive behavior. Efforts by India, Japan, Australia, and several other countries to work together for repositioning supply chains reflect their anxieties in this regard. On the other hand, China's purported intention is ostensibly to maximize the benefits emanating from the economic clout that it has come to enjoy. The fact that Chinese President Xi Jinping reached out to American and European businesses urging them to resist efforts by their countries to decouple from China[1] demonstrates China's efforts to utilize its formidable economic appeal for connecting to global businesses, notwithstanding its relations with the US has declined to almost toxic levels since the outbreak of COVID19.

Concerns over 'loss' from economic interdependence have become prominent among countries in a world order fractured by major power rivalry. Countries like Russia and Iran have been at the receiving end of the US policies in this regard. Financial sanctions imposed by the US made it difficult for both countries to have adequate leverage in accessing funds in a global financial system overwhelmingly dominated by dollar-based transactions and US institutions. Indeed, the dominance of the modern global financial system by the US and the American dollar—and its attendant implications—might have implicitly encouraged some countries to own and popularize digital currencies.[2] President Trump's arm-twisting of US trade partners

---

[1] Pottinger (2021).

[2] China has already issued its own digital currency—the digital yuan—while Russia is planning to issue digital rouble. Other countries that have issued their own crypto-currencies include Singapore, Tunisia, Ecuador, and Senegal. https://www.fxempire.com/education/article/the-next-crypto currency-evolution-countries-issue-their-own-digital-currency-443966. Accessed on 3 April 2021.

by raising tariffs on exports to the US (e.g. for China, as well as for steel and aluminum imports at large) and withdrawing preferential access for exports (e.g. GSP benefits from India) mark efforts to extract a price for economic interdependence. Concerns over China extracting a high price for the dependence that most major countries of the world have on it, become manifold, given China's aggressive intentions visible in several geographies (e.g. Indian Ocean, South China Sea, South Asia, Himalayas). The price of dependence is not just for trade and investments; it is also concerning China's proficiencies in 5G technologies and giant retail businesses like Alibaba and Tencent, emerging viable competitors to their US counterparts, and spreading deep in industrial and consumer spectrums of several countries of the world.

In retrospect, the prominence of the downsides of economic interdependence, as visible now, was inevitable in a world where the rivalry between major powers makes geo-economics take precedence over economic perspectives. The current US-China relationship, particularly after COVID19, is no more a relationship of competition for economic superiority; it has elevated into a competition for political gains, security and defense advantages, and in the superiority of beliefs and systems, as embodied by liberal ideas and democratic principles, as opposed to state control and autocracies. It is therefore perfectly logical that economic interdependence, as promoted and permeated by economic globalization since the end of the Cold War in the early 1990s, will no longer be looked at as a benign and 'win-win' bonding in the current conditions. Rather, the pitfalls of such bonding in terms of potential damage for national interests, including security and strategic interests, would be scrutinized closely not just by the two key rivals—China and India—but also other global actors looking to hedge against 'costs' of interdependence and diversifying risks.

The geo-economic perspective is expected to prevail in the world order shaping around COVID19 as alliances and partnerships restructure on political grounds and 'manage' economic and business relationships accordingly. There will be lasting effects of such a perspective on global institutions and the character of globalization.

2 Trade Bodies Will Change, as Will Trade Rules

Economic globalization in the liberal world order was premised on the functioning of institutions and rules. Among institutions, WTO played a pivotal role in setting out rules of trade between countries. Its agenda widened over time to include a variety of issues that are connected to global trade, but distinct by their complexities. These include environment, labor, investments, financial services, movement of people, intellectual property, e-commerce, and cross-border data rules. The WTO has struggled to handle these issues like global trade, and economic globalization has developed new complexities due to the advancement of technology and growth of new issues connected with cross-border commercial exchanges. The WTO's difficulties in addressing these new sets of issues have encouraged several of its members to focus on regional and bilateral trade agreements for working out common rules on the issues within a smaller group of members. The WTO's problems are going to accentuate as the notion of security impacts economic globalization in ways not visualized before.

One of the substantive challenges before the WTO would be to co-exist with trade and economic partnership agreements fashioned by geo-economics. The WTO is a product of an economic vision, aiming to maximize economic gains from trade for the world as a whole, through an increase in such gains for all participating countries. However, when economic perspectives are combined with political and security interests, geo-economics emerge, making purely economic interest-based architectures disconnected from geo-economic frameworks. An architecture like the Trans-Pacific Partnership (TPP)[3] comprising the US and several of its allies from the Asia-Pacific, pursued vigorously by the Obama Administration, is an example of trade agreements being fashioned on geo-economic lines: on this occasion, specifically for counterbalancing the Chinese influence in the Asia-Pacific. A similar view was expressed concerning the Regional Comprehensive Economic Partnership (RCEP),[4] which, while premised on the Association of Southeast Asian Nations (ASEAN) architecture, could well be a China-dominated framework for regional trade.[5] With the post-COVID19 fissures experienced by the world order and the rivalry between the US and China, more trade alliances positioned on geo-economic grounds cannot be ruled. The recent energy picked up by the Quad, comprising the US, Japan, Australia, and India, might mature into a comprehensive trade and economic partnership framework.[6] At the same time, a large number of major trade agreements, such as between the European Union and Japan, the United Kingdom and Japan, and between the European Union and Vietnam, are all agreements that reflect recognition of current geopolitical realities. In some respects, these are agreements that serve multiple geopolitical interests, foremost among which is hedging against excessive dependence on China and avoiding the disruptive consequences of US-China trade friction.

Apart from geo-economic tussles, systemic challenges also await the WTO. The WTO-led global trade order, which has been a fundamental component of economic globalization, is likely to find itself getting squeezed in a global trade space, where several trade alliances and frameworks will emerge outside of its purview. The marginalization might increase if countries start working on issue-specific trade

---

[3] The TPP now functions as the Comprehensive and Progressive Trans-Pacific Partnership (CPTPP), after the Trump Administration withdrew the US from it in January 2017. The CPTPP includes Australia, Brunei, Canada, Chile, Japan, Malaysia, Mexico, New Zealand, Peru, Singapore, and Vietnam. https://www.mti.gov.sg/Improving-Trade/Free-Trade-Agreements/CPTPP. Accessed on 3 April 2021.

[4] The RCEP includes Australia, Brunei, Cambodia, China, Indonesia, Japan, Korea, Laos, Malaysia, Myanmar, New Zealand, Philippines, Thailand, Singapore, and Vietnam. https://www.dfat.gov.au/trade/agreements/not-yet-in-force/rcep. Accessed on 3 April 2021.

[5] Obama, Barack. 2016. The then US President Barack Obama urged the US legislators to support TPP, as otherwise the RCEP, which included China as its largest member-economy, would get to significantly craft the rules of trade in the region.

[6] Aghi (2020).

agreements that they feel are best negotiated outside the WTO. This is best exempli-fied by the efforts of a large number of WTO members to launch detailed talks on negotiating trade and e-commerce issues at the WTO.[7] These members, comprising a vast cross-section of the WTO's membership, hold the view that WTO's current work agenda on e-commerce needs to be sufficiently expanded to include many modern dimensions. At the heart of the efforts is the view that WTO needs to note the reality of e-commerce being an important issue in modern trade and the fact that if current global trade rules can't allow an expanded discussion on the subject, then they can be discussed parallelly among members outside the WTO. These tenden-cies, to discuss issues on the 'sidelines', or completely bypass the WTO, are likely to increase the number of plurilateral negotiations at the WTO—a natural outcome of economic globalization no longer being visualized through a multilateral and inclusive prism. The growth of plurilateral and parallels, however, might erode the multilateral character of the WTO, which would defeat the original objective of its establishment. Indeed, multilateral or global rules, particularly in trade, are essential for the survival of economic globalization. Charring of such rules might not enable WTO to contribute to globalization the way it has till now.

3 Competition Among Powers: Malign, Occasionally Benign

The current world order is experiencing intense competition between the US and China. As mentioned earlier in Chap. 2, and also in this chapter, this competition between the world's two major powers, and their allies, characterizes the post-liberal world order. While the competition has gathered momentum after the global financial crisis in 2008 and heightened since the COVID19 in 2020, the prospects of the competition reducing do not appear bright notwithstanding the Biden Presidency commencing in the US.

It would be interesting to observe if the nature of the US-China competition will remain distinctly 'malign',[8] as it was during the Trump era. Over the last 3 years, both countries have resorted to hostile and 'war like' actions including trading insults, shutting down diplomatic missions in each other's territories, and losing no opportunity to display to the rest of the world, and each other, national armed capacities through military patrols in sensitive geographies like the South China Sea. There are clear implications of the competition remaining malign. Such competition would continue to make both countries averse to the possibility of engaging, and instead make both foci on undermining each other. The effect is bound to be felt on several global concerns and institutions, where the US and China are required to cooperate for delivering quick outcomes. Notable among them are the global

---

[7] Joint Statement on Electronic Commerce, World Trade Organization (WTO), 25 January 2019. https://trade.ec.europa.eu/doclib/docs/2019/january/tradoc_157643.pdf. Accessed on 3 April 2021.

[8] Qingguo (2021).

efforts to reduce carbon emissions and address climate change. Though the Biden Presidency has recommitted the US to the international efforts to combat climate change overturning the decision of its predecessor,[9] the US-China bitterness might still spill over in the working of the climate pact. Similarly, the US and China need to agree to cooperate on ensuring movement in the WTO. Malign competition, as it exists now, might seriously undermine the prospects of global cooperation and globalized efforts to progress, if the US and China don't begin engaging.

A further outcome of malign competition with adverse impact on global rules and cooperation arises from such competition forcing countries to 'choose'. Deep mistrust and security concerns have, as discussed earlier, led to the formation of blocs and alliances of countries that are positioned around the US and China at their core. The US effort to consolidate allies in the Indo-Pacific region, and the Chinese effort to gather partners around the BRI, are the best examples. Driven by malign competition, both the US and China would persuade countries and businesses to choose between each other, on the back of efforts to establish each other's systems and practices as 'superior', while not hesitating to flag adverse consequences of choosing the other. The maligning tendency can strengthen as both countries race to outclass each other in cutting-edge frontier technologies. Techno-nationalism, putting ownership of technological innovation and its products, central to the vision of national security and economic prosperity,[10] is being practiced by both the US and China with significant consequences. Nowhere is this more evident than the US efforts to push back Huawei from the global 5G technology space on grounds of national security concerns that accompany its use.[11] The concerns have also extended to US allies and partners being encouraged to refrain from using Huawei.[12]

A change in the character of competition between global powers to being more benign can lead to speedier delivery of global public policy outcomes. While not entirely in the space of US-China relations, competition to emerge as the more effective responder to global public health exigencies, particularly the COVID19, has led to laudable outcomes. India and China have been stretching domestic pharmaceutical production capacities to produce millions of doses of vaccines for inoculating against COVID19. The beneficiaries of such efforts have not just been their large domestic populations, but also small and poor countries in various parts of the world, who have been delivered vaccines, much before they might have been able to access them under normal circumstances. The Quad has also put concerted efforts into the production of vaccines for the Indo-Pacific region establishing its intentions for addressing global

---

[9] 'Biden puts US back into fight to slow global warming', Channel News Asia, 21 January 2021. https://www.channelnewsasia.com/news/world/biden-puts-us-back-into-fight-to-slow-global-warming-14006774. Accessed on 4 March 2021.

[10] Capri (2020).

[11] 'Huawei says US push to create a 5G rival 'would be a challenge', CNBC, 20 Feb 2021. https://www.cnbc.com/2020/02/21/huawei-says-us-push-to-create-a-5g-rival-would-be-a-challenge.html. Accessed on 4 April 2021.

[12] 'Britain wants US to form a 10-nation 5G alliance to cut reliance on China's Huawei', The South China Morning Post, 29 May. https://www.scmp.com/news/world/europe/article/3086774/uk-wants-us-form-10-nation-5g-alliance-cut-reliance-chinas-huawei. Accessed on 4 April 2021.

public health concerns.[13] While the effort might be interpreted as an attempt by the US and its Indo-Pacific allies to counter China's vaccine diplomacy, the greater objective of larger doses of vaccines reaching more people, is well-served.

Notwithstanding the virtues of benign competition, the global atmosphere of mistrust between major powers and their allies forces attention on the possibility of the virtues being compromised by circumspect, malicious intents. As the world gets ready to co-exist with COVID19 and explore options of cross-border travel enabled by vaccines, the specter of vaccine nationalism looms large. China's proposal to allow foreigners into the mainland only if they have been inoculated with Chinese vaccines, draws attention to the ugly downsides of vaccine nationalism, preventing consideration of vaccines as a global public good, irrespective of their country of origin.[14] Emphasis on nationalism for vaccines would prevent efforts to arrive at standards for mutual recognition of vaccines. Indeed, the use of nationalist principles can have large ramifications for the global fight against COVID19, if vaccines developed so far, and potential COVID19 medications developed in the future, are unable to travel seamlessly across global borders due to restrictions created by intellectual property rules. The WTO has a major role to play in this regard. It must sidestep efforts by some countries, to safeguard the interests of their pharmaceutical businesses to capture greater shares of the COVID19 preventive market, in perceived 'national interests'. These eventualities can be avoided if global institutions like the WTO are assured of US-China competition not turning into a fight for hegemonic supremacy, at least on issues that are of fundamental global concern.

4   COVID19, the New Poor, and Digitalization

Pandemics, apart from their catastrophic impacts, have also been important in driving home specific lessons. The COVID19, in this regard, is pointing towards lessons that its predecessors (e.g. the Spanish Flu, Russian Flu, and the Yellow Fever)[15] were instrumental in contributing to. These lessons include the urgency of global cooperation on public health, the greater role of states in healthcare, major technological changes, and the devastating impact of pandemics on the global poor.[16]

Much of all the lessons have been evident following COVID19. Notwithstanding major power rivalries and noticeable malign competition between the US and China,

---

[13] 'The Quad counters China's vaccine diplomacy', VOA, 12 March 2021. https://www.voanews.com/episode/quad-counters-chinas-vaccine-diplomacy-4605076. Accessed on 4 April 2021.

[14] 'Notice on Visa Facilitation for Applicants Inoculated with Chinese COVID19 vaccines', Embassy of the People's Republic of China in the United States of America, 15 March 2021. http://www.china-embassy.org/eng/visas/t1861379.htm. Accessed on 4 April 2021.

[15] The Spanish Flu occurred during 1918–19 and the Russian Flu during 1889–1890. The Yellow Fever broke out in the late 1800s. A timeline of various pandemics is available at 'Visualizing the history of pandemics', Visual Capitalist, 14 March 2020. https://www.visualcapitalist.com/history-of-pandemics-deadliest/. Accessed on 5 April 2021.

[16] WEF (2021).

global cooperation has gathered around the core objective of arresting the advance of the pandemic. This is most visible in the efforts of the Global Alliance for Vaccines (GAVI), which, along with the UNICEF, WHO, and the CEPI is administering the COVAX—the global pool for procurement and distribution of vaccines. As of 1 April 2021, the COVAX has been able to distribute more than 33 million doses of vaccines to 74 countries of the world, including several poor and low-income countries in Africa, South Asia, Southeast Asia, and the Mediterranean.[17] These efforts come notwithstanding the 'dark' shades produced by geopolitics, notably the controversy over the role of WHO in managing information about the outbreak of the pandemic in China—as discussed earlier in Chap. 2—and the competitive vaccine diplomacy between countries. If the management of the COVID19, in terms of distribution of vaccines and efforts to build preparedness for tackling future strains of the fast-mutating novel coronavirus, do acquire a global shape through the GAVI, WHO, and other supporting global agencies, it would certainly be an accomplishment. The feat would've been achieved notwithstanding the destabilizing geopolitics prevailing in the world.

Might the global cooperation over COVID19 be construed as a success for globalization? More importantly, can the success, even in a limited sense, by underpinning the virtues of global cooperation, be extended to convincing arguments about greater benefits that can accrue from global rules of trade and business? After all, the angst against globalization, as evidenced from the political outcries against it during the last decade, have much to do with the view that the global rules, while purportedly being for all, have benefitted some, at the expense of others. Populist political opinions in the West, symbolized by the growth of the 'Trump' phenomenon, argue such rules to have benefitted China, and some other countries, more than the US. Parts of this disgruntled narrative connect to the view that economic globalization has benefitted owners of capital and technology, much more than wage earners, thereby legitimizing the narrative from the vantage points of displaced and upset workers. Can the COVID19—and some of the good records of global cooperation in its respect—mark the beginning of a counter-narrative for greater social and political acceptance of economic globalization?

A lot depends on the ability of global institutions to contribute to the large economic distress arising from COVID19. Pandemics, historically, have been responsible for enhancing global poverty. COVID19 is not an exception in this regard. The latest estimates by the World Bank point to the pandemic producing millions of 'new poor' with India, South Asia, and Southeast Asia, comprising a significant proportion of the people being pushed into poverty.[18] Much of the new poverty in Asia has arisen due to the displacement of workers from labor-intensive supply chains like readymade garments, as cancellation of orders has led to the cutback of

---

[17] The latest updates on roll-out of vaccines are available at GAVI https://www.gavi.org/covax-facility. Accessed on 5 April 2021.

[18] Lakner, Christoph et al. 2021.

production and jobs.[19] In the populous countries of South Asia, such as India and Bangladesh, lockdowns imposed for curbing the spread of COVID19, have adversely affected jobs in employment-intensive industries like tourism, hospitality, transport, construction, and real estate. As industries continue to face setbacks due to new bouts of the outbreak of the pandemic, jobs stay threatened, with prospects of the displaced remaining bleak. The ability of most countries to support the jobless for long periods is limited as without global economic recovery, countries would not be able to mobilize sufficient resources. The situation is ostensibly grave. But it also provides the context and opportunities for the world to come together to propose solutions to lift people out of poverty. There is no alternative to robust and sustained economic growth in this regard. However, the experience of economic globalization of the last couple of decades, underpins the importance of the benefits of such growth to be distributed equitably. Otherwise, COVID19 will not only be remembered for exacerbating global poverty, but also for contributing to global inequality. There are already concerns over owners of capital continuing to benefit at the expense of wage earners, even during the COVID19, as revealed by evidence from garment supply chains.[20]

The new narrative for globalization needs to be inclusive and mindful of addressing the concerns of the 'have not's and 'left behind's. Might the rapid advance of technology help in this regard? Technology and its applications have multiple implications in this regard. On one hand, the digitalization of production and industrial processes has been responsible for displacing several traditional jobs. On the other hand, such applications, particularly the growth of digital functions and internet-based applications have created enormous work opportunities, including home-based enterprises, start-ups, and location-independent jobs. There might not be complete equivalence between jobs lost and new opportunities, as both would depend on several factors, including the nature of industries, their locations, process transformations, and the skills of individuals. But technology can indeed be instrumental in making the global labor market more inclusive by expanding access to the global workforce, including women, the aged, and people with disabilities, to a host of exciting opportunities. However, much of the gains visualized from digitalization in this regard depend upon the capacities of countries, social communities, and income groups to access the digital space. The importance of uniform and balanced access to the internet and online modes of communication, along with abilities to buy smartphones and computers, have been starkly brought to notice during the COVID19. Nowhere has this been more visible than in India, where, the forced shift to online schooling and tuitions, following COVID19, have seen several children from households with low digital capacities, struggling to cope up with the transition.[21] If sufficient digital

---

[19] 'World's garment workers face ruin as fashion brands refuse to pay $16bn', The Guardian, 8 Octoer 2020. https://www.theguardian.com/global-development/2020/oct/08/worlds-garment-workers-face-ruin-as-fashion-brands-refuse-to-pay-16bn. Accessed on 5 April 2021.

[20] Ibid.

[21] 'Covid risks a lost generation amid India's digital divide', Bloomberg, 17 December 2020. https://www.bloomberg.com/news/articles/2020-12-16/covid-risks-a-lost-generation-in-india-as-digital-divide-widens. Accessed on 5 April 2021.

capacities don't develop, then populous countries like India, with large young populations, might end up expanding inequalities further, through the enlarging digital divide.

5 Not the Last Word

From a celebrated journey that lasted for nearly two decades till the global financial crisis of 2008, and subsequently running into a growing problem of acceptance and legitimacy thereafter, economic globalization is currently at crossroads. A variety of critiques of globalization from multiple perspectives, including experiences of countries and institutions, underlines the contrasting aspects of the process: while countries, people, and households have gained from greater global integration, there are, undisputedly, those that haven't. On the balance, the world as a whole has become more prosperous over the last three decades. Overall global income inequality has also declined. However, inequalities within countries have increased on many occasions fueling obvious political and social discontent.[22] Such discontent is natural given that the losers from globalization are relatively easier to identify, as they are specific to communities and groups, as opposed to the gainers, who are usually not organized into distinct coalitions.[23]

Before the outbreak of COVID19, globalization was struggling to adjust to the harsh rejoinders arising from nationalist-populist political movements criticizing easy movement of goods, services, technology, and people across borders for harming national interests. These narratives got vicious and complex in the context of major power rivalry characterizing a post-liberal world order. The tension experienced by global institutions as a result of such rivalry has been a further strain for globalization. As countries gradually get organized into blocs and alliances based on political motives, and global production is pushed to adjust on geo-economic grounds, global rules of business and economic management become less relevant, compared with the bloc and alliance-specific governance frameworks.

The latest challenge for globalization is the advent of COVID19. Many argue that COVID19 wouldn't have become a global catastrophe had it not been because of porous borders and easy movements. While people-to-people connectivity might have accelerated the spread of COVID19, it needs to be noted that responses to the pandemic too, such as vaccines, have materialized at a brisk pace due to the interconnectedness of the global scientific and research community, as well as agencies, systems, and governments.

---

[22] Revenga and Dooley (2019).

[23] Displaced workers in specific industries affected by cheaper imports or immigrant labor are easier to identify and get noticed. The same doesn't apply to consumers who benefit from cheaper imports or localities and resident groups benefitting from services provided by foreign workers and professionals.

As the struggle to reign in the pandemic continues, a fractured world order, torn between power rivalries, needs to regroup for addressing the biggest health concern that the world faces since the Spanish Flu a century ago. Perhaps, the exigency will provide the ground and imperative for carving out a world order that is inherently more inclusive and people-centric than the order that has prevailed.

References

Aghi, Mukesh. 2020. A Free Trade Agreement between Quad nations: Vision or reality? Financial Express, 26 August. https://www.financialexpress.com/economy/a-free-trade-agreement-between-quad-nations-vision-or-reality/2066170/. Accessed 3 Apr 2021.

Capri, Alex. 2020. Techno-nationalism: The US-China tech innovation race, July. Hinrich Foundation, July. https://bschool.nus.edu.sg/cgs/wp-content/uploads/sites/7/2020/09/Hinrich-Foundation-NUS_Techno-nationalism-The-US-China-Tech-Innovation-Race.pdf. Accessed 4 Apr 2021.

Lakner, Christoph, Yonzan, Nishant, Mahler, Gerszon Daniel, Aguilar, Castaneda Andres R., and Wu, Haoyu. 2021. Updated estimates of the impact of COVID-19 on global poverty: Looking back at 2020 and the outlook for 2021. World Bank Blogs. 11 January. https://blogs.worldbank.org/opendata/updated-estimates-impact-covid-19-global-poverty-looking-back-2020-and-outlook-2021. Accessed 5 Mar 2021.

Obama, Barack. 2016. The TPP would let America, not China, lead the way on global trade. Washington Post, 2 May. https://www.washingtonpost.com/opinions/president-obama-the-tpp-would-let-america-not-china-lead-the-way-on-global-trade/2016/05/02/680540e4-0fd0-11e6-93ae-50921721165d_story.html. Accessed 3 Apr 2021.

Pottinger, Matt. 2021. Beijing Targets American Business, Wall Street Journal, 26 March. https://www.wsj.com/articles/beijing-targets-american-business-11616783268. Accessed 2 Apr 2021.

Qingguo, Jia. 2021. Malign or benign? China-US strategic competition under Biden, East Asia Forum, 28 March. https://www.eastasiaforum.org/2021/03/28/malign-or-benign-china-us-strategic-competition-under-biden/. Accessed 3 Apr 2021.

Revenga, Ann, and Dooley, Meagan. 2019. Is inequality really on the rise? Brookings, 28 May. https://www.brookings.edu/blog/future-development/2019/05/28/is-inequality-really-on-the-rise/. Accessed 5 Apr 2021.

World Economic Forum (WEF). 2021. COVID-19 and geopolitics—5 lessons from past pandemics. The Davos Agenda 2021, 11 January. https://www.weforum.org/agenda/2021/01/covid-19-geopolitics-lessons-pandemics-history/. Accessed 5 Apr 2021.

Correction to: Geo-economics, Globalization and the Covid-19 Pandemic: Trade and Development Perspectives from Bangladesh

Mohammad A. Razzaque

Correction to:
Chapter 6 in: A. Palit (ed.), *Globalisation Impacts*,
International Law and the Global South,
https://doi.org/10.1007/978-981-16-7185-2_6

The chapter was inadvertently published with incorrect chapter title, the chapter title has been updated from "Geo-Economics, Globalization, Geo-Economics in the Aftermath of the COVID19 Pandemic: Trade and Development Perspectives from Bangladesh"

to

"Geo-economics, Globalization and the Covid-19 Pandemic: Trade and Development Perspectives from Bangladesh". The chapter and book have been updated with the changes.

The updated version of this chapter can be found at
https://doi.org/10.1007/978-981-16-7185-2_6

© The Author(s), under exclusive license to Springer Nature Singapore Pte Ltd. 2022   C1
A. Palit (ed.), *Globalisation Impacts*, International Law and the Global South,
https://doi.org/10.1007/978-981-16-7185-2_11

Printed in the United States
by Baker & Taylor Publisher Services